"One of the most insightful and prolific scholars of anti-Americanism on the planet, Brendon O'Connor has produced an essential book for the age of Trump. With sharp analysis of politics, culture, and foreign policy, O'Connor cuts through two centuries of mythmaking surrounding anti-Americanism to help us distinguish between ideological prejudice and salutary critique."

—*Max Paul Friedman, American University, Washington, DC*

"Americans have long benefitted from the critical gaze of their foreign friends. This book – the best yet written on anti-Americanism – follows in that tradition. Brendon O'Connor is among the world's great scholars of America and its overseas perceptions. At this painful and frightening moment in American history, we need his wisdom more than ever."

—*Peter Beinart, City University of New York*

"Donald Trump was elected on a promise of American greatness, but his presidency – and the American people – has fallen into disrepute overseas. In his new book, Brendon O'Connor argues that American exceptionalism and anti-Americanism are rooted in prejudice. His book is an invaluable exploration into how this antinomy originated, and why it misleads us about America's role in the world."

—*John B. Judis, author of* The Nationalist Revival: Trade, Immigration, and the Revolt against Globalization

"How will the Trump presidency affect international understandings of America, and Americans' understandings of themselves? Almost certainly it will further fuel the growth of the seemingly polar opposites – anti-Americanism and American exceptionalism. This richly researched book traces through the growth of both sentiments, and criticises their common essentialism. Throughout, it is guided by a strong sense of history, an unfailing sense of proportion and an appreciation of contrasting outlooks and virtues."

—*Rodney Tiffen, Emeritus Professor, University of Sydney*

ANTI-AMERICANISM AND AMERICAN EXCEPTIONALISM

This book argues against the tendency to see America as the worst or best nation and instead presents a case for seeing anti-Americanism as a counterproductive prejudice. There are many reasons to criticise American policies, politics and even society, but a crucial distinction must be drawn between criticism and prejudice.

Charting the development and adaptation of this anti-American tradition, O'Connor maintains that it is important to contextualise it within the particularities of the American experience and the global reach of the United States' influence and power. He argues for a move away from stereotypes and caricatures towards more specific and profitable discussions about American actions and policies.

Offering precise and useful ways of understanding anti-Americanism and American exceptionalism that place the terms in their relevant political contexts, this volume is a useful and engaging resource for those researching or studying American politics and ideology, foreign policy, American culture and international relations.

Brendon O'Connor is an Associate Professor at the United States Studies Centre at the University of Sydney. He has published books and articles on anti-Americanism, US foreign relations, and US welfare policy. His most recent book *Ideologies of American Foreign Policy* (Routledge, 2019) was co-authored with John Callaghan and Mark Phythian.

ROUTLEDGE STUDIES IN US FOREIGN POLICY

Edited by Inderjeet Parmar, *City University*, and John Dumbrell, *University of Durham*

This new series sets out to publish high-quality works by leading and emerging scholars critically engaging with United States Foreign Policy. The series welcomes a variety of approaches to the subject and draws on scholarship from international relations, security studies, international political economy, foreign policy analysis and contemporary international history.

Subjects covered include the role of administrations and institutions, the media, think tanks, ideologues and intellectuals, elites, transnational corporations, public opinion, and pressure groups in shaping foreign policy, US relations with individual nations, with global regions and global institutions and America's evolving strategic and military policies.

The series aims to provide a range of books – from individual research monographs and edited collections to textbooks and supplemental reading for scholars, researchers, policy analysts and students.

India–America Relations (1942–62)
Rooted in the Liberal International Order
Atul Bhardwaj

Ideologies of American Foreign Policy
John Callaghan, Brendon O'Connor and Mark Phythian

Alliance Decision-Making in the South China Sea
Between Allied and Alone
Joseph A. Gagliano

Foreign Policy Issues for America
The Trump Years
Edited by Richard W. Mansbach and James M. McCormick

Anti-Americanism and American Exceptionalism
Prejudice and Pride about the USA
Brendon O'Connor

For more information about this series, please visit: www.routledge.com/series/ RSUSFP

ANTI-AMERICANISM AND AMERICAN EXCEPTIONALISM

Prejudice and Pride about the USA

Brendon O'Connor

Routledge
Taylor & Francis Group

LONDON AND NEW YORK

First published 2020
by Routledge
2 Park Square, Milton Park, Abingdon, Oxon OX14 4RN

and by Routledge
52 Vanderbilt Avenue, New York, NY 10017

Routledge is an imprint of the Taylor & Francis Group, an informa business

© 2020 Brendon O'Connor

The right of Brendon O'Connor to be identified as author of this work has been asserted by him in accordance with sections 77 and 78 of the Copyright, Designs and Patents Act 1988.

All rights reserved. No part of this book may be reprinted or reproduced or utilised in any form or by any electronic, mechanical, or other means, now known or hereafter invented, including photocopying and recording, or in any information storage or retrieval system, without permission in writing from the publishers.

Trademark notice: Product or corporate names may be trademarks or registered trademarks, and are used only for identification and explanation without intent to infringe.

British Library Cataloguing in Publication Data
A catalogue record for this book is available from the British Library

Library of Congress Cataloging-in-Publication Data
Names: O'Connor, Brendon, 1969- author.
Title: Anti-Americanism and American exceptionalism : prejudice and pride about the USA / Brendon O'Connor.
Description: Abingdon, Oxon ; New York, NY : Routledge, 2019. |
Series: Routledge studies in US foreign policy | Includes bibliographical references and index.
Identifiers: LCCN 2019004239| ISBN 9780415474283 (hbk) |
ISBN 9780415474290 (pbk) | ISBN 9780429277436 (ebk)
Subjects: LCSH: Anti-Americanism. | Exceptionalism--United States. |
United States--Foreign public opinion.
Classification: LCC E895 .O36 2019 | DDC 327.73--dc23
LC record available at https://lccn.loc.gov/2019004239

ISBN: 978-0-415-47428-3 (hbk)
ISBN: 978-0-415-47429-0 (pbk)
ISBN: 978-0-429-27743-6 (ebk)

Typeset in Bembo
by Taylor & Francis Books

For my sons, Finnegan and Sean

CONTENTS

ILLUSTRATIONS

Figures

Tables

ACKNOWLEDGEMENTS

This book emerged out of my passion for teaching and talking about all things American, particularly the politics, culture, and foreign relations of the United States of America. I am grateful that I have had such attentive and engaged students to teach at Griffith University and the University of Sydney who have listened to and critiqued my ideas on anti-Americanism and American exceptionalism. The first draft of this book was rehearsed on these students and the conversations I have had with them has made this a much stronger book. In the course of writing I had the opportunity to present my ideas in a number of seminar series as well as giving a few keynote addresses. I would like to take this opportunity to express my gratitude to the audience members who engaged with my ideas and provided comments on the work in progress. In particular, I would like to thank those who attended and participated in discussions at the Institute for the Study of the Americas, University of East Anglia, Central European University, Woodrow Wilson Center, World Affairs Council, University of Cambridge, University of Texas, Florida International University, Ohio State University, Montana State University, University of Chicago, University of Munich, Macquarie University, and University of Queensland. I would also like to thank Claire Maloney at Routledge for her support and guidance in seeing the book through to publication. Finally, I would like to thank the United States Studies Centre at the University of Sydney for supporting this book and thank Conor Wakefield and Dan Dixon for their diligent research assistance work.

PREFACE: ARE WE ALL AMERICANS OR ANTI-AMERICANS NOW?

On my virgin visit to the United States in early 1996 the first place I stayed was in Times Square. Over the next few days while walking around Manhattan Island I had a strong sensation – like many tourists before me – that I had already been to New York City. In a certain sense I had, courtesy of the films of Martin Scorsese and numerous other directors. I came to know New York better a few years later when I worked briefly in the World Trade Center for an organisation that researched drug use and HIV/AIDS. This gave me a particular familiarity with the Twin Towers, a familiarity I would soon share with millions of television viewers around the world as we all watched, over and over again, the towers being hit and then collapsing. Even today watching on YouTube, footage of the planes crashing into the towers is both spectacular and appalling. The attacks arguably grabbed global attention in a manner unrivalled by any single other event this century and, along with the assassination of JFK and the landing of the first man on the moon, are among the most dramatic televised moments in human history. These iconic events demanded attention because of their apparent uniqueness, significance, and possible consequences. Undoubtedly these events also received so much attention because they either occurred in America[1] or, in the case of the moon landing, were carried out by Americans. The September 11, 2001 terrorist attacks opened up an instant global conversation about anti-Americanism, leading over the next few years to a flood of books on the topic.[2] Therefore it is fair to contend that the 9/11 attacks, and how they were responded to, are the starting point for the contemporary debates about anti-Americanism. Conversely, in 1969 the moon landing was used as further evidence of American exceptionalism and superiority as the American astronauts fulfilled the challenge set by President Kennedy in 1961.

On October 11, 2001 President George W. Bush, giving a press conference discussing the 9/11 attacks, famously and naively stated: "I'm amazed that there's such misunderstanding of what our country is about that people would hate us. I am – like most Americans, I just can't believe it because I know how good we are."[3] When Americans were the first to walk on the moon on July 21, 1969, the world watched with amazement and American exceptionalism was widely proclaimed. The Australian Labor Prime Minister Julia Gillard recalled this feeling in a 2011 speech to the US Congress: "For my own generation, the defining image of America was the landing on the moon. My classmates and I were sent home from school to watch the great moment on television. I'll always remember thinking that day: Americans can do anything."[4] American images, ideas, and stories are a constant in the lives of most non-Americans. This led Peter Conrad, the Australian born, English based, cultural critic to write in 2014 that: "Like many others who arrived in the world after 1945, I often need to remind myself that I am not American."[5] The familiarity of outsiders with the US can lead to admiration, insightful criticism, and contempt. This leads to America being seen as an exceptional model for other nations to follow as well as a dystopia that should be strongly avoided. In fact, when travelling abroad, Americans are often surprised by how much of their culture, politics, and general news is readily available and consumed by non-Americans.

In the days following the destruction of the Twin Towers, much was written about the symbolism of targeting these particular buildings. French philosopher and provocateur Jean Baudrillard wrote that the attacks on the Twin Towers joined "the white magic of movies and the black magic of terrorism." Although Baudrillard was criticised for trivialising the attacks and for the racist connotations embedded in his statement, his words effectively described how both Americans and non-Americans have fantasised about the destruction of America's might. In countless dramas millions have been positioned to root for Americans to triumph against adversity, and, more than occasionally, to get their comeuppance. Sensational attacks on the World Trade Center existed in the celluloid world long before 2001: the Twin Towers were the target of Islamic terrorist attacks in the 1982 film *Right is Wrong*, they were partly destroyed by aliens in the 1996 movie *Independence Day,* and damaged by meteor hits in the 1998 film *Armageddon* (footage that was removed when the movie appeared on American network television in 2002). While not literally the centre of world trade, the Twin Towers were important sites for the exchange of global finances and ideas. They were largely targeted for their metaphorical symbolism in America's most famous city. The reality was that, along with symbolising the power of American capitalism, they were a tourist attraction and a shopping mall. The sheer variety of the workers and visitors in these buildings reminds us of just how indiscriminate both the 9/11 terrorist attacks and some people's reactions to them were. Many will remember the *Le Monde* editorial "We are all Americans now", but I also recall the *Guardian* headline that characterised an entirely different reaction: "A bully with a bloody nose is still a bully."[6] What disturbed me about this second response is that the strikes on the Pentagon and Twin Towers killed innocent people – airline passengers, office workers and tourists. The US government was certainly not cut down by these attacks, which killed random individuals that were rich and poor, powerful and powerless. If anything, the US government was emboldened by the 9/11 attacks. These responses got me interested in writing about anti-Americanism and American exceptionalism. I wanted to better understand the considerable number of non-Americans that sympathised with the actions and aims of Osama bin Laden and al Qaeda. In 2005 the Pew surveys found that 61% of Jordanians had confidence in bin Laden to "do the right thing regarding world affairs"; the numbers were similar for Palestinians and Pakistanis.[7] Meanwhile, "confidence in Bush to do the right thing in world affairs" amongst Jordanians stood at a paltry 1% in 2005; whereas in 2003 78% of Americans and 83% of Israelis had confidence in Bush to do the right thing.[8]

This duality of admiration and antagonism has been a long-held aspect of the world's fascination and familiarity with the US. Thomas Jefferson wrote in the 18th century that "every man has two countries, his own and France." His words were written at a time when France was at the forefront of struggles for human rights and the quest for greater philosophical understanding. By the mid-20th century it was America, not France, that was likely to be everyone's second country. A fascination with America existed well before it became a great power, a fascination that was often tinged with hope or fear. America has long been seen as humanity's "last best hope on earth",[9] and, conversely, as a nation that questionably inserts itself across the world with its military bases, corporations, and popular culture. Thus America is often perceived as the land of inspiring politicians and innovators like Washington, Franklin, Gates and Obama, but also as the home of dumb and their cousin dumber (cue: Reagan, Bush Jr, Sarah Palin, Trump, and Miss Teen South Carolina[10]). Of course we should not forget the supply side of this equation. America receives a disproportionate level of attention because of the reach and muscle of American media and American corporations, and because of the power and influence of its government.

Given the ubiquity, power, and influence of the US it is hardly surprising that it is the subject of significant hatred and even the target of violence. What was surprising was the reaction of many Americans, from the president down, to the 9/11 attacks. So many Americans seemed unaware of just how much anger and resentment their country inspires around the world. This reflected the legendary insularity of Americans that Sacha Baron Cohen has made a career out of skewering. There are any number of answers to the much asked question after 9/11 "Why do people hate America?". American meddling in the foreign affairs of other nations has caused many unfortunate outcomes. Fault can easily be found with US government policy since WWII in East Asia, the Middle East and Latin America. Others resent the global influence of American corporations and economic policies, the spread of Americanisation, or the impact of American evangelising and moralising. Given these resentments, when four planes were hijacked and thousands of people, largely Americans, were killed, many people's feelings of sympathy were mixed with thoughts that America was getting what it deserved, that Goliath had finally been paid back by David. The word "blowback" quickly entered the popular media, a term first used by the CIA to describe the unintended negative consequences of covert actions, in a report on the agency's involvement in the overthrow of the Mosaddegh government in Iran in 1953. These mixed emotions about 9/11 were at times crassly expressed as people began to tire of the American media's coverage of the tragedy. At other times they were laid out in more complex terms as the details of the US government's relationship with bin Laden was probed (which possibly dated back to the US's financial support of anti-Soviet mujahidin groups in Afghanistan during the 1980s).[11] The editor of *Le Monde* summarised his view of the world's reaction: "What's happening to [Americans] is too bad, but they had it coming."[12] I remember finding such sentiments objectionable at the time as they conflated people with governments.

The Bush administration's ill-conceived decision to invade Iraq undoubtedly boosted latent antipathy towards America. This action also poisoned much of the good will that existed towards America after 9/11. Global opinion surveys clearly show this rising negativity: in 2003 99% of Jordanians surveyed by Pew had an "unfavourable" attitude to the US, as did 71% of Lebanese.[13] One of the tragedies of the Bush era was how the administration managed to turn legitimate concerns about terrorism into mockery of Bush's approach to it – "the war on errorism" as the Punk band NO FX summarised it – so soon after the events of September 11. The Bush administration overreached and in so doing botched the arguments against bin Laden, terrorism and nuclear proliferation. Instead of maintaining a broad opposition to these threats, Bush's cowboy talk and exaggerated claims about the threat posed by Saddam Hussein deflated global public support for the fight against terrorism. Much of the negative opinion was not only directed at George W. Bush and his administration's policies but also towards the American people themselves. Responding to various waves of criticism, the *Washington Post* columnist Robert Samuelson penned a piece which opened with the line "We Americans are people too." The article adopted a rather didactic tone about the need for Europeans to be more thankful for America's global leadership. Nonetheless Samuelson does make the valid point that you can criticise the policies of a foreign government without hating its people.

The inability to separate the American government from its people was one of the more obvious flaws in much commentary about the US in the Bush era, and this challenge arises again today during the Trump presidency. In conflating the American people with their politicians, and likewise with their government's actions abroad, ironically foreigners are taking American exceptionalist thinking on board. In other words, many non-Americans buy into the mythology that the American government is, more so than other democracies, a "government of the people, by the people, for the people". It is common for peoples around the world to see their own leaders as unrepresentative chameleons while being drawn to talk about American presidents as symbolising their people. A president Reagan, Bush Jnr or Trump apparently symbolises an ignorant nation; whereas electing a president Obama means Americans suddenly do in fact care about the world's opinion of the US. The situation can be partly explained by the heavy emphasis on personal biography in American politics and the tendency of presidential candidates to link their personal narrative with national mythology. It is also perpetuated by an electoral system that offers a direct vote for the political leader as opposed to the Westminster system where members of parliament, not voters, choose the leader.

My point here is not to defend the foreign policies of recent Republican presidents, far from it, but to point out that for criticism of politicians like Reagan and
Trump or the policies of the Bush Jnr administration to be effective, it must move
beyond caricature. It must be able to provide strong evidence that reveals the special
influence the American people have on their politicians or how the ignorance of the
American people about foreign affairs is reflected in their leaders' decisions. This
book searches for evidence that Americans are more ignorant than people elsewhere
and finds some evidence to support this claim, but certainly not comprehensive
proof. One stunning data point was that Americans were the worst at guessing their
own population of all the nations surveyed in a 2002 National Geographic poll of
young Americans: they consistently significantly overestimated it. Overall the limited
data we have suggests Americans are significantly more ignorant than Western Europeans about basic global affairs and geography, a little more ignorant than Canadians or Brits and slightly better informed than Mexicans. The second last chapter of
this book addresses this question of American insularity and ignorance about the rest
of the world. There is a long tradition of stereotyping the worst, most ignorant or
most gauche aspects of America as the norm. In a reflective moment, Oscar Wilde
commented that the "English people are far more interested in American barbarism
than they are in American civilization". The origins of anti-Americanism are most
sensibly traced to the Jacksonian period (the 1820s and 1830s) in American history.
Just as expressions of anti-globalisation existed before the late 20th century, forms of
anti-Americanism existed before the 1820s. However, both anti-Americanism and
anti-globalism have a key period that was crucial in shaping their tropes and language. In the case of anti-Americanism, it was the Jacksonian period when the
American frontier dramatically expanded (often in rough and ready circumstances)
and Europe experienced an equally dramatic surge of interest in America. As a result,
there emerged a greatly increased volume of travel writing about the new nation.
This literature and commentary, widely read at the time by a public looking for ways
to understand this new force in the world, gives a great insight into perceptions of
America. In this key period, Europeans were forming their views about the nature of
America and Americans. The results were often not pleasing. Most of the commentators of the day painted Americans as unsophisticated, boastful and financially
untrustworthy. It is my contention that this anti-American outlook – with its focus
on America as an uncouth nation – reached its apex in terms of influence in the
Jacksonian era. Negative commentary in the years following tended to play off the
tropes and stereotypes about Americans that were established in this era.

One of the most widely read travel books of the Jacksonian era was Frances
Trollope's *Domestic Manners of the Americans* (1832), which lampoons the rough and
ready eating habits of Americans on the frontier, decrying the "total and universal
want of manners, both in males and females". A decade later Dickens, in *American
Notes* and *The Life and Adventures of Martin Chuzzlewit* added to the existing picture
of the ugly American by satirising Americans for their "worship of the almighty
dollar" (a phrase he coined), for being swindlers and for their love of national and
personal puffery. Dickens' American books regularly highlighted how every other

American seemed to have some trumped up title as General this or Professor that; and how people constantly told you how great a man such and such was and how wonderful America was. Proclaiming the US to be "the greatest country in the history of the world" is of course a longstanding favourite line of American politicians. At her best Trollope offered a searing critique of American hypocrisy over slavery and Dickens very effectively pinpointed the contradictions in America's claims that it was an egalitarian society. However, both helped create and perpetuate anti-American stereotypes by portraying behaviour in the backwoods and frontier as typical of the whole. This made their commentary a mixture of snobbery and insight.

America is frequently a nation of opposites: the home of much of the global pornography industry and of the most prominent anti-pornography movements; the Mecca of fatty food diners and the birth place of the raw food movement, and the home of a tradition in many ways diametrically opposed to that of Jacksonianism. Wilsonian America stands against the inward-looking populist tendencies of the Jacksonian tradition. Named after Woodrow Wilson, (president of both Princeton University and the United States), this tradition champions the promotion of human rights, international laws and institutions, and world peace. However, it can also be viewed as naïve, preachy, and culturally tone deaf. French Prime Minister Clemenceau at the Versailles Peace conference said talking to Wilson felt like "talking with Jesus Christ". Elsewhere he said "God himself was content with ten commandments. Wilson modestly inflicted fourteen points on us…of the most empty theory." Graham Greene's *Quiet American* offers in many ways a Wilsonian archetype in its protagonist Alden Pyle (at least as often seen by foreigners). Quoting book knowledge and proclaiming his wish to bring democracy to Vietnam, Pyle is introduced as a naïve American abroad; however, his idealism is soon shown to be stained by a deadly imperialism that involves the secret importing of military equipment and the bombing of civilians to create pro-American ferment in Vietnam. The most quoted line of the novel about Pyle (and implicitly about the US) is: "I never knew a man who had better motives for all the trouble he caused." In a case of life imitating art, George W. Bush quoted this line in a speech to the Veterans of Foreign Wars national convention in 2007. Bush went on to question Greene's thesis that Indochina would really have been better off without American intervention given what Bush said we know about "'boat people,' 're-education camps,' and 'killing fields.'" This is a fallacious argument because violent American intervention was in part responsible for the rise of Pol Pot and the refugee crisis at the end of the Vietnam war. What Bush typifies here is a general unwillingness by recent American politicians (and much of the American media) to admit any foreign policy mistakes by America in the present or in fact at any time in the past. Whenever Obama made mild references to possible errors of judgement, or reflected on how American policies may have stirred up foreign resentment, he was repetitively attacked as unpatriotic. From the outside, this inability to admit mistakes and apologise looks suspiciously like the continuation of what Senator Fulbright called the "arrogance of American power."

What frequently most bewilders and annoys foreigners is when Jacksonian brutality and Wilsonian pronouncements are employed simultaneously. Both are exceptionalist traditions – they both start from a view that America is a model for other nations, which can and should be imposed on other parts of the world. Wilsonians are more inclined to think American inventions exist for the benefit of higher values such as democracy and liberty and for the ultimate betterment of those invaded. Jacksonians are not particularly interested in the feelings of foreigners or higher goals. They have always been America firsters like President Trump. The Jacksonian tradition is inward looking by inclination; however, if drawn into a conflict as in 1941 or 2001 this tradition unleashes a strong drive to crush America's opponents. Bush drew on both Jacksonian and Wilsonian traditions to create a toxic cocktail of policies that were rightly criticised as self-righteous, delusional and deadly.[14] We can see this bewildering combination of ideas in his promise to "ride herd" on the Middle Eastern peace process,[15] or his claim in his second inaugural address in 2005 that the ultimate goal of US foreign policy was "ending tyranny in our world",[16] or in his government's assertion that it was bringing democracy to Iraq. However, as much as Bush deserves forceful criticism, much commentary on him and his government misfired because, rather than examining the details, commentators and media treated Bush as a half-wit and wrote off all of his government's pronouncements as insincere. Further, as evidenced by the *Daily Mirror* headline in 2004 "How can 59,054,087 people be so DUMB?", the American people were often dismissed as just plain "dumb" in the Bush era.[17] Admittedly it was hard not to be furious at the policies of Bush and Cheney. Bush's election and re-election were tragedies as far as I was concerned. However, name-calling, abuse and anti-Americanism seldom wins a political argument. A case in point is the *Guardian* newspaper's ill-fated 2004 "Operation Clark County" letter writing campaign. *Guardian* readers were encouraged to send a letter to a voter in Clark County, Ohio trying to convince them to vote for Kerry not Bush. As I document in this book, the operation misfired spectacularly. National stereotypes are hard to avoid and remain extremely popular – few would argue that Americans and the French have similar customs and sensibilities – even though the people of these two nations have more in common than is readily acknowledged. When national stereotypes become overused touchstones for analysis, they can easily reflect certain prejudices about foreigners. Americans have a unique word to describe this negative outlook towards them and their nation: anti-Americanism. It is a word that partly exists because foreigners have been so drawn to America and had so much to say about it (with much commentary being extremely negative). At the same time Americans themselves frequently overreact to criticism, showing a tendency toward "annoying patriotism" as de Tocqueville called it. This attitude leads to much commentary on America being falsely called anti-Americanism. Smug foreigners and self-righteous Americans have often shed more heat than light on the question of what makes the United States and its people tick. The reactions to September 11, 2001 were yet another chapter in this three-centuries-old story of fascination with the US. The rights and wrongs of the US were debated widely. Given the unexpected and dramatic nature of the attacks, and the emotional responses to them, it is no surprise that many of the books written in their immediate aftermath have dated badly. At the time, and since, there was much hyperbole about the epoch-changing potential of the attacks. Distance from these events gives us the opportunity to reflect on them more soberly: 9/11 did not "change everything" as some claimed. Rather, they amplified certain existing tendencies. Finally, the Bush administration's use of these attacks to justify an ill-planned war in Iraq severely dented the credibility and trustworthiness of the US in the world. The global enthusiasm generated by the election of Barack Obama showed that, despite America's many failings, the world holds a great reservoir of hope for the US to be truer to its oft-pronounced ideals. Trump's entry into the Oval Office has rightly confounded many Americans and non-Americans alike and led to a resurgence of negative sentiment towards the US in most countries. Whether this reaction should be read as anti-Americanism requires us to have a stronger understanding of what this word sensibly means, which is a central aim of this book.

Notes

1 Throughout this book I use a variety of abbreviated ways of talking about the United States of America i.e. the US, the United States, and America. I know some people find the use of the term America inappropriate but the abbreviation America to me seems quite different from the words "the Americas" or "North America". Most people seem to accept that the people of the United States of America are to be called Americans; from this it would seem reasonable to suggest that these Americans come from America. In the 21st century, people do not generally call people from the North American and South American Continents, "Americans", in the way that people from the African continent are called Africans.

2 See: Paul Hollander, *Understanding Anti-Americanism: Its Origins and Impact at Home and Abroad* (Chicago: Ivan R. Dee, 2004); Andrew and Kristin Ross, *Anti-Americanism* (New York: NYU Press, 2004); Denis Lacorne and Tony Judt, *With Us or Against Us: Studies in Global Anti-Americanism* (New York: Palgrave Macmillan US, 2005); Max Paul Friedman, *Rethinking Anti-Americanism* (Cambridge: Cambridge University Press, 2012); Ziauddin Sardar and Mary Wyn Davies, *Why Do People Hate America?* (London: Icon Books, 2002).

3 George W. Bush, "President Holds Prime Time News Conference," in the White House Archives, October 11, 2001, <https://georgewbush-whitehouse.archives.gov/news/releases/2001/10/20011011-7.html>.

4 Julia Gillard, "Transcript of Julia Gillard's Speech to Congress," *SBS* (August 23, 2013), <https://www.sbs.com.au/news/transcript-of-julia-gillard-s-speech-to-congress>.

5 Peter Conrad, *How the World was Won: The Americanization of Everywhere* (London: Thames and Hudson Limited, 2014) p. 7.

6 Charlotte Raven, "A Bully with a Bloody Noise is Still a Bully," *The Guardian* (September 19, 2001), <https://www.theguardian.com/world/2001/sep/18/september11.comment>.

7 Pew Research Center, "Confidence in Osama bin Laden," August 2017, <http://www.pewglobal.org/database/indicator/20/survey/all/>.

8 Pew Research Centrer, "Confidence in the U.S. President," August 2017, <http://www.pewglobal.org/database/custom-analysis/indicator/6/countries/11,14,64,74,81,84,106,111,166,168,233/>.

9 Thomas Jefferson called America "the world's best hope" in 1801 in his first inaugural. In 1862 President Lincoln called for America during the Civil War to preserve it status as the "the last best hope of earth", Ted Widmer, "Last Best Hope," *The New York Times*, November 30, 2012: <https://opinionator.blogs.nytimes.com/2012/11/30/last-bes

t-hope/>; In 1948 Hubert Humphrey said that America "as now, more than ever, the last best hope on earth" which he offered to "the whole two billion members of the human family". Peter Conrad, *How the World Was Won: The Americanization of Everywhere,* (London: Thames & Hudson, 2014), 7. On the last day of his presidency Ronald Reagan praised Medal of Freedom recipients as renewing "our pride and gratitude in the United States of America, the greatest, freest nation in the world—the last, best hope of man on Earth." Ronald Reagan, "Remarks at the Presentation Ceremony for the Presidential Medal of Freedom," January 19, 1989 in *The American Presidency Project,* <http://www.presidency.ucsb.edu/ws/?pid=35402>. This echoed similar themes in Reagan's 1988 State of the Union address where he proclaimed: "How can we not believe in the greatness of America? How can we not do what is right and needed to preserve this last best hope of man on Earth? After all our struggles to restore America, to revive confidence in our country, hope for our future—after all our hard-won victories earned through the patience and courage of every citizen—we cannot, must not, and will not turn back. We will finish our job. How could we do less? We're Americans." Ronald Reagan, "Address Before a Joint Session of Congress on the State of the Union," January 25, 1988, in *The American Presidency Project,* <http://www.presidency. ucsb.edu/ws/index.php?pid=36035>. On the 150th anniversary of the abolition of slavery in 2015 President Obama acknowledged Lincoln's famous words and their context and then ended his speech with his own brand of progressive and multicultural American exceptionalism as he encouraged Americas "To remember that our freedom is bound up with the freedom of others – regardless of what they look like or where they come from or what their last name is or what faith they practice. To be honorable alike in what we give, and what we preserve. To nobly save, or meanly lose, the last best hope of Earth. To nobly save, or meanly lose, the last best hope of Earth. That is our choice. Today, we affirm hope." Barrack Obama, "Remarks by the President at the Commemoration of the 150th Anniversary of the 13th Amendment," December 09, 2015, in *The White House Archives,* <https://obamawhitehouse.archives.gov/the-press-office/2015/ 12/09/remarks-president-commemoration-150th-anniversary-13th-amendment>.

10 This is one of the most watched moments in a beauty pageant history: "Miss Teen USA 2007 – South Carolina Answers a Question" (August 24, 2007), [video file]. Retrieved from: <http://www.youtube.com/watch?v=lj3iNxZ8Dww>.

11 James Scott, *Deciding to Intervene: the Reagan Doctrine and American Foreign Policy* (Duke University Press: Durham, NC, 1996); Steve Coll, *Ghost Wars: The Secret History of the CIA, Afghanistan, and Bin Laden, from the Soviet Invasion to September 10, 2001* (Penguin: London, 2004).

12 Quoted in Moises Naim, "Anti-Americanisms: A Guide to Hating Uncle Sam," *Foreign Policy* (January–February 2002).

13 Pew Research Center, "Opinion of the United States," August 2017, <http://www. pewglobal.org/database/indicator/1/survey/all/response/Unfavorable/>.

14 Anatol Lieven, *America Right or Wrong* (New York: Oxford University Press, 2004).

15 Kathryn Westcott, "Bush Revels in Cowboy Speak," *BBC,* June 06, 2003, <http:// news.bbc.co.uk/2/hi/americas/2968176.stm>; Andrew O'Hagan, "You Have a Mother Don't You?", *London Review of Books* 25, 17 (2003), <https://www.lrb.co.uk/v25/ n17/andrew-ohagan/you-have-a-mother-dont-you>.

16 George W. Bush, "President Sworn-In to Second Term," the Second Inaugural Speech from the Office of the Press Secretary in The White House Archives (Washington, D.C.: The Capitol Hill, January 20, 2005), <https://georgewbush-whitehouse.archives.gov/ news/releases/2005/01/20050120-1.html>.

17 June Thomas, "Brits to America: You're Idiots!," *Slate* (November 04, 2004): <http:// www.slate.com/articles/news_and_politics/international_papers/2004/11/brits_to_am erica_youre_idiots.html>.

INTRODUCTION

Exceptional terms for ordinary people

President Obama at a press conference in 2009 in Strasbourg France stated: "I believe in American exceptionalism, just as I suspect that the Brits believe in British exceptionalism and the Greeks believe in Greek exceptionalism." This common-sense and diplomatic response was excoriated by American conservatives: "The Obama–Clinton duo failed our country by defying America's exceptionalism and betraying our nation's history and founding fathers' revolutionary spirit that established America on the principles of freedom and democracy…I will repeat my belief that American exceptionalism is real. Let us not fear what we know to be true, instead we should always remember that our country was built upon, Judeo-Christian values and principles; and instead let us remember the sacrifices of those who have gone before us. America is unique and is the greatest country in the history of the world" (Michael Flynn, 2016 Republican Party Convention).[1]

Sarah Palin, the former Vice-Presidential Republican nominee, claimed Obama's response proved that he "doesn't believe in American exceptionalism at all. He seems to think it is just a kind of irrational prejudice in favour of our way of life. To me, that is appalling." Drawing on the medium of our age she suggested Obama is like the "politically correct" mother in the movie *The Incredibles* who wants to play down her son Dash's superpowers by telling him that "Everyone is special." Palin sympathises with Dash who mutters in response, "Which is another way of saying no one is special."[2] For believers in American exceptionalism like Palin, Americans are special in ways that others are not: they have talents, ambitions, and personalities that are better than those of people elsewhere.[3] Furthermore, they insist that the American nation is a superior model for others to emulate and follow: "through persuasion when possible and force of arms when absolutely necessary."[4] Newt Gingrich boldly asserts this superiority when he writes "America is simply the most extraordinary nation in history. This is not a statement of nationalist hubris. It is an historical fact."[5] Senator Marco Rubio has proclaimed like a broken record that: "America is the single greatest nation in all of human history."[6] It is not only conservatives who make this claim to singular greatness, Michelle Obama echoed this oft-repeated exceptionalist hubris in her widely praised speech at the 2016 Democratic Party convention when she claimed: "don't let anyone ever tell you that this country isn't great, that somehow we need to make it great again. Because this right now is the greatest country on earth!"[7] The flip side of this coin is the anti-American stance that Americans are a sub-species of the human race and that America is the worst nation on earth, ever.

When we leave the make-believe world of Hollywood, the mature reality is that Americans are ordinary people like the rest of us – they are not Supermen and Wonder Women (or supervillains), and America is just another country. Indeed, America's "Superpower" status did not enable it to bend the laws of history in Afghanistan or Iraq: the awful reminder was that attempting to reorder foreign societies with imposed values is generally counterproductive and extremely costly in terms of human lives and resources. This book is premised on the view that it is important to understand the particularities of the American experience and the incredible reach of American influence and power. Nonetheless, as thinkers from Thucydides to Mark Twain have recognised, human nature is, for better and worse, fundamentally the same everywhere. Charles Murray has written that "Americans have been different as a people, even peculiar, and everyone around the world has recognised it."[8] I reject this essentialism and the notion that Americans are an essentially distinct type. Humans are not a varied species, we are all one people. American exceptionalism and anti-Americanism cloud this understanding of Americans being like the rest of us. These are two terms that reflect how often America's virtues and vices are exaggerated. Politicians and commentators who claim America is exceptional often congratulate their nation with little regard for precision or facts, or without much knowledge about other nations. Critics of America are not immune to exaggerating their case either. Just as we should be critical about the myths Americans tell each other about being a land of opportunity and righteous leader of the free world, we should also be critical of the stereotypes about Americans that have emerged around the world. These terms are useful to examine in unison in one book because they represent extreme understandings of America that are at opposite ends of the scale: anti-Americans see the United States as a terrible model for others to follow while believers in American exceptionalism view the US as a highly admirable model. Throughout the book I will argue that debates over anti-Americanism should move beyond stereotypes and caricatures of America and Americans and instead towards more sensible and profitable discussions about what America represents and symbolises.

What is anti-Americanism/What is American exceptionalism?

Before getting into the many conversations about the supposed causes and aims of anti-Americanism I want to try to define this word. Most books on anti-Americanism claim they are interested in defining this term; however, nearly all of these works soon move on to examining the supposed causes of anti-Americanism without ever really telling us what anti-Americanism is or differentiating it from mere criticism of America and its policies.[9] Instead we are told that there are "anti-Americanisms,"[10] or that it represents a family of ideas, or they repeat a line uttered by Justice Potter Stewart in his struggle to precisely define pornography: "I know it when I see it".[11] These responses are far from satisfactory: the blatant subjectivity of the Potter Stewart position makes it open to abuse, while to talk of anti-Americanisms in the plural often casts the net too wide and therefore fails to establish a difference between anti-Americanism and what would better be called criticism of America. This is one of the weaknesses of Katzenstein and Keohane's definition in *Anti-Americanisms in World Politics* (2007), which includes too many strands of "anti-Americanism" (including even Martin Luther King's call for America to be true to its ideals).[12] I travel in the opposite direction from this definitional permissiveness in this book. The first point to make is that the term is overused and often abused. Calling opposition to the second Bush administration or the American led war in Iraq, "anti-Americanism," was often misplaced at best and disingenuous at worst. Calling unfavourable ratings of America in the PEW and other global opinion surveys "anti-Americanism" is superficial, simplistic and seems aimed at increasing the publicity of such surveys. There is an important difference between talking about anti-American sentiments and anti-Americanism. The "ism" at the end of this peculiar term has a particular significance that I will explain in detail in this book.

Both anti-Americanism and American exceptionalism are contested terms, with a variety of claimed meanings. This book aims to offer durable and precise definitions to reduce this contestation. Precision and basing one's arguments on strong evidence are doubly important in the age of Trump. President Trump's standard mode of operation is to demonise his opponents using misinformation and lies. Entirely rising above this politics of name calling and bias is challenging when the president of the United States has ridden on this tactic to the highest office in the land. Taking the high road and losing is not easy to accept. In this environment avoiding anti-American thoughts is hard. For non-Americans it is challenging not to be angry at the American people for electing such an inappropriate and ill-suited person to the most powerful leadership position in the world. It is appealing to see Trump as the result of something fundamentally and uniquely malignant about American society. As tempting as these arguments are, they often overreach. In the current political climate, it is crucial to think carefully as scholars and critics about where justified criticism ends and anti-Americanism begins. This is important not just in the case of President Trump, but also with regard to how we judge American politics and foreign policy in general, and how we view the global influence of American economics and culture. This book aims to provide a basis for protecting healthy criticism from being written off as anti-Americanism. I argue this can be done by having a narrow, concise, and pejorative understanding of what anti-Americanism is.

As for the second term in the title of this book, American exceptionalism is a powerful concept in 21st century American politics. Does American exceptionalism imply that America is different from all other nations or does it imply that America is superior? The problem with the first definition is that it is a self-fulfilling prophecy, with those that believe America is exceptional looking for evidence to support their case. For example, in 1963 when Seymour Martin Lipset published *First New Nation*, he claimed Americans were exceptional because of their higher rates of university attendance than other nations. In 1996 in *American Exceptionalism: The Double Edged Sword*, Lipset posits that crime was a standout reason for seeing America as unique. In Kurt Andersen's hugely enjoyable *Fantasyland* (2018) it is religion he says that makes America exceptional.[13] The problem is Canadians now attend university at higher rates than Americans, the El Salvadorians and Hondurans have much higher crime rates, and the Poles, Maltese and Iranians can match Americans for their level of religiosity. Seeing American exceptionalism as something that can be objectively measured is a misguided project. Furthermore, in areas where America is different, often from other OECD nations, like in the provision of government welfare, we have better words like welfare laggard to describe America's more miserly welfare state. American exceptionalism is not an objective condition, rather it is a subjective belief.[14] It is an ideology. When used by American politicians, the term and idea tend to mean that America is superior to all other nations. Neal Gabler has written that:

> The hoariest and most oft-repeated cliché in American politics may be that America is the greatest country in the world. Every politician, Democrat and Republican, seems duty-bound to pander to this idea of American exceptionalism, and woe unto him who does otherwise. This country is "the last, best hope of mankind," or the "shining city on the hill" or the "great social experiment."[15]

Such talk reflects a dangerous nationalism that Americans are often blind to or think is accepted and even welcomed by other nations. President George W. Bush claimed when justifying the invasion of Afghanistan that: "We defend not only our precious freedoms, but also the freedom of people everywhere to live and raise their children free from fear."[16] Similarly in his inaugural address he declared: "So it is the policy of the United States to seek and support the growth of democratic movements and institutions in every nation and culture, with the ultimate goal of ending tyranny in our world."[17] To some, including many Americans, these sound like worthy goals of a benevolent hegemon: the exceptional role that America has in the modern world. To many others this sounds like American imperialism dressed up with soaring rhetoric. Trump, at first glance, seems to have rejected this exceptionalist mission of the US military intervening abroad to slay monsters and promote American values. However, he has not eschewed exceptionalism entirely. Trump's Jacksonian exceptionalism sees America as the greatest society on earth: this sense of superiority and a belief in the righteousness of American might in Trump's worldview gives America the right to play by its own rules while expecting other states to largely acquiesce. Trump's call to "Make America Great Again" reflects an exceptionalist and nationalistic understanding of international relations. In Trump's worldview, making America great often seems to imply making other nations worse off (particularly in trading terms) than they previously were. This book will argue that this prideful politics undermines attempts to cooperate with others and see politics in less nativist terms. The commonplace way both American exceptionalism and anti-Americanism are used reflects an age of exaggeration and hyperbole. The aim of this book is to offer more precise ways of understanding anti-Americanism and American exceptionalism that place the terms in their political contexts, but refuse to let the loudest or most powerful voices have the last say on what these words mean.

Given the breadth of antipathy implied by the term anti-Americanism it is tempting to declare the word oxymoronic: as it is surely impossible to hate a whole nation and all its people. Some have suggested the word is merely moronic: a boo word crudely employed to silence criticism. In other words, anti-Americanism operates as a term of abuse, much as the word "communist" has been used in the United States to sideline and malign opponents. The French scholar Marie-France Toinet in a searching essay in 1990 asked "Does Anti-Americanism Exist?"[18] According to a 2004 Josef Joffe essay "most Europeans will argue that anti-Americanism does not exist."[19] Jean Paul Sartre foretold these responses with his retort in 1948 that "I am not anti-American. I don't even know what the word means."[20] However, many political words lack a certain basic logic – think of neo-conservatism. Nonetheless through their regular use and circulation meanings and importance are attached to these words. Of course, the meanings given to political terms are often contested and my argument here is that academics as professional analysers of words and concepts have an important role to play in making sense of these competing meanings. As such this book is an attempt to intervene into debates about anti-Americanism to clarify and shape the meaning of this word. When we academics declare political words like anti-Americanism or Anglosphere too confused or politicised to be used we court irrelevance. The word anti-Americanism cannot be waved away like a naughty child. It is here to stay and thus requires refinement.

Anti-Americanism is a peculiar word: we have no exact equivalent for any other nation. Anti-Icelandism is incomprehensible because not much is widely known or resented about this small island nation, but even anti-Frenchism is unknown in the English language. We have Francophobia, as well as Anglophobia, Russophobia and Sinophobia, which suggests you must be a major power to have an oppositional word dedicated to your nation. However, these phobias are not entirely equivalent to anti-Americanism which suggests a deeper level of opposition, to not just to the American people and government, but to the idea of America as a model for others. To understand this term we need to ask: why the "anti" at the beginning and the "ism" at the end of this exceptional term? And what is it *specifically* about America and Americans that elicits a special type of disdain and dislike? Firstly, to the "anti": this would seem straightforward, as to be "anti" something is to be against. However, "anti" politics often creates more heat than light. Think of debates over anti-globalisation or anti-communism – these are often rancorous debates where caricature is commonplace. Such debates are typified by strong claims, denials, and counterclaims. Hence we have anti-anti-Communists and even anti-anti-anti-Communists. If ideologies are seen by many as rigid dogmas, then anti-ideologies like anti-communism are often unsubtle attacks on caricatured dogmas. This is political discourse at its rough and readiest, and as a result is often ignored or poorly analysed by academics. This leads us into the world of ideologies and *isms* that is too frequently overlooked because it is considered too crude, with ideas deployed as weapons. Martin Heidegger in *What is a Thing?* contended that: "Every mere *ism* is a misunderstanding and the death of history."[21] This is often the case when it comes to *anti* ideologies like anti-communism and anti-Americanism where distortion and a lack of historical awareness are commonplace. Nonetheless there is a place for ideological analysis as Michael Freeden has ably shown in his corpus of scholarship which argues for the place of *isms* to help simplify discussions about important ideas. Drawing inspiration from Freeden's work, this book examines American exceptionalism and anti-Americanism as ideological concepts, an approach that clearly differentiates this book from other works on this topic.

The reason for opposition to America rising to the level of an "anti" position, akin to anti-capitalism, anti-communism, anti-Catholicism or anti-Semitism, has to do with the importance that has been accorded to the American experience, by Americans and outsiders, since the settlement of the American colonies.[22] In other words, enough people need to care (or to be more exact dislike something) for opposition to be called "anti"-such-and-such. Talking of anti-Finlandism in most parts of the world would be not just ridiculous but unlikely to be even vaguely understood by most people. Alternatively anti-Americanism makes far more immediate sense as an oppositional stance to things like American foreign policy, cultural products or leaders. Similarly, while anti-Cameronism sounds entirely contrived, anti-Thatcherism still means something three decades after Margaret Thatcher's prime ministership, because Thatcher was widely seen to be not just another prime minister, but an embodiment of significant ideas. The "ism" is tagged on the end of anti-Thatcherism because Thatcher's policies and period as Prime Minister were seen as a watershed period in British politics: she was seen to promote a more overtly ideological agenda that installed a new neoliberal economics system. Treating Thatcher as the sole change agent, like treating America as different from all other nations, is exaggerated. Prime Minister James Callaghan's decision in 1976 to prioritise tackling inflation over tackling unemployment was a key turning point against Keynesianism in the UK. Furthermore, as the scholars David Marsh and Colin Hay have shown the UK state did not shrink under Thatcher but developed a new rhetoric and new priorities.[23] Just like Thatcher was not seen as just another PM, America is viewed as more than just another country. From the settlement of America by religious minorities to the establishment of a Constitutional democracy to America's early development of mass popular culture and mass consumerism, Europeans (and others) have viewed America as a model, as a vision of the future as de Tocqueville called America in the 1830s. This rendition of American history and political culture tends to exaggerate America's differences from other nations and ignores its many similarities. It reflects what I call the ideology of American exceptionalism. Non-Americans buy into this view of America as unique with their regular refrain "only in America." Many presidents have repeated this notion that America was born different and has continued to be so. For instance, Obama in his 2011 State of the Union address asserted: "What's more, we are the first nation to be founded for the sake of an idea – the idea that each of us deserves the chance to shape our own destiny. That's why centuries of pioneers and immigrants have risked everything to come here."[24] The notion that in America people shape their own destiny has been crucial to the idea of American exceptionalism. Charles Murray suggests this idea is at the core of the concept. The problem with this argument is social mobility for the poor in America – immigrants and non-immigrants – is far less impressive than many other OECD countries including France or Germany.[25]

Pride, prejudice and precision

Debates over what anti-Americanism is have been heavily influenced by the umbrage some Americans have taken to verbal attacks, or at least perceived attacks, on their nation and its character. This is a long-standing trend that Max Paul Friedman has very convincingly traced back to colonial times.[26] In many ways, large and small, the American tendency to defensive nationalism and patriotism, what de Tocqueville called the "annoying patriotism" of Americans, leads to criticism often being falsely labelled anti-Americanism. This tendency has undoubtedly cheapened a number of important policy debates: this can be seen in debates over subjects from health care to military interventions. Reasonable arguments are too often dismissed in American debates as being "too European" or "too French" and are contrasted with supposedly muscular, virile, and exceptional American policies. On the domestic front American politicians have generally shown too little interest in learning from other like nations on how to have cheaper and more universal health care coverage. For example, Speaker John Boehner when opposing Obamacare – which brought America more into line with other more universalist health care systems – proclaimed with seemingly little interest in other national models that America had "the best health care delivery system in the world."[27] In terms of American foreign policy, exceptionalism and nationalist instincts have led to Americans not taking advice from other nations at key moments in its history. Friedman lays out in considerable detail in *Rethinking Anti-Americanism* the example of Americans writing off French advice as anti-Americanism in the early 1960s regarding the difficulties of winning a war in Vietnam. Similarly, in the lead up to the 2003 Iraq War American leaders dismissed the advice of their counterparts elsewhere who were strongly questioning the wisdom of invading Iraq. Donald Rumsfeld infamously waved away the concerns from the French and German leaders as the anti-Americanism of "Old Europe." This history makes it tempting to dismiss anti-Americanism as a contrived word deployed to avoid listening to advice from others. This is true to a large extent, but it is not the whole story. Anti-Americanism is also a useful word to explain the existence of collective prejudices against the US and its people. Hence there is a point of the *ism* at the end of this unusual word. In this sense it is worth comparing anti-Americanism and anti-Semitism. Anti-Americanism is certainly not as damaging nor dangerous as anti-Semitism, so seeing anti-Americanism and anti-Semitism as "twin brothers" as Andrei Markovits does is mistaken.[28] However, both are collective prejudices, which stereotype a people (Jews or Americans) as fundamentally different to other people, and a nation (Israel or America) as uniquely malevolent. In seeking to strengthen critiques of the failings of Americans and America this book disavows anti-American stereotyping that overreaches by presenting America as an exceptionally evil nation.

I will argue in this book that anti-Americanism is most sensibly viewed as a prejudice against Americans or America. It occurs when people move from criticising particular individuals or policies to essentialist commentary. For example, there are plenty of overweight people in America, as any local or visitor can readily see. Statistically obesity is a very serious problem in the US, as it is in many other countries. World Health Organization figures show Americans as the leader of the pack on global obesity rates. In 2016 36% of American adults were estimated to be obese compared to 35% in Saudi Arabia, 31% in New Zealand, 30% in Canada, 29% in Australia and 22% in France. Based on the evidence saying "all Americans are fat" is a clear case of anti-Americanism; just as the claim that all Americans are loud, stupid and boastful is clearly anti-Americanism. What of more complex cases such as the claim that Americans are less interested and know less about the rest of the world than people in other nations. Or that American foreign policy is uniquely self-righteous and naïve. I would argue we should use the normal markers of prejudice to judge the anti-Americanism of a claim or action. These are the key questions to ask: does a statement or action show a lack of differentiation between people, is it biased, does it fixate on the weirdest aspects of the society, is it exaggerated or one-sided, does it show an indifference to contradictory evidence, or does it fail to differentiate between the people of a nation and their government's policies. The indiscriminate nature of the terrorist attacks on the World Trade Center on September 11, 2001 make them a very easy example of anti-Americanism. In other more complex cases judgment is clearly needed. Below I set out five observations about how best to define anti-Americanism to help clear-headed judgments to be able to be made about what is and is not anti-Americanism.

1. It is important to differentiate criticism from anti-Americanism. Without this, on one hand critics of America will be unfairly demonised and on the other hand prejudiced arguments will be taken more seriously than they should be. To separate criticism from anti-Americanism a more precise definition of anti-Americanism is necessary.

2. The most precise and sensible way to examine anti-Americanism is to view it as a prejudice with the usual markers of prejudice: prejudgement, bias, lack of differentiation of different Americans or American policies, exaggeration, fixation on the worst American actions, conspiratorial thinking, and one-sided arguments. This sets a high standard for what is considered anti-Americanism

and challenges the frequent overuse and abuse of this term. However, this approach only takes us part of the way to a useful and meaningful definition.

3. Much of what is called anti-Americanism would be more precisely labelled as a variant of one of the following: anti-imperialism, anti-hegemonic sentiment, anti-capitalism, anti-militarism, anti-globalism, anti-Christian sentiment or anti-modernism. What is interesting and most useful to study is to focus on the word itself and from that obvious starting point ask what it is *specifically about America* that causes so much antipathy that this commentary is called anti-Americanism. Put simply, what is it that people see as *uniquely*, or *typically, American* that so aggravates them? For example, why is it often claimed that Americans take up capitalist ideas in a particularly extreme and vulgar fashion. This movement from specific complaints to general views about America creates the "ism" on the end of the term, which is what makes the term most interesting.

4. To get at the origins of this term and the specific things about America that have been strongly disliked a focus on the history of how America has been seen by visitors and internal dissenters is crucial to understanding this term. This approach focuses on the continuities in the term, however without ignoring various discontinuities.

5. Lastly, specific criticisms are regularly expanded into broadsides against American society in general. In other words, American failings are not just seen as singular failings but as collective failings. This tendency is partly the result of America being viewed as an idea or an ideology, a way of being, that is different from other nations.

To summarise, anti-Americanism is most usefully understood as a collective or ideological prejudice. Thus anti-Americanism does not simply mean opposition to certain American policies or Americans it connotes opposition in a broader sense against what America symbolises. James Ceaser and Andrei Markovits have both described this as opposition to what America supposedly "is" as opposed to disagreements with what America "does".[29] This understanding is a little too neat because what America does often leads to disapproval of not just particular actions but of America in general. Therefore, it is important to acknowledge that in anti-American discourse what American "does" and "is" are frequently intertwined. Furthermore, even what individual Americans do is frequently generalised to show something supposedly insightful about what America as a whole is like.

Stereotyping Americans or do Americans stereotype themselves?

The tendency to generalise about America and stereotype Americans is easy to recognise if we examine the origins of anti-Americanism. Travellers to the New World in the late eighteenth and early nineteenth centuries were forever looking for ways of summing up this new nation the United States of America. This new world nation quickly fascinated Europeans who wanted to know what was

different about America. Not surprisingly individual experiences led to generalisations: John Keats' family lost money so Americans were a nation of swindlers;
Charles Dickens although he was paid significant amounts of money for a lecture
tour of America was denied copyright payments so in his literature and essays he
satirised Americans' "worship of the almighty dollar" (a phrase he coined) and for
their financial untrustworthiness; Frances Trollope experienced the rough and
ready eating habits of Americans on the frontier leading to her decrying America as
almost totally wanting of manners and refinement. Others could not find the types
of conversation, architecture or culture they enjoyed in Europe and thus dismissed
Americans as an uncouth, unsophisticated and uncultured people. Of course not all
of those who reported back to the Old World about America caricatured it and
most travellers had a variety of positive and negative things to say, however, it was
the extremes that were remembered (and frequently the most negative extremes).
America quickly became a land of extremes in how it was described: it was over-
sold as the land of opportunity and liberty (America the exceptional) and exaggerated as a nation of cheats, boasters, and ignoramuses (America the backwater). It
was from these negative stereotypes that anti-Americanism emerged. The tendency
to generalise and stereotype when talking about the people of a particular nation is
of course a very common human trait and America is not alone in receiving this
treatment. What is significant about stereotypes about America is how powerful
and widely held they are. For example, within days of hearing about Sarah Palin's
2008 interview with Katie Couric where her foreign policy knowledge was shown
to be extremely scant, millions of people around the globe had adopted strongly
negative opinions about her as one of those typically ignorant Americans.[30] This
occurred because people near and far have a sense of this type of American who is
extremely insular but very confident. They have seen the stereotype in many
books, films, comedy sketches, and cartoons. Palin deserved the derision as she was
running for one of the most important leadership positions in world politics without a rudimentary knowledge of foreign affairs. However, whether her weaknesses
represent a people who are uniquely ignorant and insular, but overconfident is a
more complex matter. Similarly, the Australian conservative cartoonist Bill Leak
once commented that it was difficult to draw George W. Bush because he was
already a caricature.

The literary critic Peter Conrad has suggested that "Americans lend themselves"
to this stereotyping "because they are so preoccupied with the stresses of personal
identity and the collective unease of national identity, and so fond of seeing
themselves in symbolic terms. They have the habit of abstractness. Rather than
simply and unselfconsciously living, they are critical spectators of their own
lives."[31] Quickly we see the connection between what might be called Americanism and anti-Americanism. Conrad is suggesting that Americans behave as
though they are characters in a television sit-com with the camera forever on them.
Furthermore, Americans have a strong tendency of seeing their own life as a personification of the national mission and story. Barack Obama was particularly
inclined to present his life in this fashion and claimed frequently that "in no other

country on Earth is my story even possible."[32] He presented his election victory in 2008 as America fulfilling its promise and its dreams.[33] Not surprisingly this sense of American exceptionalism and grandiosity invites admirers and admonishers. Obama is far from alone in seeing himself as a personification of his nation's story. Frequently American autobiographies and biographies have the words "An American Life" somewhere in their title. Memoirs by Reagan and Sarah Palin not surprisingly use these words as do biographies about Jerry Garcia, Andrew Mellon, George Kennan, Condoleezza Rice, Burt Lancaster, Martha Washington, Ben Hogan, George Washington, Jesse Owens, Oral Roberts and Benjamin Franklin (as do many more books on less well-known individuals).[34] A noted Franklin biography is titled "The First American". Another popular title is "An American Journey" used in the title of Colin Powell's autobiography and one of the biographies of Bill Clinton (as well as several other biographies). This tendency is nowhere near as common in other countries: in fact I am yet to find in library searches one biography or memoir titled "An English Life/Journey" or "A British Life/Journey" (a title I presume the English would see as arrogant and presumptuous). My point here is that it is hardly surprising that non-Americans have created a powerful set of stereotypes and myths about Americans when Americans themselves have been so obsessed about their own national identity and what the quintessential American values are and who the true American is. At the 2016 Republican Party convention the former Happy Days actor Scott Baio said "let's make America great again. But let's make America America again."[35] As though there is an agreed upon sense of what America truly symbolises and stands for. In 2008 Palin said to an audience in Englewood, Colorado:

> We believe that the best of America is in these small towns that we get to visit, and in these wonderful little pockets of what I call the real America, being here with all of you hard working very patriotic, very, pro-America areas of this great nation. This is where we find the kindness and the goodness and the courage of everyday Americans.[36]

Barack Obama challenged certain stereotypes about who could be elected president and who truly represented America. However, not all Americans accepted a man with a white mother and black father as the face of 21st century America. One particularly ugly response was the "Birther" movement, led by Donald Trump, which claimed that Obama was not born in America (and was a Muslim). This was aimed at portraying him as not a real American. A disturbing number of Americans believed this misinformation: a *Time* magazine poll in 2010 found that 24% of Americans thought Obama was a Muslim,[37] and a 2011 Gallup poll showed that only 56% of Americans thought Obama was born in the USA.[38] Despite this racism, Obama was elected and re-elected US president and in terms of American myth making and exceptionalism, Obama seemed to be in many regards a politician from central casting. The man sent to restore faith in the American dream and America's founding values. A man for non-Americans to embrace as the reasoned leader of the free world. This sense of restoring hope is expressed in Obama's victory speech in November 2008 when he proclaimed: "If there is anyone out there who still doubts that America is a place where all things are possible, who still wonders if the dream of our founders is alive in our time, who still questions the power of our democracy, tonight is your answer."[39] In other words, Obama was saying his victory restored the American dream and American exceptionalism.

Why do people hate America?

American presidential elections, speeches, and bloopers, American foreign policy, American movies, music, food, television, computer games and celebrities are more broadly known than the politics, culture and people of any other single country. As a result, "America" is a common reference point, a *lingua franca*, a threat, a friend, and a source of anxiety for the peoples of the world. Given this breadth of influence it is hardly surprising that anti-Americanism, pro-Americanism, and widespread ambivalence toward the United States exists in all societies. This book calls for debates on America to proceed armed with information and evidence rather than cant and prejudice. As the most powerful state in the world, America will rightly be the focus of much attention and, frequently, criticism. However, there is a difference between criticism, which is healthy and necessary, and anti-Americanism, which is prejudicial and often counterproductive. A central characteristic of this prejudice is that it reduces American society and policies to a series of tropes and caricatures, ignoring the fact that this is one of the most diverse countries on earth. To return to the television metaphor, anti-Americanism is often based on an unwillingness to see America as a "variety show" with appealing, unappealing and indeed mundane features. In the realm of foreign affairs, anti-Americanism is often the result of a disinterest in differentiating between various US actions and policies, fixating instead on the worst aspects of America's role in international relations.

What are the principal causes and objects of anti-Americanism? Some obvious candidates would be: American manners, gun-slinging cowboys, Wall Street, "over here, oversexed, overpaid" GIs, Dresden, Hiroshima, gum-chewing, the Korean War, Coca-Cola, the CIA in Guatemala, Iran and Chile, Hollywood, the Vietnam War, Ronald Reagan, Cruise missiles, religiosity, support for Israel, MTV, McDonald's, Guantánamo Bay, SUVs, unilateralism, the 2003 Iraq War, George W. Bush, and Donald Trump. As these answers suggest, anti-Americanism is not just a response to what America does around the world but also what it symbolises. Just as McDonald's represents more than a hamburger company, these names and events are catch-cries for what is wrong with America and its role in the world. Every bellicose American president is a gun-slinging cowboy in the cartoon pages of the world press. Wall Street, well before Oliver Stone's movie, was synonymous with greed and corporate ruthlessness. American SUVs are not only blamed for global warming, they are seen as a sign of American arrogance.[40] Or as Amnesty International states: "Guantánamo Bay has become a symbol of injustice and abuse in the US administration's 'war on terror'."[41] As contradictory as this list is, all of the items on it have engendered animosity and at times hatred toward the US.

However, which of these animosities can fairly be called anti-Americanism and which are better seen as criticism is too often left unanswered, or if addressed, is done so in an overly partisan manner.

The structure of this book

To confront this crucial question of "what is anti-Americanism?" I attempt in the first chapter of this book to set a standard for what constitutes anti-Americanism. I outline different conceptual understandings of the term, look at the merits and weaknesses of various definitions, and conclude that anti-Americanism is best understood as a prejudice that has, at times, ideological overtones. I situate this conceptual debate in the post-9/11 context. The chapter relies upon opinion polling data, particularly the invaluable Pew surveys, to document the recent highs and lows of anti-American sentiment, but argues that these polls should be the starting point, rather than the endpoint, for understanding the concept. Two events in the early 21st century have made anti-Americanism one of the central issues of our age: the terrorist attacks of September 11, 2001 and the Iraq War. 9/11 was the most quintessential anti-American act in modern history, fulfilling all sensible definitions of anti-Americanism because of its indiscriminate malice against America and Americans. The terrorist attacks precipitated a wide-ranging debate about the successes and failings of American foreign policy and American society; some in these debates suggested that America had brought these attacks upon itself. Whether such views were anti-American quickly became the subject of even more heated debate. The second critical event in debates about anti-Americanism was the US decision to go to war against Iraq in 2003, an action that clearly led to much negativity world-wide, not only toward the Bush administration, but also toward America more generally. This decision, and the post-invasion quagmire in Iraq, gave a particular edge to debates about America. The disastrous war in Iraq and the Bush Jnr and Trump presidencies have highlighted the importance of effective criticism, and in my view also the importance of not sliding into anti-Americanism when opposing US policies, politics and culture. To defend this argument I have attempted to craft a more precise and negative definition of how anti-Americanism should be sensibly defined. From the broad and varied commentary on the topic, I have extracted five understandings of how the term is generally used. Simply stated, these competing conceptions can be characterised as anti-Americanism first as one side of a dichotomy, second as a tendency, third as a pathology, fourth as a prejudice and fifth as an ideology. By crafting a more precise definition I aim to convince readers that there are fairly easily discernible ways in which anti-Americanism can be differentiated from criticism.

Chapter 2 charts the historical course of anti-Americanism through two complementary approaches, firstly by offering a brief history of the key literature on anti-Americanism and the insights this has provided and secondly by detailing the historical development of the anti-American tradition. I will detail the latter by examining what I see as four overlapping waves of anti-Americanism: cultural, political/military, economic, and terrorist. I will argue that anti-American prejudice is most instructively understood as a tradition that began to take shape in the early 19th century when a set of negative stereotypes emerged about America that have been recycled and developed upon ever since. These negative opinions were principally focused on the alleged backwardness and boorishness of both America's culture and its people. In the early 1830s in Europe, a common view developed that America was, to use the phrase employed by Andrei Markovits, an "uncouth nation".[42] This anti-American tradition has ebbed and flowed in its usage and prominence ever since, being more obvious and visible in some periods than in others. This tradition jostles with other meta-narratives (such as American exceptionalism) for public attention. Certain presidents animate the anti-American tradition in a unique way: note the remarkable differences between how George W. Bush and Barack Obama are viewed by the European populaces.[43] The American president is seen as symbolising his nation in a manner unparalleled by any other modern democracy. America has always been a source of significant European fantasy and projection. It has been claimed that Europeans did not discover America, rather that they invented it. It is hard to deny that mythology has played an especially important role in American society and politics. The European myths regarding the first explorers and pilgrims were largely positive, with America portrayed as the Golden Land, the chosen land and even the New Jerusalem.[44] However, anti-American attitudes can be found in commentary on the early American colonies. In its earliest forms, the belittling of America (the continent as much as the British American colonies) often focused on the so-called degenerate New World environment and its supposedly inferior animals. The humid New World climate was often commented on as making people incapable of serious thought or human achievement. This ecological scaremongering about the US as a barren and deformed environment has been explored by Andrei Markovits,[45] Philippe Roger,[46] James Ceaser,[47] and most comprehensively by Antonello Gerbi.[48] Once these early environmental dismissals of America waned, the United States of America was principally critiqued as a cultural wasteland (i.e. as Europe's cultural inferior). This denunciation has been the most central and lasting strand of the anti-American tradition and has been most evident in the commonplace negative responses around the world to presidents George W. Bush and Donald Trump. There is usually an underlying cultural element to negative responses to these American leaders, with a large percentage of the world's population seeing them as uncultured, uncouth and ignorant; such mockery draws on a long anti-American tradition that has firm cultural foundations.

Chapter 3 on Australian anti-Americanism aims to answer the conceptual question of how we better differentiate between anti-Americanism and criticism. To help establish criteria to enable differentiation I analyse two case studies of Australian reportage. The first details aspects of the Australian national broadcaster's coverage of the 2003 Iraq War while the second case study examines coverage of the Korean War by the journalist Wilfred Burchett. In the case of the Australian Broadcasting Corporation's (ABC's) coverage of the 2003 Iraq War there were formal allegations from the conservative government of Australia at the time that the coverage was an example of anti-Americanism within the ABC. Internal and independent inquiries were set up to determine whether the coverage was anti-American and the vast weight of evidence which the chapter explores suggests this charge of anti-Americanism was falsely made in an attempt to silence criticism of the government's ill-conceived involvement in the Iraq War. In stark contrast, the second case is one where the term anti-Americanism is fairly used. I will detail how in the case of his reporting of the Korean War Wilfred Burchett acted as a Chinese propagandist rather than as an "independent journalist" (a label he claimed to describe his approach). My arguments about Burchett centre on him spreading false information about the American use of bacterial warfare in the Korean War. American conduct in the Korean War deserves to be closely scrutinised and criticised. Their engagement in extensive bombing campaigns against civilians in the Korean War, as they had done in Japan at the end of WWII, deserved more analysis at the time and today than it has received. However, what did receive significant coverage in the socialist press in Europe was the claim that American pilots dropped infected insects on North Korea. The best evidence we have shows that this did not actually occur; rather it was a Chinese-conceived propaganda campaign that Wilfred Burchett played an integral role in constructing and disseminating.

Chapter 4 illustrates the importance of who the American president is to non-Americans, and considers how the rise and fall of negative sentiment toward the United States tends to depend on whether a Democrat or a Republican is in the White House. The Pew surveys on global attitudes towards the US strongly support this claim.[49] A case in point is the presidency of George W. Bush, which saw an historical low point for global attitudes towards the US. There were good reasons for this: at the top of the list of complaints was Bush's extremely unwise decision to invade Iraq. Bush and his administration dismissed their critics in simplistic, patronising and unfair ways. Dissenters were said to be on the side of the terrorists or Saddam Hussein. The challenge for those who disapproved of Bush was to find fault with his knowledge, beliefs and decision-making approach without falling into long standing anti-American stereotypes. Without ignoring the degree to which the administration's policies at home and abroad have fed the stereotypical portrayal of Bush as a "know-nothing cowboy" from Texas, the chapter draws our attention to the degree to which Bush's presidential style distracted many foreign observers from the substance of his policies. This obsession with style draws on old anti-American themes that make it difficult for non-Americans to understand why so many Americans could have voted for Bush in 2004, and at times undermines the prospect for critical engagement with policy rather than personality.

In Chapter 5 the book's focus turns to understanding "what is American exceptionalism?" Since Barack Obama was asked in 2009 if he believed in American exceptionalism, like other US presidents did, the term has been very widely used in American politics and media commentary. However, academics have had too little to say on this topic. Hilde Eliassen Restad's *American Exceptionalism: An Idea that Made a Nation and Remade the World* is a recent and noteworthy exception, but in the major political science journals the topic of American exceptionalism has been largely ignored. This quietism is especially unfortunate as esteemed political scientists such as Seymour Martin Lipset and Byron Shafer were once the most prominent writers on this topic. My chapter does not simply bemoan the quietism of political science on the topic of American exceptionalism, it also offers a new way of studying the term. This new approach firstly recognises how the term is used in popular discourse and argues this vernacular understanding of the term is a more accurate way of analysing American exceptionalism than seeing the term in a comparative sense as political scientists have tended to do. Secondly, I advocate an approach that attempts to avoid the pitfalls of the comparative approach to studying American exceptionalism pioneered by Lipset, which tends to look for statistical evidence to affirm that America is indeed exceptional, at the expense of also acknowledging the ways these differences with other nations have changed over time and how America also shares much in common with many other countries.[50] I argue that American exceptionalism is best understood as an ideology that is an important component of American nationalism. In the popular press, the idea of American nationalism has been much discussed in regard to the 2003 Iraq War and the rise of Donald Trump. I would argue that nationalism is in fact a persistent feature of American politics (and the politics of all nations rightly understood). However, in academic writing American nationalism has not been investigated as much as is warranted: my chapter is a step towards addressing this weakness. Lastly, the chapter argues the term ideology is more useful than is often recognised by political scientists when analysing contemporary politics. To make the case for ideological analysis I draw on the scholarship of Michael Freeden, which is highly regarded in the United Kingdom, but rarely cited or used in American political science. The chapter aims to bridge the gap between political science and popular understandings of American exceptionalism. My starting point is that claims of American exceptionalism are ultimately claims of superiority: such claims are dangerous as they lead to hubris and hinder persistent problems like inequality being seriously addressed. My message to political scientists is that this is a contested term that you once had a lot to say about and should once again care and write about. My message to general readers of the chapter is that the notion of American exceptionalism prevents America from seeing the constitution as a living document that has strengths and weaknesses, from developing policies to address America's gaping inequalities, and from taking a more circumspect view of what America can achieve beyond its borders.

Chapter 6 on American ignorance and insularity explores three questions. First, do we have enough evidence to judge whether Americans are less knowledgeable about the rest of the world than people in other industrialised nations? Second, the limited evidence available suggests Americans are poorly informed, why is this the case? Third, does this ignorance matter and specifically is this likely to be a significant cause of US global decline? The statistical evidence I have gathered from the Pew Research Center, National Geographic and other surveys suggests that Americans in fact do seem particularly ignorant about global affairs. This survey evidence is reinforced by the small body of high-quality scholarly research on this topic.[51] The most obvious reason for this ignorance is due to America's sense of exceptionalism and innate insularity and the impact this has on all levels of education, the US media, and on national politics. On the third question of whether this ignorance about global affairs matters, I would suggest that ignorance matters more today in our globalised world than ever. In the 19th century America's self-obsession was arguably one of its strengths,[52] which saw it develop rapidly without getting too embroiled in other people's wars and conflicts. During the Cold War American ignorance about foreign affairs was dangerous to other nations, particularly in the Third World. When it came to American involvement in conflicts in Latin America and Africa during the Cold War, George Orwell's famous quote about the nationalist mindset seems to aptly describe the average American's knowledge of their nation's many Cold War interventions: "The nationalist not only does not disapprove of atrocities committed by his own side, but he has a remarkable capacity for not even hearing about them."[53] America's Cold War record did diminish American standing and often led to very reasonable claims of hypocrisy. However, the survey evidence suggests amongst America's European allies, America was always seen more "favourably" than "unfavourably" by the general public.[54] Sentiment was likely to be rather different in Iran, Guatemala, Vietnam and Nicaragua during the Cold War. In the post-Cold War era American interventions have been viewed very unfavourably across the globe, even by its European allies. The election of Trump has also been widely condemned and led to very unfavourable survey results about America's standing in the world.[55] Perceived American ignorance particularly regarding the decision to invade Iraq and inaction on climate change has played an important role in increasing and animating criticism of America in the post-Cold War period. I argue in Chapter 6 that more research is required to understand the degree of this ignorance and the role that it plays in supporting ideas that are conspiratorial and lack a strong evidential basis. There is undoubtedly an instinct, outside of America, to believe the worst about American knowledge and understanding of the world. Countless comedians have drawn upon this stereotype of the clueless American. Analysis of American ignorance can easily slide into anti-Americanism when it forgets how limited knowledge about global affairs is in so many countries. However, the desire for the American people to be more aware of their nation's global imprint and the impact of American interventions in other societies is entirely reasonable and far from an anti-American instinct.

It is common for people to claim that Donald Trump's election victory and presidency changes everything we understood about politics; furthermore, the Trump phenomenon is often contended to be unprecedented and many claim Trump's election could only have occurred in America. Chapter 7 challenges these arguments by showing how Trump is more familiar than is often contended and how the so-called Ugly American traits that Trump is seen to personify are more globally apparent than non-Americans often want to admit. Because Trump is so frequently viewed as sui generis – as unique, unpredictable, and often inexplicable – his election has been less of a source of anti-Americanism than George W. Bush's electoral success was. People around the world are disappointed in those who voted for Trump, but they are also dumbfounded about Trump's success and this confusion has tended to keep a lid on knee-jerk anti-Americanism. Most people's criticisms and frustrations are directed at the man himself. Furthermore, it is widely understood that Trump is not the only populist politician or campaign to be surprisingly successful in recent times around the world. As with Bush, Trump's personality has been the focus of constant global attention, and like Bush, Trump is viewed as personifying a number of negative aspects of American culture, particularly the tendency to boast about wealth and success. However, these perceptions about Trump have led to less anti-Americanism than they did during the Bush era because it is more apparent to non-Americans that opposition to Trump is more vocal and sustained than it was during the Bush years.

My final chapter will argue that just because Trump constantly used attention-seeking shock tactics to dominate the news cycle as a candidate and, since becoming president, to shape or change the narrative, we should be less shocked by him than most media coverage primes us to be. This is because in many ways the Trump campaign and presidency is politics catching up with popular culture. Or possibly politics is being taken over and becoming a sub-branch of popular culture. Liberal democratic theory has led us to believe that politics is guided by certain norms and principles which result in politics in democracies like the US having more exalted standards and a stronger moral code than the anything goes – entertain us! – character of modern popular culture. The Trump presidency is showing us in stark terms that the belief that the political and cultural realms are separate was a naïve myth. Recognising this, the crucial question then becomes: Can liberal democratic politics resist being ethically hollowed out by popular cultural trends? This chapter will argue that extreme cultural forms – namely punk, pornography, shock-jocks, anti-PC comedies like *South Park*, confessional television, World Wrestling Entertainment, 4chan,[56] trolling, and on-screen violence as entertainment – all made the rise of Donald Trump as a successful candidate possible and far less shocking to many voters than is often claimed. How this is integrally related to anti-Americanism is that America's unique weakness has long been seen as its puerile and uncouth popular culture: its freak shows, its soap operas, its rock 'n' roll, its violent movies, and its reality television. However, it is increasingly erroneous to see American popular culture as being significantly distinct from popular culture in many other places, furthermore popular culture is increasingly hybrid and transnational.

Finally, the chapter ends by exploring how America has become less exceptional in its foreign policy rhetoric and mindset under the Trump presidency. Trump himself has argued the term "American exceptionalism" is an "insult" to other nations and that he does not like the term.[57] This is a departure from the orthodox and almost liturgical promotion of the idea that America is exceptional: the term has become a commonplace chorus line in presidential speeches, particularly since Reagan was elected in 1980. However, Trump's nationalism is more orthodox in America and elsewhere than is often acknowledged. Undoubtedly, his nationalism is more naked, bellicose, and at times more frightening, but all presidents are nationalists and to pretend otherwise was another myth that Americans like to tell themselves. The claim that nationalism was just a European disease was never true but much circulated: the paucity of serious books on American nationalism beyond Anatol Lieven's excellent *America Right or Wrong* and a few other titles is evidence of the power of this myth. My book concludes by arguing that the problem with Trump is not solely that he is a nationalist (like all other political leaders), but the problem is his nationalism is not moderated by policy-orientated and generally more pragmatic ideas like realism and liberalism; rather it is animated by populist beliefs. This heady mix of nationalistic populism is far from just an American exception, rather it afflicts many countries in the 21st century. Across the globe, populist nationalism is a significant hindrance to saner policies being developed within nations, and to peaceful cooperation being achieved between nations.

As extreme and as frightening as Trump is, his politics, and the social, economic and cultural forces that helped bring him to power are familiar across the globe. In a number of ways this means that America is no longer on the pedestal that it had long placed itself upon. It is difficult to judge how permanent this new posture is, but the current impact is that anti-Americanism and American exceptionalism are less significant terms than they once were. In other words, as America becomes perceived from within and from the outside as just another nation with the regular problems and struggles that most nations face, despite its power and often triumphant history, seeing Americans as a unique super-species or sub-species becomes harder to sustain. Positive mythmaking and the perceived need to denigrate America in order to keep its hubris in check are not what they once were. This is because these myths are no longer as believable as they once were, about the superiority of America's constitutional system, that social and economic mobility was greater in America than everywhere else, and the supreme myth that America had a special guiding role to play in world affairs.[58] The heavy weight of evidence has undermined, significantly although not entirely, these commonplace claims. As for the desires of other nations to bring America down a peg or two, this seems less noticeable and possibly less necessary in the Trump era when the denigration of the United States is increasingly self-inflicted.

Notes

1 Michael Flynn, "GOP Convention Primetime Speech" (Convention held in Cleveland, Ohio, July 18, 2016), <https://www.prnewswire.com/news-releases/gop-convention-primetime-speech-text-embargoed-for-delivery-300300379.html>.
2 Sarah Palin, *America by Heart* (New York, NY: Harper Collins, 2013), 69; Charles Murray has argued that "Historically, Americans have been different as a people, even peculiar, and everyone around the world has recognised it…the signature of American exceptionalism – the assumption by most Americans that they are in control of their own destinies." Murray goes on to say that this is not a belief that people in other nations have, in fact "No other country comes close." Charles Murray, "Charles Murray Irving Kristol Lecture: The Happiness of the People" (Lecture at AEI Annual Dinner Address, March 11, 2009), <http://www.aei.org/publication/the-happiness-of-the-people/>. Jonah Golberg also quotes *The Incredibles* to disapprove of Obama's 2009 statement

in Strasbourg on exceptionalism in "The Bashing of American Exceptionalism," *LA Times*, November 09, 2010, <http://articles.latimes.com/2010/nov/09/opinion/la-oe-goldberg-exceptionalism-20101109>.

3 Seymour Martin Lipset in 1963 in *First New Nation* argued that Americans are more ambitious and committed to social egalitarianism than people elsewhere and that made them exceptional. Seymour Martin Lipset, *The First New Nation* (New York, NY: W. W. Norton & Company, 1963). For Charles Murray in 2009 it is Americans' optimism that makes America exceptional. Charles Murray, "Charles Murray Irving Kristol Lecture: The Happiness of the People" (Lecture at AEI Annual Dinner Address, March 11, 2009), <http://www.aei.org/publication/the-happiness-of-the-people/>.

4 Sarah Palin in *America by Heart* approvingly quotes Richard Lowry and Ramesh Ponnuru's widely circulated essay in conservative circles which claims: "Our country has always been exceptional. It is freer, more individualistic, more democratic, and more open and dynamic than any other nation on earth. These qualities are the bequest of our Founding and of our cultural heritage. They have always marked America as special, with a unique role and mission in the world: as a model of ordered liberty and self-government and as an exemplar of freedom and a vindicator of it, through persuasion when possible and force of arms when absolutely necessary." Ramesh Ponnuru and Rich Lowry, "An Exceptional Debate," *National Review*, February 18, 2010, <https://www.nationalreview.com/magazine/2010/03/08/exceptional-debate/>.

5 Newt Gingrich, *A Nation Like No Other: Why American Exceptionalism Matters* (New York, NY: Simon and Schuster, 2011), 13.

6 Peter Beinart, "How the GOP Will Help Get Obama Re-Elected in 2012," *The Daily Beast*, February 11, 2010, <https://www.thedailybeast.com/how-the-gop-will-help-get-obama-re-elected-in-2012>; Jonah Golberg "The Bashing of American Exceptionalism," *LA Times*, November 09, 2010, <http://articles.latimes.com/2010/nov/09/opinion/la-oe-goldberg-exceptionalism-20101109>.

7 Mathis-Lilley and Wade in a 2015 article list 13 times when Barack Obama called America the greatest nation on earth, Ben Mathis-Lilley and Chris Wade, "Watch Barack Obama Talk About How America is the Greatest Country on Earth in 13 Different Speeches," *Slate*, February, 20, 2015. See also Glenn Kessler, "Giuliani's False Claims about Obama's Speeches." *The Washington Post*. February 22, 2015, <https://www.washingtonpost.com/news/fact-checker/wp/2015/02/22/giulianis-false-claims-about-obamas-speeches/?utm_term=.a0163f207458>.

8 Charles Murray, "Charles Murray Irving Kristol Lecture: The Happiness of the People" (Lecture at AEI Annual Dinner Address, March 11, 2009), <http://www.aei.org/publication/the-happiness-of-the-people/>.

9 This criticism is particularly apt for Peter J. Katzenstein and Robert O. Keohane's *Anti-Americanisms in World Politics* (Ithaca, NY: Cornell University Press, 2007).

10 Peter J. Katzenstein and Robert O. Keohane, *Anti-Americanisms in World Politics* (Ithaca, NY: Cornell University Press, 2007); Robert Singh, "Are we all Americans Now? Explaining Anti-Americanisms," in *The Rise of Anti-Americanism*, eds. Brendon O'Connor and Martin Griffiths (London: Routledge, 2005).

11 Potter Stewart was struggling to precisely define pornography (See: Justice Potter Stewart, concurring in *Jacobellis v. Ohio* (378 US 134, 1964)).

12 Peter J. Katzenstein and Robert O. Keohane, *Anti-Americanisms in World Politics* (Ithaca, NY: Cornell University Press, 2007). Although Robert Singh's work on the causes of anti-Americanism also argues that there are "anti-Americanisms", rather than one coherent anti-American ideology, he has a narrower and more convincing understanding than Katzenstein and Keohane. Singh distils these anti-Americanisms down to three principal strands: the first is Leftist critiques of America's unjust and self-centred use of its wealth and power; the second is rival nationalisms and the universal pretensions of American nationalism; and the third encompasses cultural concerns about the Americanisation of cultural products, norms, and public policies. It is Singh's highlighting of the importance of nationalism in provoking anti-Americanism that makes his

contribution particularly thought-provoking (Robert Singh, "Are we all Americans Now? Explaining Anti-Americanisms," in *The Rise of Anti-Americanism*, eds. Brendon O'Connor and Martin Griffiths (London: Routledge, 2005)). Josef Joffe takes a similar line to Singh. He argues that anti-Americanism "is not criticism of American policies, not even dislike of particular American leaders or features of American life, such as gas-guzzling SUVs or five hundred TV channels. It is the obsessive stereotypization, denigration, and demonization of the country and culture. The most vicious, sustained, and direct expressions of this state of mind are found in the Arab and Islamic world" (Josef Joffe, *Überpower: The Imperial Temptation of America* (New York, NY: W. W. Norton, 2006), 77). To justify these assertions, Joffe turns to the world of newspaper cartoons, arguing that "because they trade in images and not words" they are "one of the best conduits into the unconscious" (ibid., 78). Along with noting that the most favoured image of America in the Arab and Islamic world is the bloodthirsty cannibal, Joffe also comments on the racist overtones of cartoons caricaturing Condoleezza Rice (ibid., 77–79). The excesses of these cartoons are a good example of how opportunistic anti-American prejudice can undermine important arguments, in this case about America's role in the Middle East. The opportunistic (and at times contradictory) nature of anti-Americanism is a topic on which Jean-François Revel has highlighted (See: Jean François Revel, *Anti-Americanism* (New York, NY: Encounter Books, 2003). For example, in some parts of the world America is condemned for being too sacrilegious (with its commercial culture and open displays of sexuality on MTV and the like), whereas in other parts of the world it is condemned for being too religious.

13 Martin Seymour Lipset, *American Exceptionalism: A Double Edged Sword* (New York: W.W. Norton & Co., 1996); Kurt Andersen, *Fantasyland: How America Went Haywire, a 500 Year History* (New York, Random House, 2017).

14 See Hilde Eliassen Restad, *American Exceptionalism: An Idea that Made a Nation and Remade the World* (London: Routledge, 2014).

15 Neal Gabler, "One Nation, Under Illusion," *Boston Globe*, October 13, 2009 <http://www.boston.com/bostonglobe/editorial_opinion/oped/articles/2009/10/13/one_nation_under_illusion/>.

16 George W. Bush, "Address to the Nation on Operations in Afghanistan," in *The Selected Speeches of President George W. Bush, 2001–2008* <https://georgewbush-whitehouse.archives.gov/infocus/bushrecord/documents/Selected_Speeches_George_W_Bush.pdf>.

17 George W. Bush "President George W. Bush's Inaugural Address," in *The White House Archives*, January 20, 2001, <https://georgewbush-whitehouse.archives.gov/news/inaugural-address.html>.

18 Marie-France Toinet, "Does Anti-Americanism Exist?" in Denis Lacorne, Jacques Rupnik, and Marie-France Toinet eds., *The Rise and Fall of Anti-Americanism: A Century of French Perception* (London: Macmillan, 1990).

19 Josef Joffe, "On Anti-Americanism in Europe" (Speech at Stanford University, 2005) <http://www.stanford.edu/~weiler/Josef_Joffe_on_Anti_Americanism.pdf>.

20 Jean-Paul Sartre, "Objections Noted; French Writer Answers His Varied Critics," *New York Times*, March 21, 1948, X3.

21 Martin Heidegger, *What is a Thing?* (Washington D.C.: H. Regnery Co., 1967), 60–61.

22 You could also say the same about the term "American exceptionalism". It too is suggestive of the importance that has been accorded (and claimed) about origins and development of America.

23 Colin Hay and David Marsh, *Demystifying Globalization* (London: Macmillan, 1999).

24 Barack Obama, State of the Union Address, January 25, 2011, <https://www.cbsnews.com/news/state-of-the-union-full-obama-speech-text/>.

25 Timothy Noah, *The Great Divergence: America's Growing Inequality Crisis* (New York, NY: Bloomsbury Publishing, 2012).

26 Max Paul Friedman, *Rethinking Anti-Americanism: The History of an Exceptional Concept in American Foreign Relations* (Cambridge: Cambridge University Press, 2012).

27 Louis Jacobson, "John Boehner Says U.S. Health Care System is Best in World," *Politifact*, July 5, 2012, <https://www.politifact.com/truth-o-meter/statements/2012/jul/05/john-boehner/john-boehner-says-us-health-care-system-best-world/>.

28 Andrei S. Markovits, "'Twin Brothers': European Anti-Semitism and Anti-Americanism," *Jerusalem Center for Public Affairs*, January 08, 2006, <http://www.jcpa.org/phas/phas-markovits-06.htm>.

29 James Ceaser, "The Philosophical Origins of Anti-Americanism in Europe," in Paul Hollander, ed., *Understanding Anti-Americanism: Its Origins and Impact at Home and Abroad* (Chicago: Ivan R. Dee, 2004); Andrei Markovits, *Uncouth Nation* (Princeton: Princeton University Press, 2007).

30 Based on detailed analysis of newspapers in a number of countries.

31 Peter Conrad, *Imagining America* (New York, NY: Oxford University Press, 1980), 175.

32 Barack Obama, "Democratic Party Convention" (Convention held in Boston, Massachusetts, July 27, 2004), <http://www.washingtonpost.com/wp-dyn/articles/A19751-2004Jul27.html>

33 Obama's opening words in his November 2008 victory speech were: "If there is anyone out there who still doubts that America is a place where all things are possible, who still wonders if the dream of our founders is alive in our time, who still questions the power of our democracy, tonight is your answer." Barrack Obama, "Obama Acceptance Speech in Full" in *The Guardian*, November 05, 2008, <https://www.theguardian.com/commentisfree/2008/nov/05/uselections2008-barackobama>.

34 There are other biographies that use the title or subtitle "An American Life"; these are about Ralph Bunche, D. W. Griffith, Archibald MacLeish, Jimmy Gentry, and Elizabeth Cady Stantan.

35 Scott Baio, "Transcript: What Scott Baio Said about Donald Trump," *Maclean's*, July 18, 2016, <https://www.macleans.ca/politics/washington/transcript-what-scott-baio-said-about-donald-trump/>.

36 Sam Stein, "Palin Explains What Parts of Country Not 'Pro-America,'" *Huffington Post*, November 17, 2008, <https://www.huffingtonpost.com.au/2008/10/17/palin-clarifies-what-part_n_135641.html>.

37 Angie Drobnic Holan, "Why do so many People Think Obama is a Muslim?" *Politifact*, August 26, 2010, <https://www.politifact.com/truth-o-meter/article/2010/aug/26/why-do-so-many-people-think-obama-muslim/>.

38 Lymari Morales, "Obama's Birth Certificate Convinces Some, but Not All, Skeptics," *Gallup*, May 13, 2011, <https://news.gallup.com/poll/147530/obama-birth-certificate-convinces-not-skeptics.aspx>.

39 "Louis Hartz, also insisted that the American stories of peoplehood revealed that the elites and citizens of the United States were also unhealthy, obsessed with the nation's own past, liberal or otherwise. The United States, he explained, had never experienced a revolutionary break from feudalism in the way that Europe had. As such, it had never witnessed the overthrow of one domestic political system and its replacement with an alternative. This, in turn, had led to Americans possessing an astonishing reverence for their own past in the mistaken assumption that it was this continuity that was responsible for the relative prosperity and international success of the republic. Such a view resulted, Hartz suggested, in an inability to understand the political future in terms of the discontinuity that was needed for real change. The United States was simply politically incapable of appreciating what other nations understood as the occasional necessity of dramatic political transformation. This ensured that America was destined always to look backwards to the period of the Founding even at periods of intense political introspection rather than forwards to a new polity grounded in an alternative political ideal." Ben Jackson and Marc Stears, *Liberalism and American Stories of Peoplehood: Essays in Honour of Michael Freeden* (Oxford: Oxford University Press, 2002), 83.

40 Tony Judt makes this link with sport-utility vehicles (SUVs) in "Anti-Americanism Abroad," in *The Rise of Anti-Americanism,* eds. Brendon O'Connor and Martin Griffiths (London: Routledge, 2007).

41 Amnesty International, "Guantánamo Bay – A Human Rights Scandal," *Amnesty International*, January 13, 2006, <https://www.amnesty.org/download/Documents/72000/am r510102006en.pdf>.

42 Andrei Markovits, *Uncouth Nation: Why Europe Dislikes America* (Princeton: Princeton University Press, 2007).

43 Rath Hatlapa and Andrei Markovits, "Obamamania and Anti-Americanism as Complementary Concepts in Contemporary German Discourse," *German Politics and Society* 28, 94, No. 1 (Spring 2010).

44 Malcolm Bradbury, *Dangerous Pilgrimages: Trans-Atlantic Mythologies and the Novel* (London: Penguin Books, 1995)

45 Andrei Markovits, *Uncouth Nation: Why Europe Dislikes America* (Princeton: Princeton University Press, 2007).

46 Philippe Roger, *The American Enemy* (Chicago: University of Chicago Press, 2005).

47 James Ceaser, *Reconstructing America* (New Haven: Yale University Press, 1997).

48 Antonello Gerbi, *The Dispute of the New World: The History of a Polemic 1750–1900*, Rev. ed. (Pittsburgh: University of Pittsburgh Press, 1973).

49 Kristen Bialik, "How the World Views the U.S. and its President in 9 Charts," *Pew Research Centre*, October 9, 2018, <http://www.pewresearch.org/fact-tank/2018/10/ 09/how-the-world-views-the-u-s-and-its-president-in-9-charts>.

50 On this approach see Rodney Tiffen et al., *How America Compares* (Melbourne: Springer, 2019).

51 Stephen Bennett, "'Know Nothings' Revisited Again," *Political Behaviour* 18, 3(1996), 219–233; Stephen Bennett et al., "Citizens' Knowledge of Foreign Affairs," *The Harvard International Journal of Press/Politics* 1, 2 (1996), 10–29; Shanto Iyengar et al., "Dark Areas of Ignorance Revisited: Comparing International Affairs Knowledge in Switzerland and the United States," *Communication Research*, 36(3), 341–358.

52 Fredrick Jackson Turner, *The Significance of the Frontier in American History* (Indianapolis: Bobbs-Merrill, 1893).

53 George Orwell, "Notes on Nationalism," *Essays* (London: Penguin Books, 2000).

54 Philip Everts, "Images of the U.S. – Three Theories of Anti-Americanism," Workshop on Anti-Americanism in Comparative Historical Perspective, European Consortium for Political Research, Nicosia, Cyprus, April 25–30, 2006.

55 Kristen Bialik, "How the World Views the U.S. and its President in 9 Charts," Pew Research Centre, October 9, 2018, <http://www.pewresearch.org/fact-tank/2018/10/ 09/how-the-world-views-the-u-s-and-its-president-in-9-charts>.

56 Angela Nagle, *Kill all Normies* (Alresford: Zero Books, 2017); Whitney Phillips, *This Is Why We Can't Have Nice Things* (Cambridge MA: MIT Press, 2016).

57 David Corn, "Donald Trump Says he Doesn't Believe in 'American Exceptionalism,'" *Mother Jones*, June 07, 2016, <https://www.motherjones.com/politics/2016/06/dona ld-trump-american-exceptionalism/>.

58 Peter Beinart, "The End of American Exceptionalism," *National Journal*, February 03, 2014.

1

WHAT IS ANTI-AMERICANISM?

The last respectable prejudice?

"Do I contradict myself? Very well, then I contradict myself, I am large, I contain multitudes," wrote Walt Whitman. The words from his self-referential magnum opus *Song of Myself* can also be read as a hymn to his nation (in fact the work's original title was *Poem of Walt Whitman, an American*). America seen from this Whitmanesque viewpoint is a vast and contradictory land. While this emphasis on variety and paradox would seem the obvious starting point from which to understand America, it is an outlook eschewed by anti-American commentary. This commentary reduces America's vastness to a series of stereotypes and caricatures, in which America's essence is described exclusively through negative examples drawn from history or the contemporary era. From this narrow and biased focus emerges the spectre of anti-Americanism. Selectivity and caricature have long been the tools of trade in explaining America. Oscar Wilde opined that: "English people are far more interested in American barbarism than they are in American civilization."[1] Similarly, George Bernard Shaw, whose quotes are often confused with Wilde's, ventured that "one must distinguish between civilized America and barbarian America."[2] This polarisation suggests that there are at least two Americas but it misses the bigger point that America, just like other nations, is good, bad and all that is in between.[3] The ordinariness of much of American life is lost as America is constantly fantasised, sensationalised, and caricatured. The ubiquity of cameras and smart-phones has meant that wackiness and weirdness is increasingly easy to find in the US,[4] but the disproportionate attention it enjoys in the international media reinforces certain stereotypes.[5] Meanwhile, the public thirst for American stupidity is insatiable as the recent success of Sacha Baron Cohen's *Who is America?* indicates.[6] This insatiability has a long history with James Russell Lowell writing in 1869 that "for some reason or other, the European has rarely been able to see America except in caricature."[7] Trump's 2016 drama-filled, often hyperbolic election campaign and then presidency makes the case for seeing American as a land of variety, moderation, and nuance difficult. However, more so than with George W. Bush's election and presidency, people around the world seem aware of the consistently high levels of internal opposition that Trump's presidency provokes.

How to explain the tendency to see this exaggerated and mythologised – or screen version – of America as the reality? A big part of the story is that American leaders and celebrities often portray America in a grandiose manner when delivering widely viewed speeches. America's grand founding documents, its idealistic and sweeping foreign policy pronouncements and later its celluloid dream factories have made it the most talked about country, the most desired immigrant destination and the most resented nation on earth for almost 250 years.[8] Since its founding, America has been both admired as a bold new experiment and criticised for its grandiosity, excessive self-regard and hypocrisy. Americans and non-Americans alike regularly refer to America's proclaimed exceptionalism, which, as this book argues, is a source of enormous belief in America and significant disappointment when the reality falls well short of the promise. For many refugees and immigrants, ambitious actors and musicians – and anyone else intent on making it big – America's self-proclaimed specialness, greatness and exceptionalism creates the allure that it is a dream factory for those who arrive on its shores.

For many Americans, this exceptionalist tradition is bound up in a strong patriotism and an enduring belief in the "American Dream".[9] However, many observers of America believe the opposite; rather than a dream, American exceptionalism has created a nightmarish nation whose ideas, companies and military wreak havoc wherever they go.[10] This polarised view of America as the land of opportunity on one hand and the land of destruction and injustice on the other is central to the notions of pro- and anti-Americanism. In one of the first, and still one of the most insightful books on anti-Americanism, Henry Pelling summarised the above strands of thought with the following conclusion:

> Hope and disillusion will long continue to colour the European view of America, as they did when [Samuel] Gompers crossed the Atlantic in 1909 to discover that people in Western Europe looked at his country as if in one of two distorting mirrors, either convex or concave.... To understand the Americans as they really are requires not only an appreciation of the peculiarities of the American environment, but also a recognition that, in its better features and its worse, human nature everywhere and at all times is, as Thucydides said, very much the same.[11]

America's power and imprint is so vast that it *is* challenging to talk about this nation in the considered and moderate manner recommended by Pelling. A more measured approach to America needs to illuminate both the positive and negative aspects (and all that is in between) of American culture, society, politics, and foreign policy. The anti-American outlook usually exclusively focuses on the negative and fails to recognise the variety America encompasses. The core markers of such anti-Americanism are a distorted or narrowcast focus, a reflexive dislike, and a tendency to conflate the nation's people with their government and its policies. One of the most obvious examples of this anti-Americanism is the belief aired following September 11, 2001, that "they had it coming".[12] This is the kind of comment that Todd Gitlin seems to have had in mind when he wrote: "When hatred of foreign policies ignites into hatred of an entire people and their civilization, then thinking is dead and demonology lives."[13]

My analysis in this book should not be read as a blanket defence of the US. Rather, I am making the case for a differentiated understanding of the US because I strongly believe that American foreign and domestic politics is often deleterious and dangerous and therefore targeted and intelligent critique is a necessity.[14] In making this point, I follow in the footsteps of James Madison who declared in the *Federalist Papers* # 6 that "in doubtful cases, particularly where the national councils may be warped by some strong passion or momentary interest, the presumed or known opinion of the impartial world may be the best guide to be followed." Of course the outside world is seldom, if ever, impartial, but the principle is still sound. While I strongly believe that powerful nations need to be particularly closely analysed, criticism of any nation needs to be based on an examination of detailed evidence rather than sweeping generalisations and prejudices. Given the unprecedented power and influence of the United States, close scrutiny is a necessity but a narrowcast or *a priori* view of America's motives and behaviour will inevitably lead to distortions and foreclose sensible conversations and debates. Henry Pelling made a similar point about a different time period in *America and the British Left* (1957): "The historical perspective provided by these studies inevitably suggests that dangerous distortion of the facts is likely to take place among those who commit themselves most fully to an a priori view of politics. Socialists of the mid-twentieth century seem to be often as blind to the merits of American society as Radicals of the mid-nineteenth century were blind to its faults."[15]

As the opening remarks to this chapter would suggest, I see anti-Americanism pejoratively and quite distinct from criticism. Thus, for me, distinguishing between these two outlooks is crucial. Although the call to differentiate the two is regularly expressed, few scholars provide a sound analytical basis for doing so. Instead they shrug their shoulders and declare that it is "all about interpretation." In posing the question of "What is anti-Americanism?" in this chapter, I seek to provide what I see to be desperately needed – a precise definition of Anti-Americanism. When writing about anti-Americanism, an acknowledgement of the variety and diversity of global opinions on Americans and their culture must be made. It is important to avoid generalisations about American culture and politics and its critics. Two further preliminary points are necessary before offering a definition of anti-Americanism. Writing about anti-Americanism forces scholars to put their stake to being a generalist on the line; after all, this is a debate about global opinions on 328 million Americans and their culture, politics and history. Further, given the vastness of the topic, one needs to be sceptical about coming to conclusions too hastily. Donald Trump's election as President of the US makes the need for well-targeted and effective criticism of the US as relevant as ever. Trump, anti-Americanism and American exceptionalism will be discussed in the concluding chapter of this book. In this first chapter, I begin by examining what I see as the two big issues that threw discussions of anti-Americanism back into the lime-light, namely September 11, 2001 and the 2003 invasion of Iraq and its aftermath. From these much analysed events I will move on to discuss how anti-Americanism has been measured by public opinion surveys and defined in popular commentary. I will contend that most analysis is inadequate and generally far too imprecise before finally presenting my own typology of anti-Americanism.

The two elephants in the room

September 11, 2001 and America's invasion of Iraq have led, in the past two decades, to an unprecedented level of discussion about the issue of anti-Americanism. Cataclysmic events such as terrorist attacks and wars do not engender subtle debate. In place of critical and nuanced thinking, simplistic "for us or against us" clichés abound. The terrorist attacks of September 11, 2001 and the ensuing response from much of the American media and the Bush administration started a global conversation about the virtues and vices of the United States. The attacks on the two World Trade Center buildings in New York City, the Pentagon building in Washington and the planned fourth plane attack on either the Capitol Building or the White House were immediately seen as an attack on American culture, society and politics; in other words, an attack on Americanism. Once the attacks were claimed by al Qaeda and its leader Osama bin Laden, the conflict shifted to become a portent of the ideological war between "Islamofascism" and Western/ American Civilisation. As I will discuss later, this erroneous position was not only adopted, as one might expect, by the terrorists but also by certain politicians and polemists in the West. It is this ideological dimension of the discussions which is most fascinating to me. In my mind the ideological face of anti-Americanism is where we move beyond mere individual prejudice to collective prejudice. However, as I will explore in the coming pages, viewing anti-Americanism as an ideology is problematic when those most vehemently against America frequently offer contradictory views. Further, to view the issue as a clash of ideologies – Americanism vs "Islamofascism" – or a clash of civilisations is unsound, for only a small number of Muslims in 2001 supported al Qaeda or its attacks on America. It was a grave error by the Bush administration and allies like the Blair government in Britain and the Howard government in Australia to exaggerate the extent of this support for al Qaeda and terrorism. This was done at times for electoral purposes to make life hard for their so-called "soft" political opponents; something that, with hindsight, is unforgivable. This error of judgement – based often on these immoral political calculations – created a certain momentum to "do more and more" and led eventually to the disastrous decision to invade Iraq in 2003. There was a lot of sensible and reasonable opposition all around the world to making Iraq a central target in the war on terror. Just like during the Vietnam War,[16] proponents of the war in Iraq used real and exaggerated cases of anti-Americanism to help silence dissent.[17] The tragedy of the approach adopted by Bush and his allies abroad, which linked al Qaeda not only to the Taliban leadership in Afghanistan but much more broadly to include fabricated links with Iraq, have been a significant factor in increasing anti-Western sentiment and terrorism by newly radicalised Muslims. The rise of ISIS is the most extreme example of how exaggerating and targeting terrorist connections and sympathies in Iraq created a significantly more violent strand of anti-Americanism.

In the aftermath of the violent attacks of 9/11 most governments and peoples around the world spoke out in condemnation. However, it soon became apparent that many others, including a number of prominent commentators, saw the US less as a victim, and more as a reaper of the consequences of years of unscrupulous behaviour in the Middle East and elsewhere.[18] To use a term that became commonplace in the period after 9/11, the attacks were seen as "blowback" against American policies. A *Guardian* newspaper article published just one week after the attacks bluntly summarised this response with the words "A bully with a bloody nose is still a bully."[19] There were disputed reports of Palestinians celebrating the attacks and a Chinese student of mine once told me that residents in her northern China city rejoiced in the streets. Some people across the world were simply pleased to see America made to feel more vulnerable and less invincible. These negative responses reflected a distrust of and resentment towards the US. However, like many aspects of the discussion of 9/11, the level of rejoicing in the streets after the attacks on America is the subject of misinformation and exaggeration. The internet age has led to the wide circulation of and increased belief in conspiracy theories. Just as claims that 9/11 was an inside job or fabricated are false, claims that Muslim Americans were dancing in the streets of New Jersey celebrating the attacks are lies. What is remarkable about the second claim is the now president of the United States has contended that he saw evidence of this on television on the day of the attacks. In Birmingham Alabama on November 21, 2015, Trump claimed that: "I watched in Jersey City, N.J., where thousands and thousands of people were cheering as that building was coming down. Thousands of people were cheering."[20] When challenged the next day by George Stephanopoulos on the ABC's show *This Week* with the evidence that "the police say that didn't happen", Trump persisted with his claim saying:

> It was on television. I saw it.... There were people that were cheering on the other side of New Jersey, where you have large Arab populations. They were cheering as the World Trade Center came down. I know it might be not politically correct for you to talk about it, but there were people cheering as that building came down — as those buildings came down. And that tells you something. It was well covered at the time, George. Now, I know they don't like to talk about it, but it was well covered at the time. There were people over in New Jersey that were watching it, a heavy Arab population, that were cheering as the buildings came down. Not good.[21]

There is no credible evidence to support this claim of "thousands" or even small numbers of people celebrating the 9/11 attacks in New Jersey, nor is there evidence that this was reported on television as Trump claims. His source was possibly the shock-jock Howard Stern, who perpetuated the urban myth on his radio show.[22] Trump often appeared on this show, talking to Stern about how attractive he found various famous women. As I said earlier, writing about anti-Americanism in the age of Trump is very challenging given his predilection to peddle conspiracy theories and his frequently outrageous personal behaviour. Although politics in the early 21st century was often polarised, it was generally more straightforward to understand than it is today.

Turning back to the period immediately after the 9/11 attacks, although Trump is clearly wrong about thousands of people celebrating the attacks on the streets of Jersey City, not everyone around the world was sympathetic towards America. Outside of the US, claims that America was an innocent victim were questioned. The superpower was still seen as a "bully" by many people around the world. This lack of unequivocal support for America and more significantly the general unwillingness of longtime allies to follow the American government's lead in the war on terror surprised many Americans, particularly during this time of national shock and mourning.[23] Internationally, the widespread public sympathy after the terrorist attacks on America – documented in the initial Pew global surveys – dissipated, with many people objecting to the way Americans, and more particularly the Bush administration, responded to the 9/11 attacks. People baulked at the endless media coverage lacking a sense of proportionality.[24] International support for America was further damaged by President Bush's "cowboy-talk" regarding supposed links between Saddam Hussein and al Qaeda (with little hard evidence produced), the Bush administration's dismissal of dissent by European leaders as the cowardly doubts of "Old Europe", and Bush's claims that the march to war in Iraq was inevitable and beneficial for the spread of democracy and freedom in the Middle East. Attempting to encapsulate this mood, one writer went as far as to suggest that international discussions and debates in the wake of September 11, 2001 "have increased the visceral loathing not of terrorism or of Islamic fundamentalism but of President George Bush."[25] Although this overstates the situation somewhat, a 2004 Pew survey showed that Osama bin Laden was seen much more favourably in a number of Muslim countries than Bush.[26] Other reputable surveys conducted around the same time provide evidence that the US was widely viewed as a greater threat to world peace than China, Russia or Iran.[27]

9/11 revealed to Americans the world's ambivalence towards their nation, but it was George W. Bush's decision to go to war in Iraq that tipped global opinion clearly against the US. A range of international surveys including the influential Pew surveys provided clear evidence that the war against Iraq was widely unpopular and turned people against America. As Table 1.1 shows, polls taken in the lead-up to and aftermath of the Iraq war confirm that America was at that point more unpopular globally than at any time in the history of such polls. Other surveys showed that the US was less popular than France, Germany, Japan or China.[28] While 2003 saw the unpopularity of the US spike dramatically in all the nations surveyed by the Pew Research Center, the first signs of a diminishing negative sentiment towards America was not until 2008. Even then, America's unpopularity was well above that recorded in pre-2003 surveys.

Other polls yield similarly negative results. For example, another survey showed that "Saudis expressing confidence in America shrank from 60 percent in 2000 to just 4 percent in 2004."[30]

The Pew Global Attitudes Project survey used here is the most influential ongoing yearly survey of attitudes towards the US. The assumption is that those

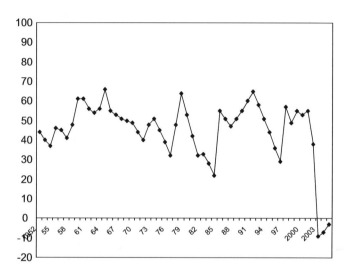

FIGURE 1.1 Opinions of the United States in four European countries, 1952–2006 (in % NET "favorable" opinion)

Source: various, including Eurobarometer, PEW, USIA[29]

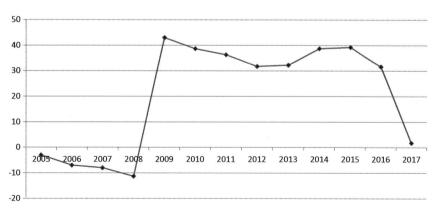

FIGURE 1.2 Opinions of the United States in four European countries, 2005–2017 (in % NET "favourable" opinion)

Source: Pew Research Center for the People and the Press

TABLE 1.1 Global attitudes toward the United States (% unfavourable)

	2002	2003	2004	2005	2006	2007	2008	2009	2010	2011	2012	2013	2014	2015	2016	2017
Britain	16	26	34	38	33	42	37	20	24	28	31	30	27	24	26	40
France	34	57	62	57	60	60	57	25	26	26	31	36	25	27	31	52
Germany	35	54	59	54	60	66	66	33	35	35	44	40	47	45	38	62
Spain	-	55	-	50	73	60	55	28	28	29	32	29	34	27	26	60
Poland	11	-	-	23	-	31	24	24	19	19	26	24	19	17	16	15
Russia	33	55	44	40	47	48	48	44	33	34	34	40	71	81	-	52
Turkey	54	83	63	67	76	83	77	69	74	77	72	70	73	58	-	79
Pakistan	69		60	60	56	68	63	68	68	73	80	72	59	62	-	-
Jordan	75	99	93	80	85	78	79	74	79	84	86	85	85	83	-	82
Argentina	49	-	-	-	-	72	62	42	41	-	-	41	44	43	-	44
Australia	-	38	-	-	-	-	48	-	-	-	-	30	-	28	34	48

Source: Pew Research Center for the People and the Press

surveyed can judge the US as a monolithic entity. The above evidence from these surveys gives an excellent indication that who the US president is and which major events have occurred significantly shape global opinion about the US, and Bush's decision to go to war in Iraq had a dramatic negative impact on how the US was viewed around the world. Attitudes towards the US became more unfavourable in every nation surveyed, except for Pakistan. Little in general changed with respect to global attitudes to the US from 2004 to 2008, however the election of Barack Obama improved attitudes towards the US in every country surveyed apart from Israel, Egypt, and Pakistan. In Western Europe opinion changed dramatically with negative sentiment nearly halving in a number of countries. Opinion in Muslim majority countries towards the US during the Obama presidency was generally more favourable than during the Bush era, but the changes were not as dramatic as with European attitudes.

During the Bush and Obama presidencies Pakistani opinion often ran counter to the dominant trends. With Pakistan, there is evidence that American foreign policy behaviour mattered more than who the US president was. US aid to Pakistan in the wake of the deadly 2005 Azad Kashmir earthquake is thought to have improved attitudes towards the US, whereas Obama's use of military drones in Pakistan is thought to have worsened opinion towards the US. Another anomaly to the general trends in the Obama era is Russia, where opinion went from being 33% unfavourable in 2002 to 81% unfavourable in 2015. The US official condemnation and economic sanctions placed on Russia as a result of its annexing of Crimea in 2014 likely account for this change in attitude. Opinion in Russia improved significantly with the election of Donald Trump who had campaigned with a more positive attitude to Russia than any American politician had shown since the embrace of "Uncle Joe" Stalin in WWII. Russian opinion here ran counter to opinion in most other nations particularly in Europe where Trump's unpopularity translated into America being seen once again as generally unfavourable. In Spain 60% of respondents and in Germany 62% had an unfavourable opinion of the US, which was a major reversal from the Obama era. Not surprisingly after Trump's claims that he would make Mexico pay for a border wall that would stop it sending its criminals and "rapists" to America, opinion hardened from 29% unfavourable in 2015 to 65% in 2017.[31] The election of Trump did not change opinion of the US significantly in Jordan or Lebanon; however, it did in Turkey where opinion had fluctuated quite significantly from 2002–2017. The Iraq war had had a very negative impact on Turkish attitudes towards the US; this dissipated in the late Obama period, but returned to a strongly negative norm when Trump came to power. In summary, these surveys do not suggest a pervasive anti-Americanism. I argue this because anti-Americanism represents a deep antagonism towards what America symbolises, whereas the ups and downs captured by these surveys demonstrate who the Americans elect as their president and what the US does in the world matters a lot to how positively or negatively non-Americans feel about the US.

Measuring a politically contested term

While the above survey results show that negative sentiment towards the US skyrocketed during George W. Bush's years in the White House, such surveys are too broadly focused to allow for detailed evaluation of this negative sentiment. A further complication is that the polling organisations never provided an exact definition of anti-Americanism. It is thus impossible to differentiate between an opinion that is simply unfavourable and one that is strongly anti-American. We can all agree that the terrorist attacks on the World Trade Center and the Pentagon were unambiguous expressions of violent anti-Americanism, but there is frequent disagreement about whether much of the broader antipathy towards America can be fairly labelled as anti-Americanism. This is not least because what one person calls anti-Americanism is defended by another as reasonable criticism. Further, it is a rare person who openly acknowledges their anti-Americanism,[32] and, like in most political debates, the caricaturing of opponents is commonplace.[33] Scholars have an important role in negotiating the way through such politicised discourses by demanding that the vague claims of anti-Americanism made by pollsters be replaced with more precision to push beyond these ambiguous assertions and inferences.

It is crucial to acknowledge the highly politicised nature of anti-Americanism. Indeed, some see it everywhere while others almost deny its existence. Conservative nationalists use it to deride any criticism of America, while some left-wing scholars see anti-Americanism as barely real. Commentators on FOX News and the like are inclined to use the term to imply that any critics of the US are sympathetic with ISIS and other similar terrorist organisations in the ongoing global war on terror. (This response repeats a familiar pattern; some Cold War warriors never tired of labelling criticisms of US foreign policy anti-American, implying that such criticisms were synonymous with support for the Soviet Union.) Recognising this usage of the term, Kenneth Minogue writes that "anti-Americanism thus often functions in argument as an incapacitating device, just like such charges as 'sexism' and 'racism'"; it is, he argues, "an attacking move in any discussion of international affairs." However, he correctly acknowledges the claim is "conventionally blocked by a denial whose point is to restore credibility to whatever point the critic of America is making."[34] Whichever side of the divide discussions of anti-Americanism fall, the traits they have in common are frequent exaggeration and polarisation. Those on one side of this debate overuse and abuse the term as a blanket condemnation of any US-focused criticism,[35] while those on the other side deny that their opinions are at all anti-American despite the fact that similar comments made about almost any other people or nation would be quickly called prejudicial. This polarised debate, although disappointing, is not particularly surprising; however, what is curious is how little scholars have contributed in terms of clarifying and elevating the discussion. The existing literature is limited and impressionistic, particularly when it comes to defining what is reasonably understood to be anti-Americanism and what is not.

The task of measuring whether the increase in negative feelings towards the US during the Bush era is anti-Americanism or simply acceptable criticism or some combination of the two is made more difficult because of the bluntness of the instruments being used. The Pew Global Attitudes Project survey is the most influential ongoing survey in the world on attitudes to America. In it, respondents are asked their attitude towards America by choosing from the following statement: "Please tell me if you have a very favourable, somewhat favourable, somewhat unfavourable or very unfavourable opinion of the United States." Respondents are asked to judge an entire nation in the same manner as they would an individual political leader or party. The assumption is that we can judge the US as a monolithic entity. Some people are clearly able to encapsulate the US thus but a great many others will make their judgements based on particular policies, actions, or elements of culture. The vastness of American society and its impact across the globe make the task of analysing responses to such broad statements as posed by Pew an imprecise undertaking. There is no doubting the influence of the Pew surveys. Their analysis has had a profound impact on commentary on anti-Americanism. While they certainly provide solid data of America's unpopularity during the Bush era in nearly all the countries where they were conducted, the poll data itself cannot provide answers to the more rudimentary question of what anti-Americanism is. Without a precise definition of the phenomenon the surveys have no chance of answering the other vital question of just how widespread anti-Americanism is. This book endeavours to answer the first question; answering the second question will always require speculation.

Anti-Americanism in popular and scholarly debate

In the months and years following September 11, 2001 a steady outpouring of newspaper and magazine articles emerged discussing anti-Americanism. A number of best-selling books also appeared, the most popular of which was Sardar and Davies' *Why Do People Hate America?* [36] Although these early contributions identified key points of conflict, they spent little time defining anti-Americanism. Similarly, a number of the luminaries of European and American academia ventured opinions on the rise of anti-Americanism, including Timothy Garton Ash, Simon Schama, and Tony Judt. These historians of the present, as Ash calls himself, neatly summarised the anti-American mood during the Bush era with historically informed articles in the *New Yorker, The Guardian* and that "other American"[37] journal of ideas *The New York Review of Books*. However, as readable as these articles are, they similarly spend little time defining anti-Americanism.

The best scholarship offers a number of ways of dividing the anti-American pie. This analysis includes Andrei Markovits' four squared division of anti-Americanism into left/right and cultural/political.[38] Moisés Naím identifies "five 'pure' types: politico-economic, historical, religious, cultural, and psychological,"[39] while Rubinstein and Smith separate anti-Americanism into the following categories: issue oriented, ideological, instrumental, and revolutionary.[40] Robert Singh distils the various sources of anti-Americanisms down to three principal strands: leftist critiques of America's unjust and self-centred use of its wealth and power; rival nationalisms and the universal pretensions of American nationalism; and cultural concerns about the Americanisation of cultural products, norms, and public policies.[41] Katzenstein and Keohane outdo all comers by suggesting six prominent types of anti-Americanism: liberal, social, sovereign-nationalist, radical, elitist, and legacy.[42] The other noteworthy division is between what Moisés Naím calls "lite" and "murderous" anti-Americanism.[43]

These divisions are useful tools with which to understand the different sources and motivations behind anti-American actions and ideas. However, my interest is to start one step further back and ask what *exactly* anti-Americanism is. A concrete definition of the term would seem necessary before we can classify it into the various strands. Such definitions have been elusive as the term is generally acknowledged by most authors as slippery. As Tony Judt and Denis Lacorne suggest in their 2005 book *With Us or Against Us*: "Anti-Americanism is above all about perceptions."[44] Given the troublesome nature of the term, which can include so many different varieties, a number of authors – Robert Singh, Andrei Markovits and Christopher Hitchens spring to mind – are drawn to the Justice Potter Stewart line of "I know it when I see it..."[45] However, since anti-Americanism is such a politicised term, this definition opens one up to the claim that you see or do not see anti-Americanism when it is convenient to your argument. Scholars must not let indignation or fear of being pigeonholed prevent them from creating more robust categories and definitions. It is also important to more precisely and rigorously define the term in order to rescue it from political abuse and misuse. In summary, the existing academic literature provides endless divisions between different so-called sources of anti-Americanism but does little to conceptualise the term and thus fails to show how it can be effectively differentiated from criticism. I attempt to fill this void with the definition that follows.

What is anti-Americanism? Five conceptions

I have extracted five understandings of how the term is used across both popular and scholarly debates. Simply stated, these competing conceptions of anti-Americanism can be characterised as: first, one side of a dichotomised worldview; second, a tendency; third, a pathology; fourth, a prejudice; and fifth, an ideology.

1. *Anti-Americanism as one side of a dichotomy.* As one half of a dichotomy, anti-Americanism is understood in a binary or oppositional fashion where people, groups or nations are seen as either pro- or anti-American. Thus anti-Americanism is simply the views and actions of those deemed not to be pro-American. This is the most straightforward, but also the most restrictive interpretation of the term.
2. *Anti-Americanism as a tendency.* A little less crude but still straightforward, this understanding sees anti-Americanism as a tendency that slides across a pro- and anti-American scale depending on the issues, the time or the place.

Opinion pollsters generally adopt this understanding with their questionnaires that aim to measure negative and positive perceptions of America. Ultimately this interpretation of anti-Americanism is too situational and partial to provide a durable definition of anti-Americanism.

3.   *Anti-Americanism as a pathology.* This understanding sees anti-Americanism as akin to an allergic reaction to all things American. It is probably the most precise and literal way of defining anti-Americanism, but if adopted, the outcome would be such a limited application of the term that almost no one's actions or thoughts apart from extremists like bin Laden's could be labelled anti-Americanism. This definition thus takes the term too far from its common usage and has limited utility.

4.   *Anti-Americanism as a prejudice.* This definition is often suggested by conservative commentators. However, scholars should take this approach more seriously because much anti-Americanism has the traditional markers of prejudice as it *prejudges*, it is often clearly *one-sided* and it offers an *undifferentiated* view of America and Americans. However, a prejudice against the powerful is arguably important in order to prevent uncritical acceptance and apathy towards political and economic dominance, making anti-Americanism possibly one of the last respectable prejudices.

5.   *Anti-Americanism as an ideology.* This is a far more complex and speculative way of defining anti-Americanism; complicated not least by the fact that the term ideology itself is multifaceted and frequently contested. At its crudest we have the anti-American ideologies of Castro and the post-1979 Iranian leaders. More complex is whether anti-Americanism in general is coherent enough to be examined as an ideology. Nonetheless the "ism" at the end makes this examination important and fascinating, albeit fraught.

Following on from these brief summaries, I will now provide a much more detailed overview of each of these five conceptions of anti-Americanism.

1 Anti-Americanism as one side of a dichotomised worldview

At its simplest, one is either pro- or anti-American. This dichotomy reduces politics down to crude polarisations. At its worst this is the "with us or against us" view of the Bush administration and the "which side are you on" demand of left-wing ideologues. It also represents the worldview of tabloid journalism where for the sake of speed and simplicity, politics is constantly polarised. An interview I gave to an Australian newspaper journalist is a case in point. Because I was writing on the topic, the journalist asked if I was anti-American. I answered no, explaining that both the terms pro- and anti-American were too simplistic to describe my views on America. I added that my outlook towards the US was one of ambivalence. However, when the article appeared in the newspaper it stated that I described myself "as pro-American,"[46] simply because I refused to be labelled as anti-American. In the mind of that journalist and others there are only two choices. This understanding may suffice in bar room conversation or within certain parts of the media but is far too broad to function as a practical definition of anti-Americanism. It overstates the degree of anti-Americanism and is thus often used instrumentally to silence or besmirch dissent by falsely labelling any critic of America an anti-American. Such quick and unsophisticated dismissals of critics can have very negative consequences as the Manichean behaviour of the Bush administration illustrated.[47]

After September 11, 2001, Bush and his administration divided the world into loyal friends and anti-American foes (or at least nations to be ignored). As a result, American policy-makers gave far less credence to alternative opinions – such as French and German concerns about invading Iraq in 2003 – than was wise. When the weapons of mass destruction were not found in Iraq, this simplistic rhetoric and behaviour made America look strategically naïve. Worse still, it contributed to the poorly planned and executed occupation of Iraq as false assumptions and cavalier thinking further propelled the Bush administration. Many fine books have critiqued the myriad factors at play in the lead up to and the aftermath of the war in Iraq.[48] Nonetheless, this arrogant and blinkered judgement of all critics as anti-American was a potent element. This definition is dangerously reductive, and is among the reasons I argue for a more precise definition of anti-Americanism.

2 Anti-Americanism as a tendency

Public opinion surveyors exemplify this understanding of the term with their ongoing questionnaires that chart the rise and fall of so-called anti-Americanism from year to year. In standard behaviourist analysis, anti-Americanism and pro-Americanism are placed at the two opposite ends of a continuum. Surveyors plot and combine responses along this continuum in order to allow for pronouncements to be made on trends in global anti-American sentiment. As mentioned earlier, the Pew Center has conducted the most widely circulated survey results on attitudes towards America this century. These results certainly painted a clear picture of the global increase in negative attitudes towards the election of George W. Bush, and even more significantly towards the Iraq war of 2003. This is starkly illustrated by simply picking two of the countries surveyed over that time. By 2003, 99% of Jordanians and 54% of Germans had an unfavourable attitude to the US. One year earlier in Jordan it was considerably lower at 75% and German negativity was at only 35%. An even greater sense of how far America's reputation fell during the George W. Bush presidency is captured by the fact that in 2005 China was viewed more favourably in all the surveyed nations other than the US, Canada and Poland. In the same year France and Germany were seen more favourably by all nations apart from US respondents, and Japan was favoured over the US by all except the Chinese and Americans. Such results were a major public diplomacy indictment of the US.

On the other hand, if you are looking for a more positive reading for America in the data, you could point to evidence that European respondents in 2005 clearly thought that it would be a "bad thing" if "China were to become as powerful militarily as the US". And quite revealingly when asked "If an innocent people were being killed by the army, the police or another tribe, in another country, who would you trust most to do something to stop the killings?", people put the US at the top of the list of seven choices of France, Germany, China, Great Britain, Japan, Russia and the US.[49] Furthermore, during the Bush era, as a people, Americans were seen favourably by the majority of respondents in Canada, Great Britain, France, Germany, the Netherlands, Russia, Poland, India, Nigeria and Japan.[50] However, in places where the US as a nation was most unpopular, the surveys generally revealed an unfavourable view of Americans as well, as was shown by respondents in Argentina, Jordan, Pakistan, the Palestinian territories and Turkey.

Whatever angle you take on this data, it undoubtedly chronicles the shifting tendencies in world opinion during the Bush presidency. The most important of these shifts is the change in how respondents across the world generally viewed America. Before the Iraq War the view of most respondents was "somewhat favourable", but from 2003 to 2008 this shifted to a majority having a "somewhat unfavourable" opinion of the US. Although it seems alarming that post-WWII allies of the US such as France, Germany, Spain and the Netherlands all had a more unfavourable than favourable attitude toward the US, the negative attitude of the vast majority of respondents was only "somewhat unfavourable" as opposed to "very unfavourable." The reporting of the survey data seems to miss this very crucial point. Furthermore, looking at the data, it seems much of what the Pew survey calls anti-Americanism could just as easily be renamed "anti-Bushism." When the Pew survey asks: "Why do you have an unfavourable view of the U.S.? Is it mostly because of President George W. Bush or is it a more general problem with America?" strong majorities of respondents in Canada and in all the Western European countries surveyed state "mostly Bush".[51] It seems quite a conceptual leap to equate visceral dislike of an individual president with anti-Americanism. My view is that the Pew Survey results showed anti-Bush and anti-American foreign policy sentiment rather than instances of true anti-Americanism. This view is substantiated by the survey results during the Obama presidency which saw a significant decline in unfavourable attitudes toward the US. In all countries surveyed in Europe (except Russia), in Asia (except Pakistan), in Africa (except Egypt) and in the Americas there was a decline in negative opinion. The story in the Middle East is more complicated with negative opinion holding reasonably firm in Lebanon and Jordan and increasing in Israel. France showed the biggest shift in national opinion: 60% of people surveyed in 2007 had an unfavourable view of the US; by 2009 this had dropped dramatically to 25%. Negative opinion also plummeted in Germany from 66% in 2007 to 33% in 2009.[52]

During the Bush era the Pew report writers used the term anti-Americanism liberally, undoubtedly in order to make their influential surveys more marketable. There was no concomitant definition of the term. Rather the 2005 report boldly opens with the statement: "Anti-Americanism in Europe, the Middle East and Asia, which surged as a result of the U.S. war in Iraq, shows modest signs of abating. But the United States remains broadly disliked in most countries surveyed, and opinion of the American people is not as positive as it once was."[53] But is it anti-Americanism? If taken to mean a negative attitude toward the US as a country, then the answer is a resounding yes. But this would suggest the "anti" in anti-Americanism means "somewhat unfavourable" rather than a narrow and intense dislike. This approach removes much of the term's intended pejorative meaning. By reducing understanding to a continuum of pro- or anti-American tendencies, this definition jumps the gun by automatically assuming that any critical attitude towards America is anti-American. I favour a definition that attempts to offer a more comprehensive and deeper understanding, rather than one that is simply based on more respondents having a negative view, rather than a positive view, of the US on a given day.

3 Anti-Americanism as a pathology

In *The Rise and Fall of Anti-Americanism* (1990), an edited collection of French scholarship, the authors argue for the adoption of a narrow approach to the term by taking the word anti-Americanism quite literally and suggesting it implies a dislike of all things American. Theodore Zeldin examines what he calls "[t]he pathology of anti-Americanism" in an essay that examines the phenomenon from a clinical point of view.[54] Marie-France Toinet writes in the same volume:

> As for the term "anti-Americanism", we feel that its use is only fully justified if it implies systematic opposition – a sort of allergic reaction – to America as a whole. It is clear that if defined in this very narrow way, anti-Americanism either does not exist or is extremely rare. Nonetheless, accusations of anti-Americanism are bandied about with ease.[55]

Seen as a pathology, anti-Americanism is an aversion to all things American, placing one at the extreme end of the tendency continuum described previously. The word pathology suggests that anti-Americanism is the preserve of the irrational fanatic.[56] Roger Kimball takes this outlook when he writes "anti-Americanism has almost nothing to do with *criticism*. It is more a pathology than a position, operating not by evidence but emotion."[57] At first take this definition holds much appeal. It is neat, precise and narrowly defined. Sensibly the advocates of this definition warn against picking out particular quotes as a way of labelling an individual as anti-American. Most famous commentators on the US have written pieces that could be construed as revealing their anti-Americanism. For example, Alexis de Tocqueville famously wrote "I know of no country, where, by and large, there exists less independence of mind or true freedom of discussion than in America." Of course such quotes need to be seen in the context of the person's general views about America. In the case of Tocqueville, it would have to be balanced against his many positive comments about the United States. In her examination of anti-Americanism, Toinet makes this very point about Tocqueville arguing that the sum of his attitudes towards America, like that of most people's, suggest ambivalence rather than anti- or pro-Americanism.[58] Similarly, Robert Singh has written that "the sole unifying and main animating feature of anti-Americanism is ambivalence: admiration co-existing with disapproval and disappointment."[59] This emphasis on ambivalence and the recognition that very few individuals or groups are disapproving of all things American is an eminently sensible understanding of most people's attitude toward the US. However, this understanding is too narrow in its conception of anti-Americanism. Under this pathological definition of anti-Americanism only a small number of people, such as bin Laden and some of his supporters, could be labelled true anti-Americans. Most people's dislikes would be considered something less than real anti-Americanism. The term would thus be reserved for only the most fanatical haters of America with everyone else labelled a critic. This is a position advocated by some who believe that they are falsely labelled anti-American such as the Indian writer and activist Arundhati Roy.[60] If one wants to make the term anti-Americanism virtually extinct, this definition is appealing. However, it is too far from the commonplace usage of the term; in my opinion academic definitions should generally seek to build on and work with the everyday usage of words rather than re-invent them anew. By all means, we should argue for more precise usages of terms but attempting to put the word out of circulation, as Denis Lacrone does when he argues we would be better off to say Americanaphobia rather than anti-Americanism,[61] is to ignore reality (and overrate the influence of academic interventions on more general discourse). The word anti-Americanism is already too set in the collective vocabulary to be easily pared back to as sparse a definition as pathology.

4. Anti-Americanism as a prejudice

In most instances prejudice is seen as wrong and thus something to combat. The current strength of this normative position has been very effective in reducing racism and other forms of discrimination. The markers of prejudice include: undifferentiated attacks, a biased outlook, an assumption of inferiority or an *a priori* belief that only bad intentions drive one's ideas and actions. Prejudice encompasses negative stereotyping, but goes beyond this to include more direct forms of hatred and vitriol. Prejudiced opinion easily leads to exaggerations and conspiratorial ideas. These generally recognised signs of prejudice are familiar in many discussions about America and it seems sensible and fair to honestly acknowledge them as prejudice, even in the case of America (the most powerful nation on earth). Moreover, at least ideally, calling anti-Americanism a prejudice places a certain responsibility on the person making the accusation to treat the notion of prejudice seriously and not just make the claim in a careless or cavalier manner.

Those denying they hold prejudiced views against America may well claim that anti-Americanism is in fact not a prejudice because you can only be prejudiced toward "oppressed" or "disadvantaged" groups and not the mighty and powerful.[62] Some people, however, choose to openly acknowledge their views are prejudicial, arguing that anti-Americanism is a legitimate or necessary prejudice. Nick Cohen, in a 2002 article entitled "Why it is Right to be Anti-American", adopts this position. He makes the following admission: "Anti-Americanism is a prejudice, and it remains crass to identify a people with their government. But with no alternative to the present regime in Washington in sight, a depressingly convincing justification for anti-Americanism remains: that there is little about modern America to be for."[63] Todd Gitlin's apposite criticism that anti-Americanism is often "an emotion masquerading as an analysis" seems fair to direct at Cohen and his defence of anti-American prejudice.[64] The Bush administration was a long way from my favoured politics, but to sweepingly dismiss all that modern America produces is to reveal a narrow focus. It is a common viewpoint on the left, from where Nick Cohen hails, that decent American politicians had been thin on the ground for a considerable time before Obama and that America had largely been a lost cause since the 1960s.[65] These arguments are remarkably selective. From a progressive point of view and for those who bother to examine the details, good and bad decisions and policies come out of the US every year at the federal, state and city levels (a lack of concern for details or counter-evidence is a characteristic trait of anti-American prejudice). Furthermore, the US environmental, women's rights and gay rights movements have been an inspiration for many around the world since the 1960s. If we move to the cultural realm there is clearly much in modern America to be "for" from a progressive position. Prejudice was evident when commentators let their disgust at the Bush administration overshadow appreciation for the good aspects of America. One might well question why millions of Americans voted for Bush, but almost as many were opposed to him: more Americans voted for Gore in 2000 and in 2004 John Kerry lost by a whisker. The election of Trump in 2016 complicates this story undoubtedly as he seems to many people around the world the personification of the Ugly American stereotype.[66] Trump represents many things that are seen as undesirable about American politics and culture; however, even more obvious than it was during the Bush Jnr presidency is the level of internal opposition to Trump. The fact that Hillary Clinton received more votes overall than Trump is pretty widely understood. The strength of dissent towards Trump in America is also widely acknowledged. The Women's March on January 21, 2017, the day after Trump's inauguration, saw the largest single demonstration in US history with around 500,000 people protesting Trump's election in Washington DC; this was widely reported and was in fact part of a wider movement of protests across the world on that day. The American media has not been perfect in reporting on Trump's failings, but since the election it has done a fairly admirable job at holding Trump accountable and because of this most of the best criticisms of the Trump administration have originated from the US itself.

My argument here is that there is a big difference between despairing over the Trump presidency or particular American foreign policy actions and dismissing American society and the American people. Such dismissive attacks often reveal a degree of prejudice that might be the result of anger, frustration and disappointment. They may also be the result of resentment, or even borne out of a sense of superiority. Whatever their source, such attacks are often prejudicial and thus deserve to be called anti-American. These prejudices might not have been particularly deep or pernicious and in many cases they were moderated or dissipated by the election of Barack Obama; nonetheless, as I argue in the next chapter, these prejudices often draw upon longstanding stereotypes about Americans. Stereotypes that are animated by American politicians such as President Lyndon Johnson, Ronald Reagan, George W. Bush and Donald Trump. The election of Trump and his presidency, for all of its horrors, does not represent America in its entirety, which is still vast and full of contradictions. The lessons learnt in the transition from Bush to Obama should not be forgotten, and it is worth considering that Trump's election may well increase the chances of America having a social democratic president elected in the future. Bernie Sanders' success in 2016 and the decidedly left-liberal opinions of people under 25 make this at least conceivable in the near future.[67] Those who declared America a "right nation" during the Bush years would not have imagined such a prospect likely at all.[68]

Viewing anti-Americanism as a prejudice as opposed to a pathology has a number of advantages. It does not allow the exceptions to disprove the rule (an argument commonly accepted in discussions on racism). Just because a person has an Aboriginal friend does not mean they are not racist toward Aboriginal people. Those accused of anti-Americanism often bring up the objection that they cannot be labelled in this way as they like Toni Morrison or Miles Davis or Trent Reznor; or they have American friends; or they were born in America; or in E. P. Thompson's case he could not be accused of being anti-American because he was "ethnically half-American" himself.[69] These objections are beside the point; those who are prejudiced toward America may be all of these things and more. However, it is the nature of one's attitudes or actions that needs to be analysed, not one's music collection or birth certificate. While views and actions need to be set in context, it is a relatively straightforward question to ask whether or not these actions or attitudes are prejudiced. Doing so helps us get to the heart of people's views about America in a way that is widely understood and allows for necessary debate.

Once prejudice is established, it is then critical to examine the breadth and degree of malice held by the individual or group. Recognising this, a number of authors distinguish between anti-Americanism "lite" and "murderous" anti-Americanism.[70] I would not see this distinction as a dichotomy but rather as a continuum, with some forms of non-violent anti-Americanism more pernicious than others. This prejudice is similar to prejudices against other nationalities, but is different in one significant regard, because America is the most powerful nation in the world. This difference counts for nothing in the case of those killed in the 9/11 attacks – violence against civilians is violence. But prejudice against American society or the government is more complicated than attitudes generally towards other nations because of the vast influence of America and the fact that foreigners know a lot about America. What people know may not always be balanced or fair but, due to the widespread dissemination of American media, it is generally a lot more than they know about any other foreign country.

Seeing anti-Americanism as a prejudice is useful, but it only gets us so far. What I am interested in here is when it can be useful to call opposition to America not just prejudicial but ideological. Viewing anti-Americanism as mere prejudice misses the fact that America is a stand-in for many of the things that are wrong with the world. The ideological approach acknowledges that the American way or Americanism has long been considered a political and moral ethos. This was apparent in the Cold War, a conflict that was not just a military, economic and geostrategic contest, it was also an ideological contest. This is one of the reasons that anti-communism was so virulent in America during the Cold War. Where ideological anti-Americanism differs from prejudice is that what America stands for and symbolises is the principal problem. When ideological anti-Americanism concerns itself with actions, it is generally argued that patterns are discernible, which show America to be the worst, stupidest, cruellest, or most malevolent nation on earth.

With ideological anti-Americanism, Americans are presented as having an inferior way of acting and being to non-Americans. The strength of this understanding of anti-Americanism is its focus on what exactly it is about America and Americans that is particularly disliked. This ideological approach puts that question at the centre of its analysis rather than the somewhat vague indications provided by general surveys. Ideological anti-Americanism tends to adopt an essentialising outlook that sees Americans as not only different but as an inferior sub-species. At a societal and governmental level, ideological anti-Americanism considers America to be a danger to other nations, and as having a faulty system of government. These objections are at times driven by a communist or Islamic fundamentalist ideology, or they may be borne out of more complex or incoherent sets of opinions about the US. Despite the insights gained from this approach, there are myriad difficulties with analysing anti-Americanism as an ideology. This is firstly because of the complexity of the term ideology, and secondly because of the contradictory nature of the various ideological objections to America: some dislike America for being too moralistic (puritanical), whereas others claim MTV, the commonality of profanities and its pornographic industries make it too libertine. Some ideological interpretations see America as essentially inward looking and isolationist; others see America as imperialist and keen to control politics and business across all parts of the earth. What is clear is that in an aggregate sense there is no such thing as a coherent anti-American ideology. However, verbal attacks that suggest that there is a dangerous, specifically American way of doing things often reveal the ideological nature of anti-Americanism. Analysing this ideological anti-Americanism is crucial because it helps us make sense of this unusual "ism".

5. Anti-Americanism as an ideology

James Ceaser has written that: "Only one opinion or ideology in the world today has a truly global reach. It is anti-Americanism."[71] To take this definition seriously one first needs to ask what ideology is. Of course there is no simple answer. My understanding of the conceptual nature of the term ideology owes much to the scholarship of Michael Freeden.[72] Although the term was coined by Antoine Destutt de Tracy to connote the study of ideas, the more negative understanding of ideology set forth by Marx and Engels in *The German Ideology* has profoundly shaped subsequent discussions. Marx and Engels presented ideology as a distortion and manipulation of reality that masks the truth;[73] the importance of this inter-pretation is apparent in the common perception that ideology is cant or propaganda that distorts or misrepresents reality. This usage is invoked when people dismiss an argument as being "just ideology" as opposed to what they believe the "evidence shows" or is "in the best interests of society" (in debates about privatisation or health-care, for instance). This pejorative understanding of the term ideology is the one used by Philippe Roger in *The American Enemy* and by Jean-François Revel in his far less sophisticated *Anti-Americanism*. For both authors French anti-Americanism is presented as an ideological attack on a distorted and imagined America: an attack that significantly misrepresents reality. This leads both authors to conclude that anti-Americanism tells us more about French fears and anxieties than it does about American society or politics.

The understanding of ideology as falsehood is never likely to disappear entirely from definitions, but it is only part of the story. The Marxian distinction between bourgeois capitalist ideology and communist truth alerts us to one of the obvious weaknesses of this conception. Clearly communism too is an ideology, as history attests. Recognising this, many modern scholars of ideology have been drawn to talk of competing ideologies, with less emphasis placed on the division between ideology and truth. During the twentieth century, scholars were drawn to increas-ingly see all major schools of thought as ideologies. The experience of the so-called "age of ideologies" – the 1920s and 1930s – particularly shaped this outlook. It was during this period that anti-Americanism emerged as a recognised concept;[74] this historical timing goes some way to explaining why anti-Americanism emerged as an "ism" rather than as a "phobia."

While the notion of competing ideologies is a more useful starting point, this outlook is often presented too simply as major conflicts between fairly fixed ideologies with names like socialism, liberalism, and fascism. This *Politics 101* approach to ideologies misses much of the subtlety and dynamism regarding how ideologies develop. In many textbook accounts of ideologies, they are presented as dogmas or systems of belief with five or so fixed components. I am disinclined to see ideologies as monolithic fixed positions; the insights gained from anthropologic studies of "ideology as a cultural system" and behaviouralist studies of belief systems have added important nuance. They allow us to see ideologies as being big and small: from the ideology of cultural systems, as Gertz puts it, to the ideologies of political parties and social movements. At the same time, I recognise that there are limits to the number of belief systems we can contemplate; we need to assemble ideas under widely recognised labels and concepts to have any chance of engaging in dialogue and politics in general. Ideologies are after all mass belief systems, not private philosophies. This points to one of the problems with trying to understand anti-Americanism as an ideology, for, as Minogue has suggested, "No one, if we get right down to it, is anti-American in quite the same way."[75] For different anti-American thoughts and outpourings to be called an ideology there needs to be a certain commonality, or what Freeden calls an ideological "core" that these ideas coalesce around. While not entirely rigid, this core gives ideologies a "flexible coherence."[76] Freeden also argues that to qualify as an ideology, a belief system needs to have discernible views on important political concepts such as freedom, democracy and equality. Anti-Americanism would seem to generally fall short of this standard.[77] While Anti-Americanism does provide a public policy position of arguing against American culture, ideas and policies, it is a rather limited outlook. Where you can see anti-Americanism clearly as an ideology is in the hands of ideologues like Fidel Castro. As a number of authors have remarked, anti-Americanism overtook Communism as Castro's dominant guiding ideology at times.[78]

At first glance anti-Americanism is clearly too incoherent to be measured as an ideology beyond specific instances. However, this view possibly misses the commonalities within much anti-American opinion. If one focuses particularly on what America symbolises rather than its actions, it becomes possible to talk of an anti-American ideology. James Ceaser's assertion that on "every continent, large contingents of intellectuals, backed by significant numbers in the political class, organize their political thinking on the basis of anti-Americanism" certainly suggests that anti-Americanism is a mass belief system.[79] This claim requires further research and analysis, the likes of which have been begun most fruitfully by Andrei Markovits with his detailed empirical work on anti-Americanism in Germany.[80] An anti-American mindset, if we can call it that, is certainly nowhere near as coherent as ideologies such as liberalism or even conservatism; but it does have similarities with nationalism, which has been called a "thin-centered ideology".[81]

To see anti-Americanism as an ideology inevitably draws one into debates about what America represents and thus to the question of what Americanism is. Richard Hofstatder's observation that "It has been our fate as a nation not to have ideologies but to be one,"[82] would seem a perfect starting point from which to understand Americanism. However, Hofstatder's quote is a siren call that quickly grounds much analysis; an exact understanding of Americanism is far from simple. Beyond vague notions such as "American exceptionalism" there is little agreement on what this ideology is; and exceptionalism itself is certainly not universally accepted as a valid way to describe America.[83] Theodore Roosevelt in 1909 popularised the word "Americanism" declaring that "Americanism signifies the virtues of courage, honor, justice, truth, sincerity and strength – the virtues that made America."[84] In his seminal book *American Exceptionalism* Seymour Martin Lipset embraces Americanism as an ideology, suggesting its core values are: "liberty, egalitarianism, individualism, populism, and laissez-faire."[85] There are a number of problems with these definitions. Firstly, the values associated with Americanism are simply too general to really define a distinct American creed; all of these so-called core values could be equally said to define Australianism if we were to invent such a term. Once these values are articulated beyond motherhood phrases like truth, courage and liberty, they become contested – the most obvious example of this tension is the constant competition between the liberal and conservative interpretations of the American tradition. American liberals and conservatives both see their version as the more authentic understanding of Americanism. Scholars like

Lipset paste over these conflicts by adopting Louis Hartz's line that America has a dominant liberal tradition; I would argue that this position pays far too little attention to the importance of an American form of conservatism that specifically emerged as the private sphere became more politicised.[86]

Americanism could also often be referred to as American nationalism. This nationalism of course borrows from long standing myths and traditions; an understanding that Richard Crockatt eloquently outlines:

> What is not in doubt is the allegiance of a majority of Americans to certain profoundly unifying symbols, attitudes, and values that can collectively be called *Americanism*. There is no more eloquent expression of this sentiment, which is sufficiently potent and historically grounded to qualify as an ideology, than the unity displayed by the American people's reaction to September 11. Equally clear is the curious mixture of attraction and repulsion that this ideology arouses in peoples around the world.[87]

Crockatt not only correctly points out the unifying aspect of this nationalist rhetoric and imaginary, he also highlights that this "ideology" is repellent to many people around the globe, including many Americans, who find jingoistic the schoolroom pledges of allegiance, the flying of the flag off one's front porch or apartment window, and the expectation that politicians display their patriotism with lapel pins.[88] It is debates over this type of hyper-patriotism that bring Americanism and anti-Americanism most easily into focus. Claims that Barack Obama is anti-American for not wearing a flag pin or for making speeches in which he apologised for certain US foreign policies are good examples of how patriotism is employed to call another anti-American. Sarah Palin, with her claims that it is she, rather than Obama, who represents real Americans, uses this tactic also. These accusations highlight the ideological nature of those claiming someone or some view is anti-American (in these cases the pointing of the finger comes from American conservative ideology); they also highlight that the definition of the "real" America (and for that matter Americanism) is open to distortion, propaganda and political manipulation. It is nonsense to say that Sarah Palin and her supporters are real Americans and Obama and those who voted for him are not. What makes Palin more American? Is it her skin colour, the longevity of her ancestors' time in America, or how often she proclaims her love and loyalty to the nation? Such notions contradict much of America's longstanding mantra against the "Old World" of nations based on bloodlines, and that America is supposedly the nation which anyone can join regardless of birthplace and social status. Conservative patriotism and the use of the term anti-American to classify Obama and his supporters seems to support the idea that ideological anti-Americanism is principally about distortion. It also reflects a binary (or Manichean) mindset. This division of good America and bad America is not only engaged in rhetoric by conservative politicians like Sarah Palin and Fox News commentators (Bill O'Reilly, formerly a popular Fox host, divided Americans into Patriots and Pinheads). This division is also employed by those who talk with cosmopolitan confidence about "typical America" and "alternative America". Such pontificating about what is typically American is often heard when people talk about their dislike of certain "American movies" or "American food", or when travellers talk about "good" parts of America one needs to visit. In such discussion Americanism can simply become a hackneyed set of stereotypes, where personal tastes overrule serious analysis. These examples, both from conservative commentary and cosmopolitan discourse, reveal the basic human tendency to seek comfort in "us" and "them" divisions and to build up the virtues of one's own preferences or political positions while exaggerating the faults of the things one does not like or of one's political opponents. Given these stereotypes, it is not surprising that politics can quickly descend into polemics. On one hand, ideological talk can be very complex, particularly in its scholarly formations. On the other hand, in the "real world", it quickly morphs into its crudest form employed on the campaign hustings or cable television. Before we move too far away from a definition of anti-Americanism I want to summarise the discussions so far and offer some conclusions.

A more durable definition

In this chapter I have argued for a critique of America that is based on details and evidence, rather than prejudices and stereotypes; I argue for analysis, not knee-jerk rejection. I have offered five different understandings of what anti-Americanism is, all of which provide various insights. Seeing anti-Americanism as one side of a dichotomy neatly encapsulates how many polemicists see the world. The view of anti-Americanism as a tendency is likely to continue to predominate in discussions on anti-Americanism, despite its analytical limitations. The rich data available from the Pew and other quality surveys provides an almost irresistible basis for discussing year-to-year variations in "anti-Americanism". From my perspective, these surveys provide solid evidence that antipathy toward the US rose significantly during the Bush years, dissipated in many countries significantly during the Obama years and has increased markedly since the election of Trump. I argue the problem with most surveys measuring favourability towards America is that they do *not* provide us with a means of distinguishing genuine anti-American sentiment from disappointment with particular US policies such as American involvement in Iraq. Furthermore, anti-Americanism for me is something more specific than seeing the US "somewhat unfavorably", which is the response much of the Pew analysis is built upon. The *tendency approach* to anti-Americanism is useful shorthand when discussing whether a particular foreign leadership is more anti-American than its predecessor. However, once we get into the details, much of the opposition called anti-Americanism is better described as something else. Seeing anti-Americanism as a pathology is at times tempting, given the simplicity of this literal interpretation; however, on closer examination, this conception means almost no one ends up being anti-American. So where the tendency approach is ultimately too general, classifying anti-Americanism as a pathology is too specific.

I have argued that the last two conceptions of anti-Americanism are the most useful to provide a better understanding of the term. Seeing anti-Americanism principally as a prejudice allows for a relatively straightforward debate over what should be called anti-Americanism and what should more fairly be regarded as criticism. This approach, however, has failed to be widely adopted in commentary on anti-Americanism because unlike most other prejudices, anti-Americanism is often associated with "intellectuals" who apparently know better than to be prejudiced. So to overcome anti-American prejudice, we first need to overcome the prejudice against seeing anti-Americanism as a form of prejudice. The strength of this approach is that it forces us to care about the details, to be well informed, and to consider counter evidence. As analytical principles these are commendable. The weakness of this approach is that it possibly misses the big picture where America is objected to as a "civilisation" or at least a way of life. This brings us to anti-Americanism as an ideology: a view that rejects what is seen as Americanism. However, due to the many interpretations of what Americanism is, there is a fairly broad range of ideas that might be called anti-American ideologies. The various strands of these anti-American outlooks seem to lack a "flexible core", making it too early to admit the term as a member of the family of ideologies. Furthermore, we are often better off to see anti-Americanism as an amalgam of other recognised ideologies.

So my way forward is to argue for an understanding of anti-Americanism that is somewhere between a prejudice and an ideology. More precisely, anti-Americanism should be viewed as an ideological prejudice. In basic terms this is the outlook that generalises, claiming that all Americans are stupid or fat or violent, all American foreign policy is evil and all American businesspeople are greedy and exploitative. Such opinions are totalising, in that they lump all Americans and/or all American actions into one basket. This is both prejudicial and ideological in a crude and obvious sense because the totality of the American population or the totality of American government (or non-government) actions are all seen as equally bad. More commonplace, in terms of ideological prejudice, is a stereotyping of America, in which a greedy businessperson or ignorant beauty pageant contestant is seen as representative of the entire country.

Why is a more precise conversation about anti-Americanism important?

Thomas Jefferson long ago wrote that "every man has two countries – his own and France." Two centuries later, this founder of America could be talking about his own nation. Today it is America that many feel has as much of an effect on their lives as events in their own nation. Undoubtedly many people around the world follow American politics and American culture more closely than politics or culture from their own countries: the Trump campaign and presidency is an excellent example of a reality television show that the whole world continues to watch. This incorporation of America into our lives, dreams and nightmares is precisely why a better understanding of the US, and those who hate it, is important. Of course there are many reasons to be critical of the US and its policies and actions. Certainly the Bush administration could have been a much fairer and wiser global leader than it was, but anti-Americanism was not a useful solution. Rather, by inflaming issues, it was often an obstacle to real debate.

My work here is a starting point for further analysis on a topic that, as I mentioned earlier, has been largely neglected by scholars. For those less convinced that this is a subject worthy of further study and analysis I offer these reasons. Firstly, prejudice in all instances should be challenged and confronted. In its most extreme form this prejudice led to the terrorist attacks of September 11, 2001. In its more commonplace expression it leads to reflexive discrimination against Americans and American ideas and products. Secondly, for negative and undesirable American policies to be effectively questioned, a more differentiated understanding of America is crucial. Thirdly, the consecration of an anti-American ideology that automatically rejects American policy and even culture is reactionary and the enemy of intelligent thought and discernment. In closing, American politics, foreign policy, and Americanisation is rightly the concern of people around the world; the challenge is how to engage with America without letting anti-American prejudices overwhelm critique in all its various forms.

Notes

1 Oscar Wilde, "The American Invasion," *Court and Society Review*, March 23, 1887. <http://www.oscarwildeinamerica.org/Resources/The-American-Invasion.pdf>.

2 Theodore Zeldin, "The Pathology of Anti-Americanism," in *The Rise and Fall of Anti-Americanism: A Century of French Perception*, eds. Denis Lacorne, Jacques Rupnik, and Marie-France Toinet (London: Macmillan, 1990), 41.

3 Similarly, Richard Crockatt argues: "Even these polarities scarcely meet the case; they are the beginning of analysis, not the end of it. The point should be clear. Simplified images are dangerous tools of analysis and are certainly dangerous politically." Richard Crockatt, *America Embattled: September 11, Anti-Americanism and the Global Order* (London: Routledge, 2003), xii–xiii.

4 Americans have not been shy about displaying weirdness from P. T. Barnum in the early 19th century to countless television programs, with the Jerry Springer Show being the most extreme and popular example.

5 Justine Webb, *Have a Nice Day* (London, Short Books, 2008).

6 For example, a totally incoherent response from 2007's Miss Teen South Carolina to the question: "Recent polls have shown a fifth of Americans cannot locate the US on a world map, why do you think this is?" has been viewed roughly 67 million times on YouTube (and the version with subtitles another 10 million times). Her muddled response seemingly provides further evidence that Americans are indeed hopeless when it comes to worldly knowledge. However, finding ignorant (or to be kind, nervous) people in a nation of 327 million people is not that difficult; so, to paraphrase George Orwell, I believe that we need to question our own prejudices and blind spots, especially when pronouncing on the failings and inadequacies of others. (See: Miss Teen America Pageant 2007, <https://www.youtube.com/watch?v=lj3iNxZ8Dww>).

7 James Russell Lowell, "On a Certain Condescension in Foreigners," *Atlantic Monthly* XXIII (1869), 89.

8 Marcus Cunliffe makes this point, stating that America "has supplied an extraordinary drama (or melodrama) peopled with scouts and trappers, Yankees and Cavaliers, cowboys and Indians, sheriffs and badmen, Huck Finns and Nigger Jims, Abe Lincolns and Huey Longs, preachers and robber barons, do-gooders and con-men, Al Capones and J.

Edgar Hoovers, hobos and work-bosses, loners and Babbitts. No other nation has produced so rich a cast of symbolic characters for modern times." quoted in Henry Fairlie, "Anti-Americanism at Home and Abroad," *Commentary* (December, 1975), 31.

9 Jim Cullen, *The American Dream: A Short History of an Idea that Shaped a Nation* (New York: Oxford University Press, 2003); Jennifer L. Hoschchild, *Facing Up to the American Dream: Race, Class, and the Soul of the Nation* (Princeton, NJ: Princeton University Press, 1995).

10 Ziauddin Sardar, *Why Do People Hate America?* (New York: Disinformation, 2002).

11 Henry Pelling, *America and the British Left* (New York: New York University Press, 1957), 161.

12 Moisés Naím writes: "In France, the editor of *Le Monde Diplomatique* summarised his view of the world's reaction: 'What's happening to [Americans] is too bad, but they had it coming.'" Moisés Naím, "Anti-Americanisms," *Foreign Policy* (January–February, 2002), 104–105. This view conflates people with governments in a manner I find highly questionable. However, the flip side of this response is the claim of American innocence. A classic example of this claim was made by Donald Rumsfeld in 2004 when he said: "I think that people who think that terrorists pick and choose discriminately don't understand how it works. The United States had done nothing on September 11th when 3,000 people were killed." Donald Rumsfeld, "Transcript of the Prime Minister The Hon. John Howard MP Joint Press Conference with Secretary of Defense Donald Rumsfeld," (Press Conference held at the Pentagon, Washington DC, July 18, 2005). The terrorist attacks of 9/11 were inexcusable, but America has certainly done a lot more than "nothing" on the world stage.

13 Todd Gitlin, "Anti-anti-Americanism," *Dissent* (Winter 2003), 103–106.

14 This point follows the advice of James Madison in the *Federalist Papers* (# 63) where he declared that "in doubtful cases, particularly where the national councils may be warped by some strong passion or momentary interest, the presumed or known opinion of the impartial world may be the best guide to be followed." Of course the outside world is seldom, if ever, impartial, but the principle is still a good one. Alexander Hamilton et al., *The Federalist Papers* (New York: New American Library, 1961).

15 Henry Pelling made a similar point about a different time period in his *America and the British Left* (1957). "The historical perspective provided by these studies inevitably suggests that dangerous distortion of the facts is likely to take place among those who commit themselves most fully to an *a priori* view of politics. Socialists of the mid-twentieth century seem to be often as blind to the merits of American society as Radicals of the mid-nineteenth century were blind to its faults." Pelling, *America and the British Left* (New York: New York University Press, 1957), 6.

16 E.J. Dionne, *Why Americans Hate Politics* (New York: Simon & Schuster, 2004); Rick Perlstein, "Operation Barbarella," *London Review of Books*, November, 17, 2005, <http s://www.lrb.co.uk/v27/n22/rick-perlstein/operation-barbarella>.

17 Max Friedman, *Rethinking Anti-Americanism: The History of an Exceptional Concept in American Foreign Relations* (New York: Cambridge University Press, 2012).

18 Grunberg writes: "Even though the 9/11 attacks clearly marked the United States as a target and victim, a majority of Europeans considered that American foreign policy had been a contributing factor (GMF survey). Sixty-three percent of the French were of this opinion, but 57 percent of the British as well." Gérard Grunberg, "Anti-Americanism in French and European Public Opinion," in *With Us or Against Us: Studies in Global Anti-Americanism*, eds. Tony Judt and Denis Lacorne (New York: Palgrave Macmillan, 2005), 63.

19 Charlotte Raven uses the words "A bully with a bloody nose is still a bully" in her article "A Bully with a Bloody Nose is still a Bully," *The Guardian*, Tuesday September 18, 2001 <http://www.guardian.co.uk/world/2001/sep/18/september11.comment>.

20 Lauren Carroll, "Fact-checking Trump's Claim that Thousands in New Jersey Cheered when World Trade Center Tumbled," *Politifact*, November 22, 2015, <http://www. politifact.com/truth-o-meter/statements/2015/nov/22/donald-trump/fact-checking-trumps-claim-thousands-new-jersey-ch/>.

21 Glenn Kessler, "Trump's Outrageous Claim that 'Thousands' of New Jersey Muslims Celebrated the 9/11 Attacks," *The Washington Post*, November 22, 2015, <https:// www.washingtonpost.com/news/fact-checker/wp/2015/11/22/donald-trumps-outra geous-claim-that-thousands-of-new-jersey-muslims-celebrated-the-911-attacks/?utm_ term=.e1b8291349b>.

22 Lauren Carroll, "Fact-checking Trump's Claim that Thousands in New Jersey Cheered when World Trade Center Tumbled," *Politifact*, November 22, 2015, <http://www. politifact.com/truth-o-meter/statements/2015/nov/22/donald-trump/fact-checking-trumps-claim-thousands-new-jersey-ch/>.

23 See Richard Crockatt, *American Embattled: September 11, Anti-Americanism, and the Global Order* (London: Routledge, 2003).

24 2,977 people were killed in the 9/11 attacks. Nineteen terrorists also died in the 9/11 attacks. Cable News Network Library, "September 11th Terror Attacks Fast Facts," *Cable News Network*, August 24, 2017, <http://edition.cnn.com/2013/07/27/us/septem ber-11-anniversary-fast-facts/index.html>. It is worth comparing the death toll to the 2004 India Ocean earthquake and subsequent tsunami which killed over 250,000 people, and which received far less media coverage internationally. BBC, "Indonesia Quake Toll Jumps Again," January 25, 2005 <http://news.bbc.co.uk/2/hi/asia-pacific/ 4204385.stm>. Even more alarming is the death toll of the Second Congo War where it is estimated that over 5 million people died from 1998 onwards and the events received barely any coverage in the international media.

25 Paul Hollander, "Introduction: The New Virulence and Popularity," in *Understanding Anti-Americanism*, ed. Paul Hollander (Chicago: Ivan R. Dee, 2004), 16.

26 Pew Research Center for the People and the Press, "A Year after Iraq War," March 16, 2004.

27 See BBC, "What the World Thinks of America," (2003), <http://news.bbc.co.uk/2/ hi/americas/2994924.stm>. Similar results were seen in the Euorobarometer survey of October 2003. See Marta Lagos, "Threat to World Peace and the Role of the USA," *International Journal of Public Opinion Research* 16(1) (Spring, 2004), 91–95.

28 Pew Research Center for the People and the Press, "A Year after Iraq War," March 16, 2004.

29 Collected by Pierangelo Isernia, cited in Philip Everts, "Images of the U.S. – Three theories of anti-Americanism," Workshop on Anti-Americanism in Comparative Historical Perspective, European Consortium for Political Research, Nicosia, Cyprus, April 25–30, 2006. Explanatory note from Philip Everts: "Combined Net scores ('favorable' minus 'unfavorable') are given for France, Germany, Italy and United Kingdom. Averages have been calculated for years for which more polls were available. Data for missing years have been interpolated. Polls were not always held in all countries and the average figure presented in the graph sometimes may hide important differences among the four countries. Given the generally fairly positive results in terms of sympathy, trust with respect to the United States that these surveys tend to produce it is somewhat awkward and biased to (continue to) use the term 'anti- Americanism' for this indicator."

30 Max Rodenbeck, "The Truth about Jihad," *New York Review of Books*, August 11, 2005.

31 This is not shown in the table but is from this data set: Pew Research Center for the People and the Press "Opinion of the United States" August, 2017, <http://www.pew global.org/database/indicator/1/survey/all/response/Unfavorable/>.

32 Friedman writes "It is the rare author who, like Rolf Winter and Alfred Mechter-sheimer, openly acknowledges his own anti-Americanism." Max Paul Friedman, "Cold War Critiques From Abroad: Beyond a Taxonomy of Anti-Americanism," *GHI Bulletin*, 34 (Spring, 2004).

33 The abuse of the term "liberal" in post-1960s US politics is a classic example. See Brendon O'Connor, *A Political History of the American Welfare System* (Lanham: Rowman & Littlefield, 2004).

34 Kenneth Minogue, "Anti-Americanism: A View from London," *The National Interest* (Spring, 1986), 43. On this issue also see Hubert Vedrine, "On Anti-Americanism," *Brown Journal of World Affairs* X, 2 (Winter/Spring, 2004), 117–122. The popular

Internet encyclopedia *Wikipedia* similarly notes this usage of the term anti-Americanism: "[T]he term is rarely employed as a self-identifier (i.e. 'I am anti-American…') as this inherently implies bias. Instead, it is used most often as a pejorative by those who feel the United States is unfairly disparaged. The term may be employed, for instance, as a slur against groups or arguments critical of American policy" <http://en.wikipedia.org/wiki/Anti-Americanism>.

35 For examples of the misuse of the term anti-Americanism in Australian politics see: Steve Lewis, "PM Forced into Another Sugar Rescue," *Australian*, February 11, 2004; Michelle Grattan, "US Aware of Latham's 'dislike,'" *Age*, April 13, 2004; Greg Sheridan, "Labor's Anti-Americanism Won't Wash," *Australian*, June 17, 2004, 11; *AAP*, "Labor Shows Knee-jerk Anti-Americanism over FTA – Howard," August 21, 2004; Janet Albrechtsen, "On Uncle Sam, Latham's Spots Aren't Changing," *Australian*, August 4, 2004.

36 This work offers a laundry list of reasons why people dislike America, and at times they rightly point out the contradictions within American society. However, their analysis is often too glib, and logic at times deserts them, such as in the following paragraph: "The rest of the world is more alert to the contradictions within America and its history than Americans themselves; more intrigued and interested to explore these contradictions than Americans are prepared to participate in such debate. As President Clinton noted in a speech at the University of California in 1997: 'We were born with a declaration of independence which asserted that we were all created equal and a constitution that enshrined slavery. We fought a bloody civil war to abolish slavery but we remained unequal by law for another century. We advanced across the continent in the name of freedom, yet in doing so we pushed Native Americans off their land. We welcome immigrants, but each new wave has felt the sting of discrimination." Ziauddin Sardar and Merryl Wyn Davies, *Why Do People Hate America?* (Cambridge: Icon Books, 2002), 59. Are they forgetting that Bill Clinton is an American, and a rather prominent one at that? We should expect much more from these bestselling authors.

37 "The *New York Review of Books* marketed itself in Europe in 2003 with a cartoon of George W. Bush in the garb of a Roman emperor, next to the slogan 'There is another America – and we need to hear from it.'" John Micklethwait and Adrian Wooldridge, *The Right Nation: Conservative Power in America* (New York: Penguin, 2004), 292.

38 Andrei Markovits, *Uncouth Nation* (Princeton: Princeton University Press, 2007).

39 Moisés Naím, "Anti-Americanisms," *Foreign Policy* (January–February, 2002), 104–105.

40 Alvin Rubinstein and Donald Smith, "Anti-Americanism in the Third World," *Annals (AAPSS)* 497, 1988.

41 Robert Singh, "Are We All Americans Now? Explaining Anti-Americanisms," in *The Rise of Anti-Americanism*, eds. Brendon O'Connor and Martin Griffiths (London: Routledge, 2005).

42 Peter Katzenstein and Robert Keohane, "Varieties of Anti-AmericanismS," (paper presented at the annual meeting of the American Political Science Association, Washington DC, US, August 31–September 1, 2005).

43 Moisés Naím, "The Perils of Anti-Americanism Lite," *Foreign Policy* (May/June, 2003).

44 Denis Lacorne and Tony Judt, "The Banality of Anti-Americanism," in eds. Tony Judt and Denis Lacorne, 1.

45 Potter Stewart was struggling to precisely define pornography (See Justice Potter Stewart, concurring in *Jacobellis v. Ohio* (378 US 134, 1964). Robert Singh, "Are We All Americans Now? Explaining Anti-Americanisms," in *The Rise of Anti-Americanism*, eds. Brendon O'Connor and Martin Griffiths (London: Routledge, 2005). Andrei Markovits, *Uncouth Nation: Why Europe Hates America* (Princeton: Princeton University Press, 2007); Christopher Hitchens, "Anti-Americanism," *Slate*, November 27, 2002 <https://slate.com/news-and-politics/2002/11/does-anti-americanism-exist.html>.

46 "States Go Under Microscope," *Courier Mail*, April 20, 2005.

47 An example of Bush's Manichean worldview is his language of a "war on terror," with its associated talk of "evil-doers," the "axis of evil" and "good versus evil." President Bush used the phrase "evil-doers" 24 times in the eight months after the September 11, 2001 terrorist attacks.

48 Rajiv Chandrasekaran, *Imperial Life in the Emerald City* (New York: Vintage Books, 2007); Thomas E. Ricks, *Fiasco: The America Military Adventure in Iraq* (New York: Penguin, 2006); George Packer, *Assassin's Gate* (New York: Farrar, Straus and Giroux, 2005).

49 Pew Research Center for the People and the Press, "American Character Gets Mixed Reviews," June 23, 2005, 59–60.

50 This was the case in all of the nations mentioned from 2002 through to 2008. See Pew Research Center for the People and the Press, "Obama More Popular Abroad than At Home, Global Image of U.S. Continues to Benefit," July 17, 2010 <http://pewglobal. org/database/?indicator=2&survey=12&response=Favorable&mode=table>.

51 Pew Research Center for the People and the Press, "American Character Gets Mixed Reviews," June 23, 2005, 45–46.

52 Pew Research Center for the People and the Press, "Obama More Popular Abroad than At Home, Global Image of U.S. Continues to Benefit," July 17, 2010 <http://p ewglobal.org/database/?indicator=2&survey=12&response=Favorable&mode=table>.

53 Pew Research Center for the People and the Press, "American Character Gets Mixed Reviews," June 23, 2005, 1.

54 Theodore Zeldin, "The Pathology of Anti-Americanism," in eds. Lacorne, Rupnik, and Toinet.

55 Marie-France Toinet, "Does Anti-Americanism Exist?" in eds. Lacorne, Rupnik, and Toinet, 220.

56 Kimball takes this outlook when he writes "anti-Americanism has almost nothing to do with *criticism*. It is more a pathology than a position, operating not by evidence but emotion." Roger Kimball, "Anti-Americanism Then and Now," in ed. Paul Hollander, 240. More hysterical on this issue is Medved who describes anti-Americanism as "the world's most dangerous, powerful and pathological hatred," which "needs to be punished and rooted out, not respectfully analyzed." Michael Medved, "World's Most Dangerous Hatred," <http://www.worldnetdaily.com/news/article.asp?ARTICLE_ID=25296>.

57 Roger Kimball, "Anti-Americanism Then and Now," in ed. Paul Hollander, 240.

58 Toinet, "Does Anti-Americanism Exist?" in eds. Lacorne, Rupnik and Toinet, 225–226. It is interesting how readily Tocqueville is claimed to be pro-American with respect to his views presented in *Democracy in America*. It reflects both an American desire for praise (like most new nations: Australians are just as needy in this regard, if not more so; see: O'Connor, "Desperately Seeking Sam," *ABC*, September 29, 2010, <https://www.abc. net.au/news/2009-04-01/31230>). This reading of Tocqueville as pro-America also reflects a shallowness of many readings of *Democracy in America*. Particularly in volume 2, Tocqueville is very critical of American culture and society in a manner that could hardly be seen as pro-America. My sense is that although he praises American political institutions, public education and civic behaviour and sees America as a vision of the future; it is a future that will be less artful and more mundane. Tocqueville here is writing a similar story to what Fukuyama will write 150 years later. America for Tocqueville is the end of history and he often mourns this fact in what will be lost (a sense of beauty and poetry is part of what he suggests will be lost).

59 Robert Singh, "Are We All Americans Now?"

60 Arundhati Roy, "Anti-Americanism: Hallowed Be Thy Name," *Arts and Opinion* 2, 1 (2003).

61 Denis Lacorne, "Anti-Americanism and Americanophobia," in *With Us or Against US: Studies in Global Anti-Americanism*, eds. Tony Judt and Denis Lacorne (New York: Palgrave, 2005), 47–52.

62 Not one of the books I have come across on prejudice has a listing for anti-Americanism in the index.

63 Nick Cohen, "Why it is Right to be Anti-American," *New Statesman*, January 14, 2002.

64 Gitlin, "Anti-anti-Americanism."

65 In the same article Cohen writes: "However worthy individual thinkers and protesters may be, there are now no convincing radical movements in America, and haven't been for years." Cohen, "Why it is Right to be Anti-American."

66 Brendon O'Connor, "There Are Six Types of Ugly American and Donald Trump Is All of Them," *Sydney Morning Herald*, November 3, 2016, <http://www.smh.com.au/ comment/there-are-six-types-of-ugly-american-and-donald-trump-is-all-of-them -20161102-gsgtrk.html>.

67 "A 2011 Pew study found that while Americans over 30 favored capitalism over social-ism by 27 points, Americans under 30 narrowly favored socialism. Compared with older Americans, Millennials are 36 points more likely to prefer a larger government that provides more services over a smaller one that provides fewer." Peter Beinart, "The End of American Exceptionalism," *The Atlantic*, February 3, 2014, <https://www.theatlantic. com/politics/archive/2014/02/the-end-of-american-exceptionalism/283540/>.

68 Micklethwait and Wooldridge, *The Right Nation: Why America is Different*.

69 Paul Hollander, *Anti-Americanism: Irrational and Rational* (New York: Transaction, 1995), 334.

70 Ivan Krastev, "The Anti-Americanism Century," *Journal of Democracy* 15, 2 (2004), 5

71 James Ceaser, "The Philosophical Origins of Anti-Americanism in Europe," 45.

72 Michael Freeden, *Ideology: A Very Short Introduction* (Oxford: Oxford University Press, 2003); Michael Freeden, *Ideologies and Political Theory* (Oxford: Clarendon Press, 1996).

73 The idea that ideology was a tool of the powerful and thus that the study of ideology is crucially the study of power relations has also long been central to Marxist thinking. See Terry Eagleton, *Ideology: An Introduction* (London: Verso, 1991), 5–7.

74 Tony Judt, *Past Imperfect* (Berkeley: University of California Press, 1992), 190–191.

75 Minogue, "Anti-Americanism," 44.

76 Michael Freeden, "Editorial: Fundamentals and Foundations of Ideologies," *Journal of Political Ideologies*, 10, 1 (2005), 3.

77 Michael Freeden, "Editorial: Ideological Boundaries and Ideological Systems," *Journal of Political Ideologies*, 8, 1 (2003); Freeden, *Ideology: A Very Short Introduction*; Freeden, *Ideologies and Political Theory*.

78 Mark Falcoff, "Cuban Anti-Americanism: Historical, Popular, and Official," in ed. Hollander, 197.

79 Ceaser, "The Philosophical Origins of Anti-Americanism in Europe," 45.

80 Andrei Markovits, *Uncouth Nation: Why Europe Dislikes America* (Princeton: Princeton University Press, 2007); Andrei Markovits, "European Anti-Americanism (and Anti-Semitism): Ever Present Though Always Denied," *Center for European Studies Working Paper Series #108*, Harvard University, 2004.

81 Michael Freeden, "Is Nationalism a Distinct Ideology?" *Political Studies* XLVI (1998), 748–750.

82 Quoted in Michael Kazin, "The Party of Fear," *The Nation*, February 20, 1989. Hof-stadter's words echo G. K. Chesterton's much quoted "America is the only nation in the world that is founded on a creed. That creed is set forth with dogmatic and even theological lucidity in the Declaration of Independence."

83 Ian Tyrrell, "American Exceptionalism in an Age of International History," *American Historical Review*, 96, 4 (1991).

84 Theodore Roosevelt quoted in Toinet, "Does Anti-Americanism Exist?" 219.

85 Seymour Martin Lipset, *American Exceptionalism* (New York: Norton, 1996), 19. Amer-icanism or what books on American Government often call "American political cul-ture." The most extensive textbook discussion of American political culture in such textbooks is outlined by two British scholars: David McKay in *American Politics and Society*, 8th edition (Oxford: John Wiley & Sons, 2013) and Robert Singh in *American Government and Politics* (London: Sage, 2003). McKay (2009) offers an overview of what he sees as the widely agreed upon core elements of American political culture: "liberty, egalitarianism, individualism, democracy, populism and the rule of law under a con-stitution" (p. 7). This is similar to Lipset's (1996) list but McKay cites Samuel Hunting-ton, *American Politics* (Cambridge, Harvard University Press, 1981) as the source for this list. Robert Singh in *American Government and Politics* (2003) also emphasises Americans' strong and broad commitment to their political culture; making the point that the strength of this ideology can also be seen comparatively: "Even in the UK," he writes "it

is possible to advocate the abolition of the monarchy without being called 'un-British' (unpatriotic, perhaps, but to be described as un-British strikes an odd tone). The reason is that the relationship between national identity and political values is far less intimate" (p. 11). Whereas dissenters in the US are called un-American or anti-American. Following Huntington (1981) and Lipset (1996) Singh argues there is an ideology of "Americanism" based on: freedom, equality, individualism, liberalism, democracy, property, and constitutionalism (p. 9). This makes "Americans" according to Singh "among the most, not least, ideological people in the world." (p. 11). Singh acknowledges what he calls the "multiple traditions" approach of Rogers Smith, Gary Gerstle and Desmond King that places racial conflict more central in the narrative of American political culture and how this leads to an emphasis on conflict rather than consensus. However, Singh's narrative like McKay's is one of a powerful consensus of political values in America. The famous conservative Political Scientists James Q. Wilson and John Dilulio argue these are the core elements of American political culture: liberty, equality, democracy, civic duty, individual responsibility.

86 Books that go a long way to rebuffing Hartz and providing a more balanced understanding of the role of conservatism in America include: Theodore Lowi, *The End of the Republican Era* (Norman: University of Oklahoma Press, 1995); Anatol Lieven, *America Right or Wrong* (New York: Oxford University Press, 2004); Micklethwait and Wooldridge, *The Right Nation.*

87 Although I am less confident than Crockatt about what exactly Americanism might be, he is dead right to suggest that anti-Americanism is not simply a rejection of the American creed or the American example; it is commonly tinged with feelings of disappointment that America has not lived up to its ideals and rhetoric. Crockatt, *America Embattled*, 38.

88 Katha Pollit, "Put Out No Flags," *The Nation*, <https://www.thenation.com/article/put-out-no-flags/>. Todd Gitlin, *The Intellectuals and the Flag* (New York: Columbia University Press, 2006).

2

A HISTORY OF ANTI-AMERICANISM

Why do people hate America? The simple answer is American power. America's military, economic, and technological primacy, coupled with its political and cultural pre-eminence, provides much to fear, resent and dislike. Former Secretary of State, and Chair of the Pew Center, Madeleine Albright advanced this view when explaining the rise of anti-American sentiment in the early 21st century, something that is clearly charted by the Pew surveys. She contended that anti-American attitudes "simply go with the territory of being the world's only superpower, with unmatched economic and cultural influence. In many ways, we are viewed as the rich guy living on the hill... We have seen this coming since the end of the Cold War."[1] According to this theory, as Mr Big, America is damned if it acts and damned if it does not. In other words, anti-Americanism is the "price of power." America's power, and thus America's pre-eminence in the international media and global imagination, is crucial to understanding anti-Americanism. However, this explanation reveals only part of the story and as such, has considerable weaknesses. Firstly, it does not account for the fact that anti-Americanism existed well before America was a major economic or military power. Secondly, as James Ceaser has argued, the "natural source" of anti-Americanism,[2] namely power, does not account for the virulence of anti-Americanism; beyond its power "America has become a symbol for something despised on philosophical grounds" and this leads not just to rivalry but to sheer contempt.[3] Lastly, Albright's thesis does not allow for the fact that the conduct of the powerful is crucial to whether they are viewed favourably or unfavourably. This renders highly questionable Walter Laqueur's argument that "[t]o be hated is a consequence of being great and powerful. It can be remedied not by becoming gentler, only by becoming weaker."[4] The Pew surveys show that shifts in US foreign policy have a discernible impact on how the US and its people are viewed abroad; the decision to go to war against Iraq in 2003 saw a vast increase in ire towards the US; conversely America's decision in 2005 to provide aid relief to Indonesia and Pakistan in the wake of the tsunami and earthquake disasters markedly lessened antagonism in those countries. The surveys show that Obama's decision to withdraw American troops from Iraq made a big difference to attitudes about America around the world. This was a decision that did not make America weaker, it made it stronger, financially and morally. However, it also seems fair to suggest based on the Pew surveys that the Obama administration's increased targeting of Pakistan with deadly drones created greater negative sentiment towards America. As this book will argue policies do matter a lot in shaping anti-American sentiment, but so do underlying historical perceptions about America.

To understand this interplay between historical tropes, the rise of US power, and particular events, an historical approach is essential. This chapter will chart the historical course of anti-Americanism through two complementary approaches, firstly by offering a brief history of the key literature on anti-Americanism and the insights this has provided and secondly by detailing the historical development of the anti-American narrative. I will detail the latter by examining what I see as four overlapping waves of anti-Americanism: cultural, political/military, economic, and terrorist. All have both American and foreign sources; at times anti-Americanism is clearly a reaction to the actions and policies of America while at other times it tells us much more about the concerns and agendas of foreigners regarding what America represents for them. Thus, locating the key sources of anti-Americanism at either the feet of American policy-makers or critics of America will never fully explain the phenomenon; it is the interplay between American actions and the perception and retelling of these actions that is critical, and in need of more analysis. While it is true that anti-Americanism can be a simple reaction to what America *does*, more often than not it moves beyond this to become a reaction to what America supposedly *is* or what it symbolises.

A history of the literature

The results of a library catalogue search for books on the subject of anti-Americanism yields results that only go back as far as the 1960s. These first books to feature anti-Americanism in their titles were impressionistic rather than scholarly in their approach. One such example is Thomas Morgan's 1967 *The Anti-Americans*. Essentially a travelogue through the countries of Brazil, Japan, Indonesia, Egypt, Kenya, and France, the book contains global anecdotes of resentment towards America. Attempting to gauge global opinion on America through conversations with the "common people" has been a well-worn trend in feature articles over the years. In keeping with its author's background as a journalist, *The Anti-Americans* offers a series of anecdotes about non-Americans' impressions of the US and its people. The journalist Art Buchwald took a more novel approach, placing an ad in the London *Times* asking readers to tell him why they did not like Americans. The responses led him to conclude that "if Americans would stop spending money, talking loudly in public places, telling the British who won the war, adopting pro-colonial policy, back future British expeditions in the Suez … stop chewing gum, dress properly, throw away their cameras, move their air bases out of England ... turn over the hydrogen bomb to Great Britain ... not export Rock'n Roll, and speak correct English,"[5] then the two peoples could get along.

Although these journalistic approaches to the topic are often highly readable and not without insight, they do not effectively define the topic or offer any real background to its emergence. For this deeper level of analysis, we would generally turn to scholarly works. Unfortunately, the direct study of anti-Americanism was largely ignored by scholars before September 11, 2001, and as a result very few books were published on the topic. The principal scholarly (although highly polemical) exception is Paul Hollander's *Anti-Americanism: Critiques at Home and Abroad, 1965–1990*, which was published in 1992, and then updated and reissued as *Anti-Americanism: Irrational and Rational* in 1995. The best scholarship in the 20th century about anti-Americanism tended not to include the word in its titles, possibly explaining why a new generation of interested scholars has ignored the handful of books that should be considered classics and vital reference points for future works. One book particularly deserving of this status as a key early exploration of anti-Americanism is Henry Pelling's *America and the British Left* (1956). Serious analysts of anti-Americanism are still attempting to answer Pelling's fascinating question of how did anti-Americanism in Europe move from being a largely conservative position in the 19th century to a predominantly left-wing position in the 20th?

Outlining his inquiry Pelling writes:

> The purpose of this study is to show how the fund of Radical goodwill for America and its institutions, which made a contrast with the prejudices of the 'educated' classes in the middle of the nineteenth century, was gradually dissipated in the succeeding decades, until by the middle of the twentieth century the bulk of so-called 'anti-American' feeling was to be found among the adherents of the Left in British politics.[6]

Pelling's study charts the growing disillusionment with America felt by leftists and radicals across Europe.[7] His book recognises that with increased power comes increased scepticism and scrutiny;[8] furthermore, this scrutiny has often led to disappointment as the hopes and expectations for America have not always been realistic. Pelling insightfully described the source and nature of this disillusionment thus:

> It arises from the fact that the United States is by tradition not a nation-state but a community of people who have chosen to associate together and dedicate themselves to a 'proposition.' The explicit idealism of the American constitution will always lead other peoples to expect much of the United States: the danger is that it may often lead them to expect too much.[9]

In the 1990s two important works on anti-Americanism were produced: Richard Kuisel's *Seducing the French* (1993) and Tony Judt's *Past Imperfect* (1992). Both books are essential works for those wanting to understand the origins and development of French anti-Americanism. In the French popular imagination, according to Kuisel, America represented an undesirable future that was more commercial and individualistic and less artistic and romantic than France. In short, in France, American society has long been seen as an inferior model. Thus according to Kuisel it was the supposed threat of Americanisation in France that produced anti-American sentiment. Like Philippe Roger in his dense and quirky *The American Enemy* (2005), Kuisel suggests that this antagonism toward America tells us more about French than American identity.[10] Judt's book is particularly insightful for understanding the origins of anti-Americanism as an ideology of sorts, and the connection between anti-Americanism and anti-Semitism. This last subject has also been provocatively covered by Andrei S. Markovits in his *Uncouth Nation* (2007).

In *Past Imperfect*, Judt argues that disappointment and even disillusionment with America has long been the flip side of high hopes and possibly unrealistic expectations about America. With his characteristic skill and insight, Judt takes us into the world of French anti-American attitudes in the 1920s and 1930s. He argues that, like earlier 19th century criticism, anti-Americanism in the 1930s was largely conservative in its origins, with strong romantic overtones. American society was criticised for becoming something akin to Chaplin's *Modern Times* writ large, with its materialism and industrialism seen as a real threat to the beauty and variety of Western culture.[11] Furthermore, for most of these detractors, Europe was and always would be the soul of Western civilisation; however, for some anti-Americans, the Orient was romanticised as the antidote to the American way. Important criticisms of American materialism, corporatisation, and conformity that emerged in this period were pushed to the side-lines after 1945 with the discrediting of the European right and the rise of the communist threat. Furthermore, in the 1930s a particular strand of anti-Americanism had become an extension of anti-Semitism. In the minds of certain critics, Jews were associated with rootless modernity and capitalism, with the worst outcome of these forces being America. Summing up this tendency, Judt translates French right-wing columnist Robert Brasillach's answer to the question of what separated France from America. "The answer is threefold: its hypocrisy (a frequent charge), its dollars, and international Jewry." Judt goes on to note that "[a]s the last bastion of Jewish power in the world, the United States was the enemy of revolutionaries and reactionaries, anti-modernists and socialists alike."[12] This list of enemies points to the plasticity of America as a target for criticism, blame and grievance, with its antagonists frequently projecting onto it the objects of their prejudice.

Another neglected book on the topic of anti-Americanism is James Ceaser's *Reconstructing America* (1997), an incisive, although at times discursive book that details America's long history of being symbolically depicted as inferior, particularly by Europeans. Ceaser further points out that this powerful image of symbolic America is generally a distortion that is in fact little more than a plaything of European elites and intellectuals. *Reconstructing America*'s many targets, from postmodernism to the state of American political science, could tempt some to write it off as a conservative jeremiad, but this would miss the force of its central argument that anti-Americanism begins in Europe as a false dichotomy between the European and American paths to modernity. A broader audience has since found Ceaser's work in two later pieces – in the magazine *The Public Interest* and in an edited book by Hollander that came out after 9/11 – that more directly reiterate his position on anti-Americanism.[13] At a philosophical level Ceaser suggests that in Europe a Heideggerian critique of America as rootless and technologically driven has been married to a leftist critique of America as materialist and commercial, and that this has become the dominant intellectual view of America, thus fortifying the pre-existing attitude of America as inferior to Europe.[14] More simply stated, Ceaser's thesis is that: "Anti-Americanism rests on the singular idea that something associated with the United States, something at the core of American life, is deeply wrong and threatening to the rest of the world."[15] Ceaser illustrates this with a quote from a journalist character of the novelist Henry de Montherlant: "One nation that manages to lower intelligence, morality, human quality on nearly all the surface of the earth, such a thing has never been seen before in the existence of the planet. I accuse the United States of being in a permanent state of crime against humankind."[16]

A curious fact about the 20th century literature on anti-Americanism is that there was little explicit study of Cold War anti-Americanism. It could be argued that the Cold War ushered in ideological anti-Americanism as the main variant of the tradition, underpinned by socialist and communist rhetoric about America as a ruthless, imperial nation. Whether this commentary is best thought of as anti-American or as criticism has never been explored in a scholarly manner. Paul Hollander, a staunch anti-communist who escaped from his native Hungary in 1956 has surprisingly little to say about Soviet anti-American rhetoric – perhaps the antipathy between the nations was seen as so obvious that he did not regard it as necessary to study in the context of anti-Americanism. Instead, most of his writing deals with American anti-Americanism and the condemnations from Third World and European intellectuals. Hollander also spends a lot of time focusing on Americans who travelled to Nicaragua in the 1980s, whom he labels dissidents. Jean Kirkpatrick unfairly dubbed this grouping the "blame America first" crowd. Richard Kuisel's book has a Cold War focus but instead of looking at leftist opinion he asks whether the rightist President de Gaulle is fairly viewed as anti-American. In a thoughtful and revealing manner, Kuisel argues that de Gaulle did not have a "visceral dislike" of Americans or their institutions; rather, his main gripe was with American hegemony and mass Americanisation. De Gaulle seemed to share with many of his countrymen a stereotypical view that the United States was "soulless, materialist and ahistorical," and his response to the American challenge was to strengthen French independence and self-reliance.[17] It has been argued that the lesson France took from the 1956 Suez Crisis was never again to be dependent on the Americans, whereas the lesson that Britain took was never to be on the opposite side from the US in an international conflict. Given these attitudes, it is interesting that Kuisel concludes that "de Gaulle's affirmation of national pride served in the long run to dampen French combativeness towards the United States and subdue the country's assertiveness in world affairs." Further, this re-building of

French pride and de Gaulle's promotion of economic growth and technological advancement increased "domestic Americanisation" in France (as evidenced by the rise in "American-style consumption" and the "proliferation" of American products).[18] Henry Fairlie has suggested that: "It is the impact of Americanization that is at the core of anti-Americanism."[19] I would agree that this concern remains constant and ongoing, while concerns about American foreign policy actions rise and fall depending on the circumstances or the president of the day. Further, a fear of Americanisation creates an underlying nervous anxiety that explains some of the emotionality, and at times highly personalised ridicule, in non-American responses to US politicians like George W. Bush, Ronald Reagan or Donald Trump. Often underlying both the response to Trump and America is a particular dismay that success has been achieved by such a seemingly inferior nation, allegedly populated by an unsophisticated people.

It is worth spending more time examining Paul Hollander's *Anti-Americanism* which was first published in 1992 and followed by a second edition in 1995 (which includes a long introduction where Hollander dismisses his critics), because it was the 20th century's most recognised book on the topic. As I mentioned earlier, Hollander was for many years the sole scholar who gave his field of specialty the name of anti-Americanism. The book provides many examples of anti-Americanism and is driven by the sophisticated proposition that anti-Americanism is part of a global ambivalence about modernity. Hollander, like Pelling, suggests that anti-Americanism is the result of unrealistic expectations about the moral purity and capacity of the US.[20] He writes:

> Much of the profound aversion to America has been produced by the belief that great opportunities have been squandered, with a resounding failure to live up to splendid ideals. The bitterness generated by such frustrated, often youthful idealism was particularly clear and widespread in the 1960s.[21]

Through this prism, anti-Americanism becomes much more complicated than simple opposition to the United States. Some have even claimed that many anti-Americans simply want America to be true to its real self.[22] With many feeling jilted by America's failure to live up to their expectations, cries of hypocrisy are thus at the core of much anti-Americanism. I agree with Hollander's claim that anti-Americanism is often the result of a basic human need to blame and resent others for one's own misfortunes. However, rather than ending analysis there as Hollander does, one needs to take the next logical step and analyse whether the US is being used as a scapegoat, or whether these grievances are justified.

Hollander's frequently acerbic and scornful tone undermines what could have become the classic study of the subject. His insults are not reserved for the views of terrorists or dictators, but also for fellow academics who hold positions different from his own. Given that Hollander's book is fixated with highlighting the exaggerated criticisms made of America, it is hard not to see this as both hypocritical and detracting. Both editions of *Anti-Americanism* also suffer from their Cold War context. Hollander, a Cold War Warrior and émigré from the Eastern bloc, is rather too eager to lampoon leftists. This predilection leads Richard Crockatt to ask whether Hollander, by definition, considers any left-wing criticism of the United States to be anti-Americanism.[23] Furthermore, blinkered by the Cold War context Hollander originally predicted that anti-Americanism was likely to peter out once the Cold War ended.

In *Anti-Americanism* Hollander posits a division between what he calls rational and irrational anti-Americanism; this is reiterated in his generally more commendable introductory piece in the more recent *Understanding Anti-Americanism* (2004). Hollander does acknowledge that anti-Americanism can "be thought of as originating in the justified grievances of nations, groups, or individuals who have over time been victimized or harmed by the United States or offended by what is seen as its inhumane policies and unjust social order."[24] However, he largely sees anti-Americanism as an irrational phenomenon that clings on to past grievances and conspiracy theories about America. Central to this understanding is the need for anti-Americans to stereotype America to feel better about their own nations or themselves as individuals.[25] Thus anti-Americanism is frequently intertwined with nationalism or claims of internationalism which seek to challenge America's place as a leader in the political, economic and cultural spheres. Like most theories of rival nationalism, resentment plays a significant role in Hollander's understanding.

Hollander's division of rational and irrational anti-Americanism is very problematic. Much of what he labels rational anti-Americanism should simply be called criticism. Classifying people like Stanley Hoffman as rational anti-Americans seems a counterproductive exercise that only serves to render the term anti-Americanism rather meaningless. In terms of irrational anti-Americanism, it is tempting to agree with Hollander's suggestion that much anti-Americanism is irrational, especially after he presents some of the choice thoughts of Jean Baudrillard on America.[26] However, arguing about the degree of rationality contained in anti-American sentiment seems unnecessarily distracting. As I argued in the opening chapter of this book, in examining anti-Americanism, the central question should be whether so-called "anti-American" comments or actions display prejudice against America or Americans, not whether they are rational or irrational.

Moving on from Hollander, 21st century scholarship on anti-Americanism can be broadly split into two opposing camps. The first are those who see it as a demand-driven phenomenon largely created outside of America in response to local factors within the countries concerned. Based on this interpretation anti-Americanism is a conscious or subconscious misrepresentation of America for instrumental purposes or to feel superior. The second group are those who describe anti-Americanism as supply-driven, or in other words, a direct response to American actions and policies. Recent books by Paul Hollander, Barry and Judith Colp Rubin, Jean-François Revel, Philippe Roger, and Andrei Markovits largely present anti-Americanism as being a demand-driven caricaturing of America that distorts and misinterprets America for domestic political purposes. Those who see anti-Americanism as largely demand-driven tend to have a much more pejorative understanding of anti-Americanism and see it as largely a reaction to what America supposedly "is." By contrast those who see it as supply-driven see anti-Americanism in less pejorative terms, describing it as the grievances that arise from US actions, that is, a result of what America "does."[27]

The textbook term for supply-driven anti-Americanism is "blowback," a term first used in a political sense by the CIA in reference to America's involvement in the 1953 overthrow of the Iranian Prime Minister Mohammad Mosaddegh. Blowback "has since come into use as shorthand for the unintended consequences of covert operations,"[28] including claims that the CIA's support of the Afghan mujahideen and Osama bin Laden resulted in perhaps the most stunning incident of anti-American blowback – the terrorist attacks of September 11, 2001.[29] Chalmers Johnson popularised this term with his book *Blowback*, originally released in 2000 and largely focusing on reactions to US foreign policy in East Asia. However post-9/11, it went on to become a best seller, based largely on its title, a hastily written new introduction, and a dearth of any other recent material on anti-Americanism. Books that have taken up the blowback theme to varying degrees include Noam Chomsky's *9/11* and Gore Vidal's *Perpetual War for Perpetual Peace*. Ziauddin Sardar and Merryl Wyn Davies have extended the blowback metaphor to include resistance to American culture in *Why do People Hate America?* and in their *American Dream, Global Nightmare*. From the academy we have Andrew and Kristen Ross' edited volume *Anti-Americanism* which similarly sees anti-Americanism as largely the result of American misdeeds abroad and at home.

My starting point is premised on the assumption that much of what is called anti-Americanism is better called something else such as anti-imperialism, anti-capitalism, or elitism. Here we are focusing on the history of what it is about America in particular that has been seen in a prejudicial manner. This can result from grievances that are both justifiably *and* unjustifiably held. This understanding attempts to give the study of anti-Americanism an analytical edge that simply focusing on opposition does not achieve. The history of America's engagement with the outside world provides a rich tapestry to detail this anti-American prejudice. My telling of this history begins with the hatred of the nation that arose before the colonies of America were a material power of considerable note.

Early anti-Americanism

There have always been those who disliked and even hated America from its beginnings as a set of colonies and then as a nascent nation. For those drawn to see all conflicts through the lens of power, it could conceivably be argued that America, offering refuge from Europe and its old-world rules, was a powerful threat to European elites. In truth anxieties and concerns about colonial America went beyond power relations, drawing on the baser human instinct of mistrust and fear for anything new and different. This is particularly apparent in the 18th century European view of the American natural environment as deformed and hostile. The most prominent anti-American botanists in fact never travelled to America; instead they dismissed a fantasised version of the American environment as inferior and undesirable for Europeans.

The two most cited promulgators of this so-called "degeneracy theory" were Count de Buffon and the Dutch abbé Corneille de Pauw. De Pauw, the more extravagant of the two, claimed that American animals and people were deformed, with animals lacking tails or having too many legs. Further, he claimed that animals and people transported to America from Europe would not fare well; dogs apparently lost their ability to bark and women lost their fertility at a much earlier age than they would otherwise.[30] As James Ceaser has noted, this denouncement of America as inferior to Europe was in part motivated by the German government's fear of mass German emigration; as a member of Frederick the Great's court, de Pauw was called on to serve the patriotic purpose of convincing Germans that the new world was inferior.[31] De Pauw was also known to have influenced the thinking of Kant, who claimed the American climate made people "too weak for hard work, too indifferent to pursue anything carefully, incapable of all culture, in fact lower even than the Negro."[32]

De Pauw's influential theories were complemented by the work of Count de Buffon who is "generally considered the greatest biologist of the eighteenth century."[33] Buffon's scientific status lent much weight to his endorsement of the degeneracy thesis. His writings were more nuanced than de Pauw's and he was persuaded to modify his arguments after receiving evidence to the contrary from Benjamin Franklin and Thomas Jefferson. The seriousness and prevalence of the degeneracy theory is illustrated in Jefferson's attempts to disprove it, most notably in his *Notes on the State of Virginia* (1785) where he dutifully recorded American temperatures and the size and weight of American and European animals, such as the impressive American mammoth, to prove the anti-Americans wrong.[34] Jefferson was in many ways a repository of European criticisms of his native land and a consummate respondent. At great expense he sent the skin, skeleton and horns of a moose to Paris where it could be assembled for Buffon "to prove once and for all that the American moose was indeed unique and definitely bigger than its European counterparts."[35] Jefferson also conceived one of America's most impressive public buildings, the Library of Congress, as a symbol for the value Americans placed on ideas and learning. The reality of scientific evidence combined with first-hand experience of America saw theories of America as a biologically degenerate land with a hostile climate fade away,[36] but in their place, and starting soon after, grew the notion of America as a land that was, if not physically degenerate, most certainly culturally so. As the author Knut Hansen put it, America was a "backward country culturally,"[37] or at the very least a country with a culture inferior to that found in Europe.

Culture: America has no class

The double entendre of "no class" goes to the heart of European laments about American culture. It is a recurring theme of European commentary that without the ruling "class" to act as necessary guardians of quality and taste, American culture lacked "class." The aristocratic de Tocqueville, while seeing much to admire in American democratic ways, worried that without a wealthy leisure class America would never develop an appreciation of the arts and literature. In a fashion all too typical of American cultural critics, he quickly dismissed American literature while remaining seemingly unacquainted with the most admired American authors of his time, such as Edgar Allen Poe, Henry Wadsworth Longfellow, or Washington Irving.[38] Frances Trollope picked up on this lack of class in her *Domestic Manners of the Americans*, a travelogue of sorts written after her failed plans to build a grand shopping "Bazaar" in Cincinnati, Ohio. Written on her return to England, Trollope's book soon became a widely read classic that reinforced many of the prejudices held by upper-class Europeans. It also played to the fears and concerns many Europeans had about the rise of their own unsophisticated middle and working classes. John Moser recognises this when he writes: "Anti-Americanism has traditionally been as much (if not more so) an expression of elite distrust of ordinary Europeans as it has been a gesture of defiance against a powerful rival."[39] Trollope portrayed America as a Republic of rudeness where people had no appreciation of proper manners, and she saw the egalitarian ethos of Americans as the most common cause of this rudeness.[40] De Tocqueville was also concerned about the apparently poor manners of Americans and wrote that "there is too much mobility ... for any definite group to establish a code of behaviour and see that it is observed."[41] Richard Boyd and Brandon Turner have suggested that "by virtue of the rough-and-ready character of American society, its lack of respect for forms and rules, and a disdain for anything smacking of aristocratic breeding," Americans often appeared unmannerly.[42] America's lack of a class structure, its newness, and the physical (and possible social) mobility of people all gave reasons for many Europeans to believe that its culture was backward.

One of the best examples of the view that America was a land without culture, history, or class was expressed by the American born Anglophile Henry James who lamented that in America, there was:

> No sovereign, no court, no personal loyalty, no aristocracy, no church, no clergy, no army, no diplomatic service, no country gentlemen, no palaces, no castles, nor manors, nor old country-houses, nor parsonages, nor thatched cottages, no ivied ruins, no cathedrals, nor abbeys, nor little Norman churches; no great Universities nor public schools – no Oxford, nor Eton, nor Harrow; no literature, no novels, no museums, no pictures, no political society, no sporting class – no Epsom, nor Ascot![43]

Without these markers of real culture, James considered life in America barely worth living. In such an equation where the age of building and the storied nature of tradition counted for sophistication, the new world would always lack the class and depth of Europe's traditions.[44]

Early forms of anti-Americanism pitted an idealised version of European culture against a stereotype of an uncultured but brazen America.[45] Beyond plain rivalry, 19th century criticisms of America also attacked American materialism and industrialism as perils to European sensibilities and the European lifestyle. In these critiques, Europe was depicted as the aesthetic bulwark against rampant American materialism and industrialism.[46] No longer predominantly just the preserve of a conservative elite, this 19th century critique of a cultured Europe and a philistine America is today possibly a more broadly held view in Europe than ever. The writings of Andrei Markovits, Josef Joffe, Philippe Roger, and Barry and Judith Colp Rubin show that amongst the guardians and keepers of "European culture," America was often looked down upon as backward, uncouth, and largely uncultured. The defence and protection of both European high culture and cultural traditions in itself is not a prejudicial position, and in many instances should be applauded. However, defenders of European culture have regularly seen it as necessary to disparage and dismiss American culture and this is where prejudice and in fact ignorance often guides arguments that are plainly anti-American.

American religiosity played a major role in some European critiques of uncouthness, with America portrayed in the 19th century as being both too religiously experimental and unruly and therefore not truly spiritual. Once again America lacked the necessary sophistication, in this instance in its general practice of worship. The bishop and statesman Talleyrand's famous comment that America has "thirty-two religions and only one dish...and even that [is] inedible" sums up this negative attitude succinctly.[47] In German literature this supposed lack of spirituality was put down to American materialism; Nikolas Lenau claimed that "The American knows nothing, he seeks nothing but money. He has no ideas."[48] Heinrich Heine claimed that "money is their God."[49] Charles Dickens famously declared that Americans worship the "Almighty dollar." Powerful and longstanding tropes emerged out of these perceived cultural deficiencies: Americans were too busy, too commercial, too levelled, too common, too banal, too culturally homogenous, and too dumb to appreciate the finer and most important things in life. America, if one believed these stereotypes, was therefore inferior to Europe.

This negative cultural critique has been sustained for over two centuries. During the 20th century it became overlaid at certain times and in certain places with anti-Semitism as America was seen as the new home of the Jewish people and this led to further claims that America was becoming more and more restless, rootless and commercial.[50] However, as more sophisticated analysts have noted, these complaints about American popular culture, commercialisation, consumerism, capitalism, and standardisation are ultimately laments about the forces of modernity itself. Modernity is of course as much European as it is American in origin, but having America to blame for the so-called "excesses" of modernity has often proved alluring to Europeans. The German-Israeli historian Dan Diner describes America as

> the counter-world to Europe, a complementary continent of occidental civilization and a screen upon which to project all the images and metaphors arising from its contrast to Europe; a screen upon which to project isolated portions of self-hatred owing mainly to modernity, but blamed only on the New World.[51]

This dichotomised view of Europe and America was never a one-way process as Godfrey Hodgson has aptly reminded us;[52] one example is Theodore Roosevelt's critique of the Europeanised American (he may well have had Henry James in mind) who in Roosevelt's view lacked the manliness and courage of "real" Americans. Donald Rumsfeld, during the lead up to the ill-conceived invasion of Iraq in 2003, embarrassingly referred to Western European reluctance to support the invasion as the weaknesses of "Old Europe," as opposed to the support of "new" European nations like Poland. This putdown of a tired and redundant "Old Europe" relied on stereotypes and stigmas that did not serve America well in a time when a lot more diplomatic dialogue might have helped America avoid entering a disastrous war.[53]

Andrei Markovits based on a study of nearly 1,500 European newspaper articles in the early 21st century argues that the tradition of disparaging American society and culture is alive and well in Europe. The study avoided overtly political articles, focusing instead on articles with American cultural and business topics. Markovits argues that American products and methods are routinely referred to as inferior; he also claims that the articles regularly make gratuitous remarks about America and Americans that have little to do with the subjects of the articles themselves.[54] For Markovits the source of much of this prejudice is resentment at America's success. In other words, what gives European anti-Americanism its edge is the resentment at the success of this new know-nothing nation, which lacks history, refinement and a respectable culture. In their book *Hating America*, the Rubins suggest that Latin America exhibits a similar attitude to American success, viewing "itself as an extension of European culture. Since America was considered to be so inferior, its success must be attributed to exploitation and evil actions."[55] Such a mindset can easily exaggerate America's perniciousness while paying scant attention to the crimes of local dictators or former colonial powers such as Spain. Some would argue that anti-Semitism in the Middle East operates in a similar fashion.

Political/military: Too powerful and too naïve

> "I never knew a man who had better motives for all the trouble he caused."
> *Graham Greene,* The Quiet American

The United States "is the only nation in the world where scholars can earn a doctorate without demonstrating competence in any foreign language."[56] American high school students have the worst knowledge of world geography of any Western nation. On hearing these two facts, many would nod their heads sagely, and lament what they perceive as the continued insularity and ignorance of the American nation. In reality the first fact is unequivocally false and the second is open to debate. You do not need proficiency in another language to complete a PhD in Australia, New Zealand or the United Kingdom. As for the geographical knowledge of young Americans this is pretty weak, as National Geographic's international surveys reveal, particularly when compared to young people in Germany and Sweden. However, compared to Canadians and Brits, young Americans are weaker but not by large margins. More generally as Josef Joffe highlights in *Überpower* "America's high schools, so another standby goes, breed vast illiteracy and ignorance of the world. Here, too, the facts are more complex. In various comparative studies, as in PISA 2000 and 2003 [OECD assessments], U.S. high schoolers end up in midfield along with France, but ahead of their contemporaries in Belgium, Spain, Germany, Switzerland, and Italy."[57]

The assumption of American ignorance is a standard trope in the anti-American tradition. Evidence of this ignorance is generally not hard to find in America; however, the key question to ask is whether this ignorance is actually particular to America. In his book *The Seven Sins of American Foreign Policy*, Loch Johnson puts ignorance forward as one of the key sins that results in the misdirection of American foreign policy. Johnson's book provides alarming signs of American university students' lack of global knowledge; however, I wonder whether Australian students would fare any better. Johnson's broader message seems sensible and worth supporting; that given America's power, it is desirable that American students learn about the geography, culture, history and languages of other nations. However, this already happens at universities such as Georgetown, which do an excellent job of educating students keen to take on a career in foreign affairs. Undoubtedly more should be done to foster the study of the Middle East and Arabic in American universities, but the same complaints about lack of study in these areas are frequently aired here in Australia, suggesting this is a global issue rather than being endemic to the US.

Tropes about American insularity and ignorance with respect to foreign affairs (geography, international politics, foreign languages) often attach themselves to the myth that America was a largely isolationist nation for most of its history. According to this myth, America focused almost entirely on its own domestic affairs until WWII, when only the cataclysmic event of Pearl Harbor drew the nation into the global conflict. This telling of history however may be more conventional than wise. A generation of diplomatic historians often associated with the so-called Wisconsin School has shown that America was deeply involved in the affairs of its Latin American neighbours from early on in the republic's history. Furthermore, a sizeable part of the territory in the north and south of the US was gained through conquest and diplomatic negotiations. This history of the activism of 19th century US foreign policy is particularly well told by Walter Russell Mead in *Special Providence*. However, the dominant view is that beyond the American continent, America sat largely on the side-lines of history until WWII, or at the very least until its late entry into WWI. America's lack of a colonial empire – aside from those gained rather late in the piece from the conquest of islands in the Caribbean and the Philippines in the Spanish-American War 1898 – contributed to this understanding. If America's default foreign policy outlook is seen as isolationist it is easy to say Americans are not very interested in foreign affairs, or knowledgeable about international relations. Walter Russell Mead addresses this myth in *Special Providence* where he argues that America tended to simply adopt a different approach to foreign affairs than that of the European powers. According to Mead, the American approach was more democratic and commercial, which was also written off as inferior, particularly in elite continental European diplomatic circles where the preference had long been for a realist approach to international affairs, which views relations between states as principally entailing the management and balance of power relations. This was best directed by all-powerful statesmen like Metternich, Bismarck and Talleyrand, and certainly not by legislative bodies such as the US Congress. America was thought to have it all wrong with its democratic system, separation of powers and naïve moralism.[58] The German-educated Hans Morgenthau brought many of these deeply held views on the continent to his studies of US foreign policy. He tended to view America's main challenge in international relations not externally but rather in combatting the rather naïve views that Americans themselves held on foreign politics – Morgenthau argued instead for a less moralistic approach to international affairs.[59] Realist scholars like Morgenthau have tended to be far less interested in commerce and economics than diplomatic and military affairs. For such scholars, historically America has been seen as too commercial and too economically oriented. In the 19th and early 20th century, elites in Europe tended to view commerce as a grubby and lowly pursuit, fit for merchants but not diplomats. Evidence of this attitude to commerce can be seen in the fact that Oxford University did not offer an MBA until 1996 when the Said Business School was established, whereas Harvard began their MBA program in 1908.

The common interpretation in Europe, and elsewhere, of an isolationist America is often coupled with a perception of America as ignorant, naïve and moralistic in its foreign policies once it does emerge on the world stage in WWI and WWII (with the world stage largely meaning Europe). The charge of moralism is particularly associated with Woodrow Wilson and his 14 point plan for world peace. Latin Americans could easily add hypocrisy to the list of criticisms of American foreign policy. Graham Greene's *The Quiet American*, and *The Ugly American* by William Lederer and Eugene Burdick draw on these anti-American tropes of US foreign policy-making with their satirised characters who reveal the full folly of Americans abroad. Chalmers Johnson recently wrote that "Greene is unsurpassed on Americans as imperialists, 'impregnably armoured by … good intentions and … ignorance.'"[60] The other vital ingredient in the anti-American narrative highlighted by these two books is what Senator J. William Fulbright called the "arrogance of power."[61]

The myth of America as isolationist led to America not always being seen as a great power before WWII. This wilfully overlooked the realities of American power, such as America having the largest economy in the world from the 1870s onwards, and that America was rapidly becoming the world's most populous country aside from China and India. After the US entry into WWII, America was suddenly vital in both the Pacific and European arenas. The suddenness of this reality is illustrated by the fact that both Australia and New Zealand, two countries thoroughly dependent on US military efforts during the war, did not even have Embassies in Washington DC until WWII. During the war the wealth and style of

America military personnel fighting abroad was not always liked,[62] but was largely tolerated as it became obvious that American involvement was essential for an Allied victory. Although American military power was resented in the UK, France and elsewhere after the war, the unfolding drama of the Cold War undoubtedly muted this resentment. Without the dichotomising effect of the Cold War, virulent anti-Americanism could have been expected in Japan and Germany, particularly in the former in response to the dropping of the Atom bomb.

The Cold War was of course both a global power struggle and an ideological struggle. America once again was seen to symbolise a model or a system, namely capitalism or democratic capitalism, depending on who is telling the tale. As the Cold War came into focus, anti-Americanism moved from being predominantly a conservative position to being increasingly associated with communists and other leftists. At its apex, from the end of WWII until Stalin's death, Soviet anti-Americanism produced one of the most ideologically pure forms of anti-Americanism history has known. Nonetheless, as John Chiddick has argued, Cold War anti-Americanism was not always so pure or uncomplicated. Chiddick divides Cold War anti-Americanism into three camps: root and branch, positional, and non-aligned. Root and branch anti-Americanism covers those who took up systematic opposition to the US in the form of Stalinism or Maoism. This position is not only that of leaders such as Kim Il Sung or Albania's Enver Hoxha, but that of much of the 1960s New Left who championed Ho Chi-minh and Castro against the so-called American military industrial complex. Iran's Ayatollah Khomeini could also be placed in this root and branch camp, although from a fundamentalist Islamic position rather than a communist or socialist viewpoint. A particularly interesting point from Chiddick is the considerable shift some of the New Left made from their anti-Stalinist progressive beginnings and theoretical openness to becoming supporters of the most virulently anti-American regimes such as China under Mao, a regime that even the Soviet Union by the 1960s was distancing itself from. Such regimes were supported by the New Left because they provided the most anti-American option available, with a blind eye being turned to the issue of human rights in particular, and undemocratic government in general in the Communist world. This unfortunate history, which has had quite an impact on scholarship on US foreign policy, can be largely explained by the polarising impact of the Vietnam War on the New Left, as *Washington Post* columnist E. J. Dionne recognises:

> Critics of American foreign policy have nearly always been labelled 'anti-American' by their foes; being cast into the political darkness is one of the risks of dissent. But rarely have dissenters cooperated so willingly to validate the claims of their enemies. By embracing anti-Americanism as a noble cause, the farther fringes of the New Left divided and set back the anti-war movement.[63]

Chiddick's second grouping – positional anti-Americanism – largely describes the posture of various Arab states during the Cold War. Although states like Iraq, Syria, and Egypt had no great ideological affinity with communism or objection to capitalism, they saw the Soviets as the best strategic partners because of America's increasing support of Israel from the 1960s onwards. Lastly, there is non-aligned anti-Americanism, which although often categorised as anti-Americanism would be better called criticism or neutralism. Nehru in India, the French neutralists, and much of the Labour left and nuclear disarmament movement in Britain typify this position. At best, when it avoided claims of moral equivalency, this last grouping offered a humanist voice of moderation throughout the Cold War.

The Cold War immeasurably complicates our understanding of anti-Americanism because of the breadth of US involvement across the world, including the deployment of military bases and installations within many other sovereign nations worldwide. Cold War grievances and their legacies are multiple. American behaviour was often self-interested, ill-conceived and at times brutal. Nonetheless, this behaviour needs to be understood in the context of the enemies America faced. The example I am most familiar with is the Korean War, which saw America kill hundreds of thousands of civilians in the firebombing of most of North Korea's cities.[64] However, these highly questionable tactics were part of a complicated war. America was opposed in Korea by forces led and supported by three of the cruellest leaders of the 20th century: Mao, Stalin and Kim Il Sung. In Mao's case he was prepared to send hundreds of thousands of under dressed and under-resourced Chinese (preferably ex-nationalist troops) to their graves in bitterly cold northern Korea. As Mao's recent biographers, Jung Chang and Jon Halliday, argue, this was in order to kill a few thousand Americans, apparently because Mao, like Osama bin Laden, believed that the American government had no real stomach for war and that, facing the loss of their troops, they would soon capitulate.[65]

Even given the bloody and complicated experiences of the 20th century, the old views of America as inexperienced persist. A classic illustration of this occurred during negotiations between NATO allies over the question of intervention in Bosnia during the 1990s. British Conservative Party Defence Secretary Malcolm Rifkind apparently lectured American representatives including WWII veteran Bob Dole that "you Americans know nothing about war."[66] A more obscure, but even more beautifully illustrative example came during a protest in Russia opposing US intervention in Kosovo. A demonstrator held up a sign which asked "USA where were you in 1389?" The simple answer of course was nowhere; the United States had not even been conceived of.[67]

Economic Imperialism: The American mosquito

If American diplomacy was still seen as naïve at the end of the Cold War, and even more so since the intervention in Iraq, American global commercial activity is certainly no longer overlooked or underrated. The image of the exploitative Yankee became a standard indictment of both American "transnational" corporations and also of the American government through its supposed control over pernicious economic institutions such as the GATT, the WTO, the IMF and the World Bank. As a result a new set of anti-American tropes have been developed which now include Uncle Sam as the bloodsucking corporate mosquito. In a May

2005 edition of *Metall*, the magazine of Germany's largest trade union, American companies are depicted on the cover as mosquitoes with the headline "Die Aussauger" (the bloodsuckers).[68] This negativity was paralleled by comments from the German Social Democratic Party chairperson during the 2005 German election campaign that "American capitalists" would descend on German companies like a "swarm of locusts."[69] These references to the insect world remind me of Bertrand Russell's 1966 essay "Peace through resistance to U.S. imperialism" where he compares American global trade policy to the animal kingdom. Russell scorns: "Like vultures the handful of the rich batten on the poor, the exploited, the opposed."[70] Such trenchant criticism from a socialist like Russell is to be expected; however, when national leaders from wealthy capitalist European nations sound similar to Russell on subjects such as US corporations, American conditions, and US imperialism, one realises how readily available anti-American tropes are for politicians and activists the world over. The image of the ruthless Yankee capitalist is one of the strongest and most enduring of these tropes.

The philosophy expressed by President Calvin Coolidge's oft-quoted adage, that: "The business of America is business," has undoubtedly been central to American domestic and international policy-making. Walter Russell Mead has called the business-first approach to foreign policy the Hamiltonian tradition. It has always been a key, and arguably the key, driver of US foreign policy. Andrew Bacevich does an effective job of reminding readers of this abiding continuity in US foreign policy in his *American Empire* (2002).[71] Historically, criticisms of American commerce and industry have been commonplace in Europe on both the right and the left, as I argued earlier in this chapter. However, the hand of US capitalism and industry has been felt much more heavily in Canada and Latin America. As a result, America's neighbours have developed an extensive set of economic grievances that have gone on to create the strongest version of economic anti-Americanism.

In his work on Canadian anti-Americanism Kim Nossal writes that debates about "free trade" with the US have historically brought to the fore strong economic fears and antagonisms in Canada. He contends that "In 1891, the campaign [for free trade] inspired a torrent of anti-American sentiment, as manufacturing interests distributed propaganda with slogans like 'Keep Out the Wolves.'" Nossal writes that "The victory of the Conservatives under Robert Borden in the 1911 elections cast a long shadow in Canadian politics, legitimizing the anti-American tradition in Canada that viewed free trade as the harbinger of the death of the nation."[72] This notion of free trade killing sovereignty is still alive and kicking at least in Australian academia; one of the first published books dealing with the US–Australia free trade agreement negotiated in 2004 was polemically titled *How to Kill a Country*.[73] In Alan McPherson's writings on Latin America he discusses the history of economic relations including US involvement in the regrettable 1954 overthrow of Guatemalan President Jacobo Arbenz.[74] This and other actions in Latin America created a legacy which saw the US increasingly viewed as responsible for the underdevelopment or overdependency of many Latin American nations. However, as bad as US actions at times were, scapegoating of the US also seems quite apparent. Recognising this, the Rubins provide the following example to capture this attitude: "The crown jewel of Mexican anti-Americanism is the National Museum of Interventions, opened in 1981. But though Spanish colonialism had lasted 300 years, the focus is mainly on the depredations, real or imagined, of the United States."[75]

The US clearly is not and never has been a colonial power in the classic territorial sense. A brief comparison with the British Empire reminds us of this: between the two world wars the British Empire covered more than 13 million square miles, roughly 23 percent of the world's land surface; with the UK itself only accounting for 0.2% of the world's land mass. Whereas, the US accounts for 6.5% of the world land mass with its formal dependencies accounting for a mere 4,410 square miles of territory.[76] As a result America has been criticised largely not as a colonial power but as a neocolonial power. The more intangible nature of so-called neocolonialism leads to the US often being seen as all-powerful, with claims of neocolonialism often having a conspiratorial edge. Cold War politicking and US interference abroad, the relationship between powerful American companies like the United Fruit Company and the US government, and the influence of the US on the decisions of the IMF have contributed to this conspiratorial mindset, at times quite justifiably.[77] However, there are two sides at least to most of these stories; furthermore, differentiation is also once again crucial in understanding the breadth of US economic activities. A tendency to focus on the worst of America's actions while not providing a broader context for them has become an all too common part of the neocolonial critique, with Noam Chomsky the intellectual standard bearer of this tradition in recent years.[78]

It is often claimed that the US seeks to underhandedly control the world's resources in a neocolonial fashion. In the Middle East the common claim is that America desires control over the region's oil. Once again the evidence shows that the American government and American companies are heavily involved in the oil industry not only in the Middle East but around the world. This is not surprising given how vital a resource this is for the US economy. However, claims about America controlling the world's oil resources are more rhetorically than empirically based. The common argument that America went to war in Iraq to control that country's oil reserves is not supported by the current evidence. In the Middle East claims about American oil politics, and neocolonialism sound very similar to or are in fact interwoven with conspiracies about the manipulative power of Jewish money and Jews.[79] Anti-Americanism in its most extreme forms as expressed by al Qaeda and its supporters draws upon this neocolonial claim that America controls the Middle East politically and economically. Thus resistance to this supposed control justifies violence and even terrorism.

Anti-American terrorism

The terrorist anti-Americanism symbolised by the September 11, 2001 attacks has undoubtedly made the subject of anti-Americanism much more serious than the parlour room denouncements of American manners and culture of an earlier era.

The 9/11 terrorist attacks were quintessential anti-American acts, which satisfy all of the competing definitions of anti-Americanism. In targeting the Pentagon and the World Trade Center, the terrorists deliberately attacked two famous symbols of American power as well as indiscriminately killing civilians who were predominately Americans. However while 9/11 marked a new wave of anti-Americanism, the concerns of the previous waves have continued largely unabated and often combine to create a heady mix of grievances. The beginnings of terrorist anti-Americanism can be traced to earlier events such as politically motivated attacks on, and murders of, Americans in Beirut from the 1970s onwards, the Iranian hostage crisis of 1979–1980, the 1993 detonation of a van bomb in the underground car park in the World Trade Center, the 1998 car bomb attacks on the US embassies in Nairobi and Dar es Salaam, and the 2000 suicide bombing of the USS *Cole* in Aden Harbor, Yemen. All of these attacks were principally motivated by anti-Americanism.[80]

Following 9/11 many theories abounded about why the attacks had occurred.[81] Jean Bethke Elshtain noted a tendency to not take Osama bin Laden and al Qaeda at their word and instead look for deeper and possibly more complicated reasons for the attacks. For Elshtain this tendency is largely due to the inability of most commentators to take religious messages such as al-Qaeda's declared *jihad* against America seriously; as a result they see such statements as "window dressing" with many commentators seeming to believe that "the heart of the matter lies elsewhere, in leftover colonial ire or antiglobalist chagrin."[82] Elshtain's argument that more attention needs to be paid to the statements and actions of al Qaeda and other radical Islamic organisations was an important intervention in the post-9/11 discourse, too often characterised by commentators and politicians bringing their own political baggage to bear on why the attacks occurred. More recently Peter Bergen, one of the most astute analysts of bin Laden, wrote: "Statements from bin Laden and al Zawahiri have always been the most reliable guide to the future actions of jihadist movements around the world."[83]

Both Bergen and Elshtain rightly highlight the importance of religious motivations in their analyses, something that many other analysts of international relations seem ill-equipped to deal with. I will argue here that it is the intersection of religious and territorial concerns that animates most of the statements and actions of anti-American terrorists. In bin Laden's case the territorial grievances he regularly refers to are key motivational causes for his followers, but bin Laden's own antagonistic relationship with Saddam and Arafat complicates a territorial understanding of his motivations.

In analysing the 9/11 attacks two key questions are: why did these terrorists so hate America? And were there specific US actions that directly created this hatred? It seems that both official assessments in America, Australia and Britain *and* radical interpretations from some leftist academics cast the net far too wide. George W. Bush, John Howard and Tony Blair all said that those responsible for the 9/11 attacks hate America and like-minded nations because of their freedoms and liberties – in short because of their way of life. Certain left-wing scholars have cited colonialism, poverty, globalisation, and 20th century American foreign policy as the causes of the attacks. However, a series of speeches, interviews and video comments by Osama bin Laden and other al Qaeda leaders reveal a seemingly more delimited and specific set of reasons for targeting America than is acknowledged by much of the standard commentary.[84] These speeches state their grievances directly and with considerable repetition; they condemn America for its "occupying of the country of the two Holy places," for its alliance with the Jews in oppressing and killing Palestinians and occupying the sacred al-Aqsa mosque and Dome of the Rock in Jerusalem, and for its policies in Iraq which have supposedly led to the death of 600,000 children (later claimed by bin Laden to be one million children).[85] Al Qaeda clearly states that these policies justify the killing of Americans, with once again the clear aim being America's retreat from the Muslim world. Bin Laden bluntly states that "what happened on September 11 is nothing but a reaction to the continuing injustice being done to our children in Palestine, Iraq, Somalia, southern Sudan, and elsewhere, as well as Kashmir and Asia."[86] While this statement refers to a wide variety of conflicts, the underlying message is consistent – let Muslims govern their societies without outside interference.

Bin Laden and others in the al Qaeda leadership seem to believe that America can be forced to retreat and that it has far less stomach for war than the Soviets whom al Qaeda helped to defeat in Afghanistan. Until the fall of the Soviet Union the Soviets were seen by bin Laden as a greater and in fact more formidable enemy than the United States. This is not to say that bin Laden was a supporter of the US in the 1980s; it is known that he personally boycotted US products throughout this period. Bin Laden's view of the Americans as cowards can be seen in his 1996 statement entitled "Declaration of War":

> When the explosion in Beirut took place [in] 1983…you were turned into scattered bits and pieces at that time; 241 mainly Marines [and] soldiers were killed. And where was this courage of yours when two explosions made you to leave Aden [after the attack on the USS *Cole*] in less than twenty-four hours! But your most disgraceful case was in Somalia, where – after vigorous propaganda about the power of the United States and its post-cold war leadership of the new world order – you moved tens of thousands of international force[s], including 28,000 American soldiers, into Somalia. However, when tens of your soldiers were killed in minor battles and one pilot was dragged in the streets of Mogadishu you left the area carrying disappointment, humiliation, defeat, and your dead with you.[87]

This claim that Americans can be forced to retreat is repeated by bin Laden elsewhere and is clearly similar to the belief systems of other terrorist organisations that violence is an effective way to gain enemy withdrawal.

In a comprehensive study of suicide terrorism from 1980 to 2001, published in the *American Political Science Review* (APSR) in 2003, Robert Pape concludes that the aim in nearly all of the 188 cases during this period was territorial. In most attacks, territory (or greater self-rule) was ceded in response to the suicide terrorism, further fuelling terrorists' belief that terrorism is an effective method of attack.[88] However, the question of territorial disputes and bin Laden is more complicated than Pape's analysis suggests. Furthermore, Pape's suggestion that religion can be put to one side when explaining al Qaeda's motivations is mistaken. Religious motivations were thoroughly interwoven with bin Laden's main territorial aim which was his fantastic goal of establishing an Islamic fundamentalist caliphate that spread from Spain to Indonesia. This goal and his own history complicates his relations with Middle Eastern leaders and particular nationalist causes.

The problem with seeing bin Laden simply as an anti-American nationalist are firstly that al Qaeda's relationship with the central nationalist issue in the Arab world is complicated by its longstanding strained relations with the Palestine Liberation Organization (PLO). Bin Laden's mentor Abdullah Azzam split with the PLO in the 1970s, seeing it as too secular and narrowly nationalist. Bin Laden himself also had little regard for Yasser Arafat. Secondly, bin Laden was highly suspicious of Saddam Hussein and his territorial ambitions. Apart from seeing Saddam as a rival in his bid to create a Pan Arab nation, bin Laden also saw the Iraqi leader as too secular. When Saddam occupied Kuwait in 1990, bin Laden suggested to the Saudi government that he organise a *mujahid* to fight and expel Saddam's forces. The Saudi government refused, instead letting America and other western forces use Saudi Arabia as a launching pad from which to attack Saddam's military in Kuwait. In my estimation, this set of events was the major catalyst for bin Laden declaring *jihad* on America.

To conclude my analysis I will return to Robert Pape's claim of religion as a side issue. Pape's work has seen him widely cited on contemporary terrorism; his work displays some of the strengths of contemporary American political science with its emphasis on causation and data rather than on speculation and normative assertion.[89] In *Dying to Win* (2005), Pape's database of suicide terrorist attacks lists 315 cases. Analysing these attacks, he looks for broad comparative understandings of the logic and goals of suicide terrorists. This is classic behaviourist research. The first obvious weakness is Pape's lack of attention to history, particularly the historical and cultural differences between various terrorist organisations. His data leads him to conclude that "nearly all suicide terrorist attacks have in common a specific secular and strategic goal: to compel modern democracies to withdraw from territories that the terrorists consider to be their homelands."[90] In short their goals are nationalist, not religious but, to me, such clear-cut nationalist goals are more suited to the definition of a group such as the Tamil Tigers rather than al Qaeda or ISIS. Nonetheless Pape claims al Qaeda fits his pattern because it is an organisation whose principal desire is the expulsion of US troops from the Persian Gulf and the reduction of US power and influence in the region. Even if we accept this analysis, it seems reasonable to assert that al Qaeda did not only want to simply take over territory but also wanted to replace the current "US-controlled" regimes in the Middle East with Islamic fundamentalist rule.

Pape also fails to deal with the global nature of al Qaeda's struggle, which is another reason why a nationalist or narrowly territorial description is ill-suited. The connections between Muslims across the globe, a subject enticingly written about by Olivier Roy, makes al Qaeda very different from the Tamil Tigers. If we look at the second generation of al Qaeda recruits in particular, many of these people are not born in Muslim nations, and some have little or no family connections with Muslim countries.[91] In summary, anti-American terrorism is a heady mix of religious beliefs and territorial grievances, with the power of religion as an organising force for loyalty and outrage crucial to understanding bin Laden and al Qaeda. The US has become the chief target of this hatred, because of its policies and its association with the "apostate" leaders in the Middle East.[92]

Lastly, how can anti-American terrorism be best responded to? Pape's position shifts dramatically between 2003 and 2005. In his 2003 *APSR* article he supported a hard-line position, akin to the Israeli position with the Palestinians, arguing for an approach that sends terrorists a clear message that there is no hope of success. In *Dying to Win* Pape shifts to the suggestion that America pull out of the Middle East and engage in its traditional policy of off-shore balancing. This policy has gained renewed support amongst realist scholars in America and elsewhere. Of course there are no simple solutions to such dilemmas. Nonetheless, seeing such problems in largely strategic and territorial terms is likely inadequate. Such problems as the Iran stand-off or dealing with al Qaeda and ISIS are made particularly difficult by the impact that religion brings to bear on them. The factor of religion makes leaders and people alike more messianic and fatalistic, characteristics not readily dealt with by Robert Pape's rational actor model of politics.

Conclusion

During the George W. Bush administration, tropes that drew on the long history of anti-Americanism were often recycled and put into battle. This lazy thinking fuelled conspiracy theories about Bush's foreign policies which continue to be circulated widely on the internet. Although I disagree profoundly with many of the policy positions taken by the Bush administration, I also oppose the conspiratorial nature of much commentary on 9/11 and Bush's foreign policies thereafter. Chief amongst these conspiracies is the claim that 9/11 was an "inside job" or that the terrorist attacks were allowed to happen by the Bush administration to provide them with a justification for invading Iraq or most incredibly that the attacks were fabricated and never really occurred. Many of these conspiracy theories suggest that foreign policy after 9/11 was directed by a "neoconservative" cabal. The neoconservatives were often portrayed as a cunning cabal of Jews and other Washington DC insiders who wanted to force democracy and American values on the world. Economically it was often claimed that the neoconservatives wanted to control the Middle East to safeguard Israel and oil reserves for America; at the same time politically they were said to want every country to become self-governing democracies almost overnight. Lastly, it was claimed that terrorism is either something the neoconservatives needed in order to justify their own grand ambitions or a phenomenon they profoundly misunderstood. This analysis is not entirely without justification, but taken in its entirety leads to the common paradox often at the heart of anti-Americanism:

namely that of Americans being naïve and stupid, while simultaneously managing to be the opposite – all-powerful and supremely manipulative. The ultimate poster boy for this combination in the early 21st century was George W. Bush; today it is Donald Trump.

Critics of the Bush era need to understand the neoconservatives and Bush for what they are, examining their history and backgrounds, and the details of what they stand for.[93] Such analysis would require one to face up to the pluralism of American politics. Although the neoconservatives had considerable influence on the Bush administration's disastrous decision to invade Iraq, they were only one faction within American politics, competing against a number of other powerful factions and forces.[94] Few familiar with the history of the neoconservative movement before 9/11 would have described Donald Rumsfeld and Dick Cheney as neoconservatives, or, for that matter, Colin Powell or Condoleezza Rice; whether after 9/11 any of these individuals should be called neocons remains debatable. Furthermore, the most astute works on the neoconservatives see this movement as having long effectively publicised its ideas but struggling to represent a coherent set of ideas that can be implemented as policy action.[95] An accurate depiction of foreign policy under President Bush, particularly in Iraq, would emphasise the often contradictory and incoherent nature of the administration's policies, rather than presenting its foreign policy as being run by a tightly coordinated neoconservative cabal. The more we learnt from insider accounts of the Bush administration, the more commonplace disputes across, and within, departments and agencies seemed.[96] The more we learnt about the Iraq War, the more mismanagement and conflict was apparent within the Bush administration's occupation plans and strategy.[97] I discuss this at the end of a chapter on the history of anti-American tropes to emphasise that powerful stereotypes about American naivety, stupidity and greed have been created over two centuries that often hinder commentators and critics from focusing on the evidence and the facts at hand, on details and debates, and this leads to simplistic analysis and ill-founded conspiracies. Such tropes create what George Orwell called "prefabricated" arguments, which are the enemy of true thought and analysis.[98] As I will argue in the following chapters, an attention to the details provides many strong reasons to criticise American foreign policy without slipping into hackneyed anti-Americanism.

Notes

1 Gérard Grunberg, "Anti-Americanism in French and European Public Opinion," *With Us or Against Us*, eds. Tony Judt and Denis Lacorne (New York: Palgrave Macmillan, 2005), 61.
2 James Ceaser, "The Philosophical Origins of Anti-Americanism in Europe," *Understanding Anti-Americanism*, ed. Paul Hollander (Chicago: Ivan R. Dee, 2004), 45–46.
3 Ibid., 46–48.
4 Walter Laqueur, *No End to War* (London: Continuum, 2003), 161.
5 Richard Kuisel, *Seducing the French* (Berkeley, University of California Press, 1993), 8.

6 Henry Pelling, *America and the British Left* (New York: New York University Press, 1957), 4.
7 See David. Hecht, *Russian Radicals Look to America* (Cambridge, MA: Harvard University Press, 1947); Halvdan Koht, *The American Spirit in Europe* (Philadelphia: University of Pennsylvania Press, 1949).
8 Pelling, *America and the British Left*, 160–161.
9 Ibid., 161.
10 Kuisel, *Seducing the French*, 1–14; Philippe Roger, *The American Enemy* (Chicago: University of Chicago Press, 2005).
11 Tony Judt, *Past Imperfect* (Berkeley, CA: University of California Press, 1992), 190–191.
12 Ibid., 194.
13 These are an article "A Genealogy of Anti-Americanism," *Public Interest* (Summer, 2003) which was also reworked as the opening chapter entitled "The Philosophical Origins of anti-Americanism in Europe," in *Understanding Anti-Americanism*, ed. Paul Hollander (Chicago: Ivan R. Dee, 2004).
14 Ceaser, "The Philosophical Origins of anti-Americanism in Europe."
15 Ibid., 47–48
16 Ibid., 48
17 Kuisel, *Seducing the French*, 31.
18 Ibid.
19 Henry Fairlie, "Anti-Americanism at Home and Abroad," *Commentary* (December, 1975), 39.
20 Paul Hollander, "Introduction: The New Virulence and Popularity," in ed. Paul Hollander, 7, 10, 35.
21 Ibid., 10.
22 This viewpoint is espoused by Stanley Hoffman in "America Goes Backward," *New York Review of Books*, June 12, 2003 and see also Paul Hollander, *Anti-Americanism: Irrational and Rational* (New York: Transaction, 1995), 396.
23 Richard Crockatt, *America Embattled* (London: Routledge, 2003), 47.
24 Hollander, *Anti-Americanism: Irrational & Rational*, 334–335.
25 Ibid., 334–335, 343.
26 See Hollander, "Introduction: The New Virulence and Popularity," 3–5.
27 Latin American specialist Alan McPherson challenges this view of seeing anti-Americanism as irrational and suggests:

> If anti-Americanism is immediately identifiable with emotional language such as 'resentment' and 'hate,' it is because emotions stem from frustration, from the lack of solutions to the overwhelming inequalities in the world. The great majority of those hostile to U.S. power are expressing unprecedented desperation in their desire to prevent or reverse the erosion of their wealth, their traditions, and their arable land. These are all problems that they trace back to US-led globalization, and that link is very serious. Emotions, in other words, are rational responses.
>
> *(Alan McPherson, "Myths of Anti-Americanism: The Case of Latin America," Brown Journal of World Affairs X, 2 (Winter/Spring 2004), 145)*

> However, like most thoughtful writers on this topic he sees this viewpoint as a double-edged sword that leads people to conflate

> various forms of US power and imagine, without bothering to gather evidence, that they are tied together. As a result, those who see all U.S. power abroad as malevolent grow conspiratorial in their thoughts, easily manipulated in their strategies, and desperate in their tactics.
>
> *(Ibid., 145–146)*

The dilemmas raised by McPherson are profound ones and deserve serious treatment as his recent work has been exploring. (See Alan McPherson, *Intimate Ties, Bitter Struggles: The United States and Latin America since 1945* (Potomac Books: Washington DC, 2005.)

28 Quoted in Chalmers Johnson, *Blowback* (London: Time Warner, 2002), xii.
29 Ibid., xii–xvii. This finding is disputed by Jean Bethke Elshtain, *Just War Against Terror* (New York: Basic Books, 2003), 80. See Coll, *Ghost Wars*.
30 James Ceaser, *Reconstructing America* (New Haven: Yale University Press, 1997), 22–26.
31 Ibid., 26.
32 Barry Rubin and Judith Colp Rubin, *Hating America: A History* (New York: Oxford University Press, 2004), 12.
33 Ceaser, *Reconstructing America*, 27.
34 Ibid., 45; Rubin and Rubin, *Hating America*, 13
35 Gaye Wilson, "Jefferson, Buffoon, and the Mighty American Moose," *Monticello Newsletter* 13, 1 (Spring 2002).
36 Conceivably, it could be argued that Mike Davis' writing on California and its ecology draws upon this degeneracy tradition.
37 Hollander, *Anti-Americanism: Irrational & Rational*, 392.
38 Garry Wills, "Did Tocqueville 'Get' America," *New York Review of Books*, 51, 7, September, 2005.
39 John Moser, "European Anti-Americanism and American Anglophobia," in *Anti-Americanism* (Vol. 3), ed. Brendon O'Connor (Westport: Greenwood Press, 2007).
40 The Rubins state that in the development of anti-Americanism in the 19th and early 20th century "The British put a little more emphasis on excessive equality, the French on intellectual and cultural poverty, and the Germans spoke much of spiritual barrenness." Rubin and Rubin, *Hating America*, 42.
41 Alexis de Tocqueville, *Democracy in America*, ed. J. P. Mayer (New York: Harper, 1988), Vol. 2, Pt. 3, Ch. 14, 606.
42 Richard Boyd and Brandon Turner, "Anti-Americanism and the American Personality," in *Anti-Americanism* (Vol 1), ed. Brendon O'Connor.
43 Crockatt, *America Embattled*, 55, 56.
44 Adolf Hitler expressed his sense of European cultural superiority with the put down: "A single Beethoven symphony contains more culture than all that America ever created." Josef Joffe, *Überpower: The Imperial Temptation of America* (New York: W.W. Norton, 2006), 105.
45 Judt, *Past Imperfect*, 188–189.
46 Ibid.; See also Dan Diner, *America in the Eyes of the Germans* (Princeton: Markus Wiener Publishers, 1996).
47 Antonello Gerbi, *The Dispute of the New World: The History of a Polemic 1750–1900*, Rev. ed. (Pittsburgh: University of Pittsburgh Press, 1973), 326–327.
48 Rubin and Rubin, *Hating America*, 17.
49 Ibid., 29.
50 Judt, *Past Imperfect*; Andrei Markovits, *Uncouth Nation* (Princeton: Princeton University Press, 2007).
51 Diner, *America in the Eyes of the Germans*, 5.
52 Godfrey Hodgson, "Anti-Americanism and American Exceptionalism," *Journal of Transatlantic Studies* 2 (1), 2004.
53 See Max Paul Friedman, *Rethinking Anti-Americanism: The History of an Exceptional Concept in American Foreign Relations* (Cambridge: Cambridge University Press, 2012) for the long history of American stereotyping of European leaders and therefore ignoring cautionary advice from them.
54 Markovits, *Uncouth Nation*.
55 Rubin and Rubin, *Hating America*, 120.
56 Loch Johnson and Kiki Caruson, "The Seven Sins of American Foreign Policy," *PS* (January 2003), 5.
57 Joffe, *Überpower*, 86

58 Walter Russell Mead, *Special Providence: American Foreign Policy and How it Changed the World* (New York: Alfred A Knopf, 2001), 38–9, 44, 49, 54.
59 Hans Morgenthau, *In Defense of the National Interest* (New York: Alfred Knopf, 1951), 91. See also Martin Griffiths, *Realism, Idealism and International Politics* (London: Routledge, 1992), 54–58.
60 Johnson, *Blowback*, 241.
61 J. William Fulbright, *The Arrogance of Power* (New York: Random House, 1966).
62 At times anti-American tensions broke out in allied nations such as in a November 1942 riot where American and Australian troops fought in the streets of the Australian city of Brisbane for a number of hours. Although the beginnings of the riot were more complicated than just resentment of American troops and the legend has often exaggerated the fighting, it nonetheless exposed clear tensions between American troops and Australian soldiers and men in general. See John Hammond Moore, *Over-Sexed, Over-Paid, and Over Here* (Brisbane: University of Queensland Press, 1981), 217–228.
63 E. J. Dionne, *Why Americans Hate Politics* (New York: Simon and Schuster, 1992), 52.
64 Curtis LeMay interviewed in *Strategic Air Warfare*, eds. Richard Kohn and Joseph Harahan (Washington DC: Office of Air Force History, 1988), 86–89; Bruce Cumings, *North Korea: Another Country* (New York: Free Press, 2003).
65 Jung Chang and Jon Halliday *Mao: The Unknown Story* (London: Vintage, 2006).
66 Nick Cohen, "Why is it Right to be Anti-American," *New Statesman*, January 14, 2002.
67 Will Englund, "In Many Forms, Places, Hatred of America Lives," *Baltimore Sun*, September 28, 2001.
68 It is not uncommon to hear it claimed that most of the major multinational corporations in the world are US owned or controlled, despite this being factually incorrect. *Fortune* magazine lists 126 out of the top 500 MNCs as US corporations; with China being not that far behind with 120 of the top 500 and the Japanese owning 52 of these companies. See *Fortune*, Global 500, 2018, <http://fortune.com/global500/>.
69 Michael Werz and Barbara Fried, "Modernity and Anti-Americanism," in *Anti-Americanism* (Vol. 1), ed. Brendon O'Connor.
70 Bertrand Russell's essay "Peace through Resistance to U.S. Imperialism," in *Readings in U.S. Imperialism*, eds. K. T. Fann and Donald Hodges (Boston: Porter Sargent, 1971), xii.
71 Andrew J. Bacevich, *American Empire: The Realities and Consequences of U.S. Diplomacy* (Cambridge, MA: Harvard University Press, 2002).
72 Kim Nossal, "Canadian Anti-Americanism," in *Anti-Americanism* (Vol. 3), ed. Brendon O'Connor; also see J. L. Granatstein, *Yankee Go Home? Canadians and Anti-Americanism* (Toronto: HarperCollins, 1996), 48–49.
73 Linda M. Weiss, Elizabeth Thurbon and John Alwyn Mathews, *How to Kill a Country: Australia's Devastating Trade Deal with the United States* (Sydney: Allen & Unwin, 2004).
74 Alan McPherson, "Latin American anti-Americanism," in *Anti-Americanism* (Vol. 3), ed. Brendon O'Connor.
75 Rubin and Rubin, *Hating America*, 121
76 Niall Ferguson, *Colossus* (London, Penguin, 2004), 15.
77 See for example William Finnegan, "The Economics of Empire," *Harpers*, May 2003.
78 See Noam Chomsky, *9/11* (New York: Seven Stories Press, 2002). and Noam Chomsky, *Imperial Ambitions* (New York, Metropolitan Books, 2005).
79 Bin Laden's criticisms of America propound conspiracy theories regarding the Jewish influence over America. In a variety of speeches he talks of the Jewish-crusader or Zionist-American alliance, and in a video dated 2000 he goes much further, describing America as a puppet of Israel. Osama bin Laden, "Al-Qa'ida Recruitment Video," (2000), in *Anti-American Terrorism and the Middle East*, eds., Barry Rubin and Judith Colp Rubin (New York: Oxford University Press, 2002), 178. Other al Qaeda members reiterate similar views to bin Laden as do other radical Islamic organisations such as the World Islamic Front and Islamic Jihad.
80 Rubin and Rubin, *Anti-American Terrorism and the Middle East*.
81 Ken Booth and Tim Dunne, eds., *Worlds in Collision* (Basingstoke: Palgrave, 2002).

82 Elshtain, *Just War Against Terror*, 86.

83 Peter Bergen, *The Osama bin Laden I Know* (New York, Free Press, 2006), xxvi.

84 Ibid.; Rubin and Rubin, *Anti-American Terrorism and the Middle East*.

85 Rubin and Rubin, *Anti-American Terrorism and the Middle East*.

86 "Interview with Osama bin Laden," (December 27, 2001), in Ibid., 265. Elsewhere bin Laden condemns the UN promoted division and separation of East Timor from Indonesia (see "Broadcast by Osama bin Laden," (November 3, 2001), in Ibid., 259).

87 Osama bin Laden "Declaration of War," (August 1996), in Ibid., 140.

88 Robert Pape, "The Strategic Logic of Suicide Terrorism," *American Political Science Review* 97, 3 (2003), 343–362.

89 The weaknesses of Pape's *Dying to Win* (New York: Random House, 2005) are not unlike the failings in his first book *Bombing to Win: Air Power and Coercion in War* (Ithaca: Cornell University Press, 1996) where he often gets only half the story right. A classic example of this in *Bombing to Win* is Pape's claim that the US air force had strict rules of engagement in the Korean War that prohibited the firebombing of cities. This was true for the early part of the war, but the policy was overturned and the US eventually firebombed most North Korean cities, a fact Pape ignores. See Curtis LeMay interviewed in *Strategic Air Warfare*, 86–89; Bruce Cumings, *North Korea*.

90 Pape, *Dying to Win*.

91 Olivier Roy, *Globalised Islam* (London: C. Hurst, 2002).

92 None of this is to deny that US policies in Iraq have worsened this problem and vastly increased both "lite" and violent forms of anti-Americanism.

93 John Callaghan, Brendon O'Connor and Mark Phythian, *Ideologies of American Foreign Policy* (London: Routledge, 2019); Danny Cooper, *Neoconservatism and American Foreign Policy: A Critical Analysis* (London: Routledge, 2012).

94 John Micklethwait and Adrian Wooldridge, *The Right Nation: Conservative Power in America* (New York: Penguin, 2004).

95 Francis Fukuyama, *America at the Crossroads* (New Haven: Yale University Press, 2006).

96 Greg Sheridan, *The Partnership* (Sydney: University of New South Wales Press, 2006); Lawrence Wright, "How 9/11 Might Have Been Prevented," *New Yorker*, July 10 & 17, 2006; Bob Woodward, *State of Denial* (New York: Simon & Schuster, 2006); Bob Woodward, *Bush at War* (New York: Simon & Schuster, 2002); Bob Woodward, *Plan of Attack* (New York: Simon & Schuster, 2004); Ron Suskind, *The Price of Loyalty* (New York: Simon & Schuster, 2004); David Frum, *Right Man* (New York: Random House 2003).

97 George Packer, *The Assassins' Gate: America in Iraq* (New York: Farrar, Straus and Giroux, 2005); Rajiv Chandrasekaran, *Imperial Life in the Emerald City* (New York: Vintage Books, 2007); Thomas E. Ricks, *Fiasco: The America Military Adventure in Iraq* (New York: Penguin, 2006).

98 George Orwell, "Politics and the English Language" in *Essays* (London: Penguin, 2000).

3

ANTI-AMERICANISM VS. CRITICISM

Reporting on the 2003 Iraq War and the Korean War

Examining anti-Americanism in the Australian context provides insights into both how the term can be misused in attempts to undermine valid criticisms of US foreign policies and how it can be used to better understand the anti-American prejudices of individuals. This chapter will illustrate the benefits of using a precise definition of anti-Americanism as a means of countering the misuse of the term. Two case studies will be examined, looking at Australian press coverage of the 2003 Iraq War and Korean War. The first case study examines the Australian government's allegations of bias in the Australian national broadcaster's coverage of the 2003 Iraq War; the second examines the role Australian journalist Wilfred Burchett played in promoting anti-American sentiment, particularly during the Korean War. Anti-Americanism was directly alleged and denied in both case studies: in the case of the Australian Broadcasting Corporation's (ABC's) coverage of the 2003 Iraq War, claims of anti-Americanism were unjustifiably made and fairly denied, whereas Burchett's journalism and conduct during the Korean War was a clear case of anti-Americanism. Thus, these two cases are instructive to examine in order to better negotiate one of the crucial conceptual distinctions in the study of anti-Americanism, namely how to differentiate between anti-Americanism and criticism. Furthermore, the Iraq War case study illustrates how the term anti-Americanism can be instrumentally employed as a disciplining term to silence criticism of America. Alternatively, the Burchett example shows how opponents of the US government can overreach and spread lies and inaccuracies in an attempt to undermine US credibility.

To fairly and usefully comment on these claims one needs an understanding of what distinguishes anti-Americanism from criticism and scepticism. As such, scholars need to analyse the discourse on so called anti-Americanism, and must attempt to elevate such discussions by developing more precise definitions of anti-Americanism. As I have argued throughout this book, scholars have done too little to date to define what anti-Americanism actually is as an analytical term. Instead they tend to quickly move beyond this question to examine grievances against the US. Here, I have tried to provide more conceptual rigor to discussions of the term anti-Americanism, suggesting there are five ways the concept of anti-Americanism is commonly understood and used. These are: to view it as a simple dichotomy between pro-American/anti-American positions; to see it as a tendency along a scale; to view it as a pathology where everything American is strongly disliked; to understand it as a prejudice; or to interpret it as an ideology like anti-communism or anti-globalisation. Another possibility would be to see anti-Americanism as a term that is often instrumentally employed to silence criticism, but this is a political tactic rather than a way of interpreting the world. What I seek to argue here is that the Australian Communications Minister Richard Allston and his government labelled journalists from the Australian Broadcasting Corporation "anti-American" because these journalists were rightly asking critical questions about the ill-conceived and poorly planned 2003 Iraq War. The use of the term anti-Americanism in this case is not justified and is a good example of the disciplining nature of the term. Max Paul Friedman in his excellent *Rethinking Anti-Americanism* shows this is the most commonplace way the term anti-Americanism is used in discussions of US foreign relations. While I mostly agree with Friedman, in some cases the term is in fact an accurate classification. For example, calling the Australian journalist Wilfred Burchett "anti-American" is justified as Burchett was ideologically committed to strongly favour the Chinese and Soviet communist systems over the American system. This resulted in Burchett seeing the foreign policies of communist nations as far more noble and righteous than American foreign policies. This led to a selection bias in his books, which often resulted in him recycling Soviet and Chinese propaganda. His work fits the category of anti-Americanism as a prejudice that I discussed in Chapter 1. His writings have all the traditional markers of prejudice as it prejudges, it is clearly one-sided, and it offers a biased view of American foreign policy. This is particularly true of his Korean War coverage where he behaved as a Chinese and North Korean propagandist, not as the independent journalist that he and his supporters claimed that he was.[1] This form of anti-Americanism can go beyond mere prejudice to take on an ideological character, which is interesting albeit more complicated to consider. Burchett's defenders claimed he merely wrote from the "other side," which arguably plays an important function as it is useful to know how the communist protagonists viewed various conflicts. Moreover, others would remind us that, in the 1950s and beyond, American anti-communists often exaggerated the reach and power of Soviet communism and communist ideas outside of the USSR and China; in response, some defenders of Burchett would argue for moral equivalencies. However, there are clearly weaknesses to these defences of Burchett. It seems clear that he helped fabricate evidence that the Americans were engaged in biological warfare in Korea and in the case of the USSR and China, he defended the morally indefensible treatment of their own people. As I will outline in this chapter, Burchett represents a clear case of anti-Americanism; whereas the ABC case study represents a strong example of the political misuse of the term anti-Americanism to attempt to silence and discipline critical opinion.

Two case studies in anti-Americanism

My first case study examines the Australian government's claims of anti-American bias by an Australian Broadcasting Corporation (ABC) current affairs program. This study questions where criticism ends and anti-Americanism begins, and whether allegations of anti-Americanism were used instrumentally to rebuff criticisms of a controversial war. The second case study examines the career of Australian journalist Wilfred Burchett, particularly his activities during the Korean War. I argue that Burchett's obvious anti-Americanism was coupled with a strong determination to discredit the US whilst attempting to maintain his reputation as an independent journalist. With ongoing evidence of his role as a communist propagandist,[2] this legacy looks very shaky indeed.

Seen together these case studies remind us that in times of war, reporters play a crucial role. Neutral coverage and reportage from behind enemy lines is often invaluable in informing discussion about the nature of conduct during a war. However, the government of the day is likely to expect a certain level of loyalty from its own national media, both at the war zone and on the home front, and will be tempted to portray criticism as disloyalty. This strong temptation raises thorny questions for democracies, as attempts are made to discredit critical reporters and their news agencies. When the critical commentary is centred on American military actions, it has and will continue to be frequently labelled anti-American, at times fairly and at times unjustifiably. Whether that label is reasonably used is the subject of the rest of this chapter.

Anti-Americanism as polemic name-calling

In May 2003 the Australian Federal Minister for Communications Richard Alston issued a media release. Titled "Alston seeks urgent investigation into *AM*'s Iraq coverage," the release strongly criticised coverage by the ABC's flagship current affairs show *AM* in the first month of the 2003 Iraq War. The statement was accompanied by an 18-page analysis of this coverage, prepared by the Minister's office. The media release led with the Minister's dissatisfaction with *AM*'s coverage but at least half of the media release detailed a quote by the ABC's Director of News and Current Affairs, Max Uechtritz, in which he called the military "lying bastards." Citing multiple explanations for the quote from Uechtritz, the Minister questioned whether Uechtritz's views as head of ABC News and Current Affairs had been allowed to infect the ABC coverage of the Iraq conflict. Uechtritz's rather unsubtle comments had been made at a media conference in Singapore and were not intended for public consumption.[3] Although Uechtritz's words provided an easy target in the media release, the accompanying 18-page critique dealt entirely with comments on the *AM* show regarding Iraq War commentary by ABC journalists. In response to the Minister's complaints two inquiries were undertaken to adjudicate on the specific claim that the coverage was "biased, and in particular anti-American."[4]

The ABC is a government funded non-commercial television, radio and internet media outlet which broadcasts across the Australian continent via national and regional programs. It is modelled on the British Broadcasting Corporation (BBC) and enjoys a similar public affection and regard for the quality of its coverage. Like the BBC, it also faces the accompanying concern voiced by conservatives of a left-liberal bias on political issues. Despite these tensions the ABC's general reputation is strong as a broadcaster of quality non-partisan radio and television news and current affairs. It has a charter that sets out the nature of its independence from the government and the expectations of its coverage. Senator Alston claimed that the ABC's coverage of the 2003 Iraq invasion by the *AM* program appeared not to have met these "appropriate standards." To illustrate this, the document from the Minister's office detailed 68 alleged examples of biased coverage. The document included the underlining of certain words and phrases and provided a commentary on the words of various *AM* journalists.[5] Alston's two central assertions were that the coverage was biased because journalists, instead of reporting the facts, had engaged in editorialising by offering their own opinions, and that these opinions were "anti-American."

The context of these criticisms is that Australia was one of a small number of traditional US allies to support the invasion of Iraq and commit combat troops. Although small in number these troops were nonetheless symbolically important,[6] and were committed to war in Iraq in the face of significant opposition from within both the Australian federal parliament and the broader populace. Public concern culminated in huge protests on the weekend of February 14–16, 2003, when approximately 500,000 people took part in anti-Iraq War rallies across Australia, including Australia's largest ever demonstration of around 250,000 people in Sydney.[7] Furthermore, the Iraq War failed to receive bipartisan political support. Along with the Vietnam War and the sending of troops to Malaya in 1955, it was only the third time in Australian history that the main opposition party had not supported a government position of troop deployment overseas. The Australian Labor Party (ALP) leader Simon Crean in his March 18, 2003 parliamentary reply described the Prime Minister John Howard's decision to send troops thus:

> The Prime Minister today, in a reckless and unnecessary act, has committed Australia to war. The Prime Minister has his moment of truth, and what did we see? We saw capitulation and subservience to a phone call from the United States President. This is a black day for Australia and it is a black day for international cooperation.[8]

As strong as they were, Crean's criticisms took a step back from Mark Latham's earlier parliamentary attack on a US-led war in Iraq. Latham, who was to become ALP leader in late 2003, described President Bush on February 5, 2003 as the "most incompetent and dangerous president in living memory." He further claimed that "Bush's foreign policy looks more like American imperialism than a well thought through and resourced strategy to eliminate terrorists." He also dismissed the Australian Prime Minister John Howard as a "yes-man to a flaky and dangerous American president."[9] These remarks and others by ALP politicians prompted US Ambassador to Australia J. Thomas Schieffer to briefly enter the political fray to express his disapproval of anti-Bush and anti-war ALP rhetoric.[10] It was in this politically charged environment that the *AM* program began its coverage of the 2003 Iraq War.

Senator Alston called for his inquiry into the ABC coverage in May, possibly sensing a weakening of public opposition to the war in the wake of the swift defeat of Saddam's forces. The first half of 2003 had seen public opinion swing by a slim majority in support of the war.[11] Alston's criticisms can also be seen as part of a broader campaign by the conservative Howard government against the ABC. The government considered the ABC hostile towards them and had already called an earlier inquiry into the ABC's coverage of the 1998 waterfront dispute where contract stevedores trained in Dubai by the Patrick Company were deployed to replace Maritime Union of Australia workers on the Melbourne docks.

Alston's analysis was passed on to the ABC's internal Complaints Review Executive (CRE), headed by Murray Green. In response the CRE analysed every edition of *AM* broadcast on the Iraq invasion, and compared tapes and transcripts with transcripts from press briefings at the White House, the Pentagon and central command in Qatar. The CRE also compared *AM*'s coverage with that of other media before releasing its response on July 21, 2003: two of the 68 allegations made by Senator Alston were upheld but the broadcaster was cleared of systemic anti-American bias in *AM*'s coverage of the Iraq War. The first complaint that was upheld was this statement by the ABC's Washington correspondent John Shovelan: "Oh the civility of this US military. The daily Pentagon briefing begins with an illustration of its mercy and kindness." Senator Alston had claimed the comments were "dripping in sarcasm."[12] Shovelan's comments were made on April 9, 2003 after a briefing by Victoria Clarke, Assistant Secretary of Defense-Public Affairs where she claimed that the US seeks to avoid unnecessary loss of lives with its precision bombs and that the US goes to "extraordinary lengths" to help the injured in Iraq from all sides. In his rebuttal, of what amounted to a censure by Green, John Shovelen offered the following defence of himself:

> Unfortunately while context has been left out of many of the complaints, I may have been guilty of leaving the context out here. But I disagree with Mr Green's findings that the item was to quote the Minister "dripping in sarcasm". In the US there was a debate about whether the US military was taking a far too civil or humanitarian approach to the war. ... It was the only piece to my knowledge, certainly on *AM* which pointed out the Pentagon's approach, beginning daily briefings with "good human interest stories" (which by the way were summarily dismissed in the US media), its deliberate policy of showing its smart weapons technology in the best light and failing to provide any information when its bombs went astray. ... Three months on the Pentagon hasn't released its findings into bombs which went astray in Baghdad

markets or the Palestine Hotel incident in which two independent journalists were killed by a tank shell. ... I don't shrink from the fact it was a highly critical piece. But just because it is, doesn't mean it is "dripping in sarcasm".[13]

Green found that Shovelan's comment was "sarcastic in tone and, in my view, excessive." However, Green adds that, "There is no justification, however, to extrapolate this item in order to demonstrate a pattern of endemic anti-Americanism."[14] In other words, a few critical, and possibly cynical, remarks do not add up to an anti-American bias in the coverage. The other complaint that was upheld was in relation to speculation as to why the president did not watch the opening air offensive against Iraq on television. Once again evidence of "endemic anti-Americanism" was not found by Green.

After the Minister indicated that he was not pleased with the outcome of the CRE review, the next step in the ABC's complaints-handling process was for the external Independent Complaints Review Panel (ICRP) to further review the Minister's complaints. In August the ICRP received the Minister's submission "Rebuttal of the ABC Response to a Complaint about the *AM* Program's Coverage of the Iraq Conflict." The ICRP reported its findings in October.

Ironically while the ICRP dismissed the Minister's contention of "over-emphasis" and "lack of objectivity" for *AM*, they did note that the language used by the Minister himself in his 68 complaints often contained loaded words. The ICRP gave an example of one of the complaints and also quoted other complaints that included "beating up a story," "putting the boot in," "gratuitous barbs," "cynicism," "ridicule" and "immature and irrelevant abuse," stating that many of these remarks were directed personally at the *AM* presenter Linda Mottram.[15] Such hyperbolic criticism hardly provided a good example of sober and non-inflammatory analysis, and certainly lacked the cool objectivity the Minister had demanded of the ABC. Alston attacked the ABC's coverage of concerns over a possible refugee crisis on the borders of Iraq, even though this had been reported as a genuine fear by the US government and most aid agencies in the Middle East. He also complained about the statement that the Turkish parliament had rejected US war efforts, a known fact that was widely reported.[16]

The ICRP found no evidence, overall, of biased and anti-American coverage as alleged by the Minister, and also did not uphold his view that the program was characterised by one-sided and tendentious commentary by program hosts and reporters. The five-member panel said there was no overall bias in the ABC's coverage of the Iraq War, which it found to be "competent and balanced." The ICRP stated that it was mindful of the line of demarcation between straight news reporting and programs of analysis and interpretation. They placed *AM* firmly in the latter category. Such programs cover analysis, comment and opinion but unlike newspapers, radio and television do not always clearly make this distinction.

In terms of a number of individual *AM* broadcasts the ICRP upheld the contention that there were statements by the presenter or a reporter that displayed serious bias. These 12 statements, nine of which emerged from on-air conversations between Mottram and *AM*'s Washington correspondent John Shovelan, included the two upheld by the initial CRE report. The ICRP also upheld five other complaints as "non serious" breaches of ABC editorial guidelines which warn against the use of emotive language and editorialising as well as a failure to identify sources.[17]

Why did the ICRP uphold ten more complaints than the CRE? The differences seem largely about semantics, but context also plays an important role. The CRE report gives full transcripts to flesh out the complaints, often placing the alleged "bias" in a much broader context, thereby seriously diluting its effect and impact. In some of the complaints rejected by both reports, the transcript seems to negate the complaint entirely. The ICRP does not justify its decisions in the detailed manner of the CRE. For example, the CRE report places complaints 54 and 55 in the journalistic context of the day. Centred as they were around the deaths of three journalists from American fire, Mottram's alleged "bias" and "anger" becomes much more understandable when viewed alongside the outraged comments of her international colleagues. As journalists, Mottram and her team would not only have been shocked by the unnecessary deaths of colleagues but also would have been comparing their reports to those being filed elsewhere around the globe. Compared to the outrage and suspicion voiced in these reports, Mottram's "bias" seems mild indeed.

The Minister's initial demands for an inquiry had centred on his claim that his office had "received a number of complaints of bias, and in particular anti-American coverage by the ABC, particularly the *AM* program." Alston's case is seriously undermined by the details of these complaints, obtained later by the ABC's *Media Watch* program using Australia's freedom of information laws. These details reveal that the "number of complaints" were ten in total, with nine making no mention of the *AM* program at all. The single complaint about *AM* came directly from Brian Loughnane,[18] the federal director of Alston's own political party, the Liberal Party of Australia. This revelation exposes Alston's allegations as gross political manipulation, lacking any honesty and real credibility.

This manipulation and lack of credibility did not prevent Alston from announcing that the judgments of the IRCP report were "a brutal reality check" for the ABC. A more honest analysis was offered by media commentator Mark Day when he said "when the umpire's call is three to one against you, it's hardly a victory."[19] Mark Day goes on to express the view that the whole issue was built around Alston's lack of understanding of editorial processes. Day says that what Alston saw as bias and "relentless negativism" can equally be explained as part of the daily editorial process. While Shovelan undoubtedly made a few sarcastic comments, in general the ABC was carrying out its mission of reporting without fear or favour. While this sometimes portrays the US in a less than flattering light, it does not qualify as anti-Americanism. In general, this incident highlights how the charge of anti-Americanism is used as a disciplining tactic in political debate. This was a war for which the Australian government volunteered its troops, not brought on by a direct attack on either Australia or its allies. For these reasons a sceptical outlook by the press seems entirely appropriate. Claims of anti-Americanism are thus not well founded. With the advantages of hindsight, there were very good reasons to be sceptical of the motivations for invading Iraq and the way the American led forces were going about occupying the country. Thomas Ricks, one of America's most respected military reporters has called Operation Iraqi freedom a "fiasco" and this seems entirely fair. The ongoing destruction that resulted from the replacement by the Americans of Saddam Hussein's regime reminds us that in fact not enough questions were asked in 2003 about why this war was necessary and what its result would be. The ABC's *AM* programme should be praised for its scepticism given that the record of regime change throughout the world has been very destructive since WWII.

Wilfred Burchett and anti-Americanism

My second case study is of Australian journalist Wilfred Burchett's coverage of the Korean War and tells quite a different story, showing that claims of anti-Americanism, although usually denied, are at times very appropriate. I focus on Burchett's activities during the Korean War to illustrate the depth of his anti-Americanism, and argue that from near the beginning of his career, he became instinctively anti-American and pro-Communist in a manner that was both prejudicial and ideologically driven. Burchett was the first unsupervised Western reporter to cover the atomic bombing of Hiroshima. His account of the devastation this bomb wrought stands as an iconic piece of reporting with its famous opening line "I write this as a warning to the world" printed as a banner headline by *The Daily Express* on September 5, 1945, a month after the first atomic bomb had been dropped on Japan. He risked his life to cover this harrowing event, a pattern that would be repeated throughout his career as he took on risky assignments to cover foreign wars. This legendary opening to Burchett's international career and his subsequent involvement in war zones saw him lionised by some as a consistently brave and independent reporter who covered stories from the "other side." His supporters chose the tags of "rebel" and "liberal."[20] Burchett certainly took on this role, choosing to portray himself as a champion of the underdog and as an independent voice, and denying Communist Party membership throughout his career.

Despite these independent claims, any objective analysis of Burchett's career, largely played out in the Cold War arena, would describe his reportage as characterised by an anti-American, pro-communist stance.[21] For his critics such as Robert Manne, Burchett's coverage of the "Atomic plague" not only made him a journalist of note, but also marked the beginning of his career as an unreconstructed anti-American. Manne writes: "Burchett claims to have been appalled by the attempts of the US Army Command in Japan to disguise the medical effects of the atomic bomb at Hiroshima. From this moment, until his death, a rancorous anti-Americanism became a fundamental element of his political thought and journalistic mission."[22] Burchett's scepticism and hostility toward the US is obvious in his writings from the early Cold War. His coverage of the conflicts between the Americans and the Soviets in Germany is staunchly pro-Soviet.[23] This worldview is outlined in his journalism of the time and his book *The Cold War in Germany* (1950). It is also repeated in his three books of memoirs *Passport* (1969), *At the Barricades* (1981) and the posthumously released *Memoirs of a Rebel Journalist* (2005). His efforts as a propagandist for the Soviet cause are apparent from his writings in Germany where he attempted to downplay and discredit the claim that Soviet troops had raped a large number of German women.[24] Burchett's views on post-WWII Europe are unremarkable and could be written off as Stalinist cant. However, they contain arguments that have gone on to have a longer shelf life than popular support for Stalinism in the West. Burchett's belief in the Soviet Union as a post-WWII bastion of peace and the socialist ideal now reads as obviously foolhardy, but his portrayal of the Marshall Plan as a disingenuous imperialist plan to control Europe is still widely debated.[25] In his popular work *The Clash of Fundamentalisms* Tariq Ali calls the Marshall Plan "one half of the 'Siamese twins' of American imperialism."[26] The other striking and oft-repeated feature of Burchett's writing on Germany was the way he labelled enemies of socialist causes Fascists or neo-Nazis.

Burchett's commitment to the Stalinist cause was confirmed in his coverage of the show trials in Hungary and his criticism of Tito.[27] From reporting on the wonders of communism in Eastern Europe, Burchett travelled in the early 1950s to Communist China, where he once again found a communist society deserving of fulsome praise. Burchett wrote in a letter to his father from China in early 1951 "I would do anything at all for this people and their government because they represent the fullest flowering of all the finest instincts of humanity."[28] The extent to which he was willing to support the Chinese position in the Korean War shows how much this loyalty blinded him.

Burchett's coverage of the Korean War is the most controversial period of his career. The war itself was a complex event involving international, regional and internal conflicts. The recently ended Japanese occupation of the Korean peninsula added another layer of complexity. Claims of neocolonial intentions carried particular weight given both this history and America's occupation of Japan. Furthermore, there is no doubt that the conduct of the United States and its allies during the Korean War deserved more scrutiny than it received at the time, particularly since the war was being fought as a defensive effort under the legal banner of the United Nations. "In the first month of their operation alone, the Strategic Air Command groups dropped 4,000 tons of bombs. Besides high explosives, the bombers used napalm."[29] Although the targeting of civilians and the firebombing of cities was prohibited in the early stages of the Korean War,[30] eventually most northern Korean cities were destroyed.[31] In retirement, Curtis LeMay, the former head of US Strategic Air Command during the Korean War commented: "we eventually burned down every town in North Korea… and some in South Korea too. We even burned down [the South Korean city of] Pusan – an accident, but we burned it down anyway."[32] Also deserving of attention was the belligerence of the UN commander in chief, General MacArthur, especially his want to use nuclear weapons on the Chinese and North Koreans, a position he promoted until his dismissal by Truman.[33]

The under reporting of both the high rate of casualties and the ethics of the US bombing campaign seem to be the result of a combination of factors. Firstly, the press was more compliant in the main,[34] with journalists like Burchett being the exception to the rule (and as I will argue not a particularly credible exception). Dissenting views on the Korean War in the West were also undoubtedly hindered by a climate of fear about communist sympathizers, with America's McCarthyism being the worst example of the excesses of this outlook. Secondly, much of the discussion of the Korean War is set in the context of the Cold War, and the tensions and tactics between the US, USSR and China. This focus led to the Korean War being regularly described as a limited war. This definition was cemented by the fact that fighting was contained within the boundaries of Korea, and also by the fact that the US did not use maximum force on all occasions. US Korean War veterans talk of America fighting a war "with a hand tied behind its back."[35] This "limited war" framing has tended to obscure discussion on the ethics of the US campaign. Undoubtedly the secretive and mercenary nature and conduct of both the North Korean and Chinese governments also hindered a more sympathetic account of the "other side" in the conflict. Mao showed a near total disregard for his soldiers in Korea. It was a war in which the Chinese leader was prepared to lose hundreds of thousands of Chinese lives (preferably ex-nationalist troops) to kill a few thousand Americans. For Mao, his troops were an expendable resource – the pawns in the game of a war of attrition that would eventually see the US withdraw as the American public reacted to the growing death toll of US soldiers in the conflict.[36]

Burchett's reportage during the Korean War came with the blessing and support of the North Koreans and the Chinese. He saw the war as entirely America's fault and his coverage portrayed North Korea and China as blameless. The partiality of Burchett's view of the "other side" is evidenced in his coverage of Chinese and North Korean atrocities. Although he worked in the POW camps of North Korea he makes no mention of the killing and torture of US and South Korean soldiers, facts well documented in a number of studies.[37] Instead when describing the North Korean POW camps he wrote: "This camp looks like a holiday resort in Switzerland. The atmosphere is also nearer that of a luxury holiday resort than a POW camp."[38] Elsewhere he wrote, "The 'overwhelming consensus' was that no group of POWs had been so well treated in modern history."[39] As Robert Manne has written, these camps were as bad as any during the 20th century. Manne notes that, "According to this report in the first year of the Korean War 'food, shelter and medical attention' in the North Korean and Chinese camps was so inadequate that 1600 United Nations POWs died."[40] R. J. Rummel estimates that the "North Koreans killed from 5,000 to 12,000 ROK POWs" and were responsible for the "murder of 5,000 to 6,000 American POWs."[41] To claim that such events happened in conditions akin to a luxury hotel is propaganda with no basis in truth. This misrepresentation of the North Korean POW camps seems worrying, but the most significant propaganda role Burchett was to play in the Korean War was in spreading the claim that the American military was engaged in an extensive biological warfare campaign in North Korea and China. The claims, made by the governments of

North Korea, China and the Soviet Union, were spread by Burchett and other Soviet-bloc propagandists, and remain one of the best examples of anti-American propaganda during the 20th century.

The claims began in May 1951 when the North Korean Minister of Foreign Relations sent a cable to the UN President alleging the US military was using bacteriological weapons. In 1952 the Chinese started making similar claims with Zhou Enlai claiming that the "US had sent 448 aircrafts on no fewer than 68 occasions between February 29 and March 5 into Northeast China to airdrop germ-carrying insects. The human diseases alleged to have been spread were plague, anthrax, cholera, encephalitis, and a form of meningitis."[42] Moscow radio on February 18, 1952 broadcast that the US was spreading smallpox and typhus bacteria and also secretly sending lepers to northern Korea. By March 8 the Chinese were claiming the "United States had dropped insects, rats, shellfish, and chicken feathers containing disease germs on Chinese as well as North Korean territory."[43] Wilfred Burchett was central to communist efforts to spread these claims. Initially he spread the claims via his reporting of the war and later reiterated them in his 1953 *The Monstrous War*, with his subsequent autobiographies also retelling this story.

Throughout 1952 the claims the US was engaged in germ warfare was the most significant story in the Chinese press regarding the Korean War; the allegations received more coverage between mid-March and mid-April 1952 than the entirety of Korean War coverage to that date. The Soviet press was also to take up the issue with considerable alarm, and the story was also reported by Burchett and Alan Winnington in socialist and communist newspapers in Western Europe, with the claim becoming a major source of resentment towards America amongst the Communist Party of France (CPF) in 1952. The CPF was instrumental in organising a large rally in 1952 in Paris when the commander of US forces in Korea, General Ridgway was in France for NATO negotiations. Thousands of French protesters turned out to condemn the US, dubbing Ridgway the "Bacterial General" for America's supposed use of germ warfare in Korea.[44]

The UN and other international organisations remained sceptical of the claims, largely because the North Korean and Chinese governments, despite their regular reiterations of the claims during the Korean War, had refused to allow international organisations like the International Committee of the Red Cross or the World Health Organization to investigate. The Americans, particularly Secretary of State Dean Acheson, called for such investigations claiming the Americans had nothing to hide. However, the Chinese and North Koreans claimed such organizations were biased towards the US and denied them access to investigate the supposedly infected areas. At the same time, Burchett and other pro-communist sympathizers drew upon the "expertise" of "international commissions" of lawyers and scientists, established to lend credibility to these allegations. The most noted of these was the International Scientific Commission, an organisation that Burchett regularly cited as the authority confirming the germ warfare allegations. However, the members of the commission seemed never actually to have visited the sites where the germs were supposedly dropped; they instead relied on testimonies and samples brought to them.[45] Further, like Burchett, the members of the Commission from the West (notably its spokesperson Dr Joseph Needham) were committed communists and far from neutral investigators.[46]

The linchpin in the campaign was the testimony of 25 captured US pilots that they had in fact dropped biological weapons. Since the Korean War it has been claimed by a number of pilots that Wilfred Burchett was involved in transcribing and editing these confessions.[47] This claim was repeated by a number of the captured pilots in a court case in Australia in 1974,[48] and it seems likely that the confessions by the US POWs were obtained as a result of torture and various threats. The wording of some of the confessions is straight out of standard Chinese press reports of the period, with the pilots using such improbable wording as US "imperialists" and the "capitalist Wall Street war monger."[49] Burchett's close proximity to apparently tortured POWs and his alleged threatening of prisoners who argued with him[50] belies his claimed independence.

In most of Burchett's writings on what he calls the "microbes war" he relies on second hand information. However, his imagination and enthusiasm to support the claims lead him to claim a personal sighting of bugs supposedly dropped by the American military. Burchett writes:

> One [bug] was an inch-long with a trailing abdomen and pincer like jaws, the other was smaller, like a very slim house-fly. They were obviously not at home in the water and as the sun dried their wings, some of them shook themselves and flew off. We all did our best to avoid contact except for one of the ferrymen. Using scraps of paper, he gingerly edged a number of each into a small bottle, corked it and asked my interpreter to take it to the nearest laboratory. Ferrymen and passengers agreed that they had never seen either type of fly in the area before.[51]

This claim is made in *The Monstrous War* and repeated in the more recently released extended autobiography *Memoirs of a Rebel Journalist*. He also fabricates conversations with the captured pilots who, he states, confessed to dropping germs on Korea. In one of many revealing moments he writes, "I talked to all the airmen at length and on several occasions. I am convinced that the statements they made are accurate and were made of their own free will."[52] Elsewhere Burchett writes that an American POW ate a fly to prove that there were no germs dropped on North Korea and died the next day after suffering terrible fevers.[53] This story is repeated by the Australian academic Gavin McCormack, one of Burchett's strongest defenders; McCormack goes on to quote the findings of the International Scientific Commission as though it is a credible source on this allegation. The real story behind this soldier's death remains unknown. One might hazard a guess that he either did not exist or was killed by his captors.

Over the years, scholars have tended to remain more open-minded than organisations such as the UN and until recently there long remained a lingering possibility of the allegations being true.[54] However the opening of Soviet archives has finally debunked the claims as a well-coordinated hoax.[55] The Soviet archival evidence proving the claims of biological warfare to be a hoax were first translated by the Japanese newspaper *Sankei Shimbun* and have subsequently been published and analysed in *Critical Reviews in Microbiology* and also by the *Cold War International History Project*. Milton Leitenberg in his article in *Critical Reviews in Microbiology* writes, "In January 1998, 12 documents were obtained from former Soviet archives that provide explicit and detailed evidence that the charges [of germ warfare] were contrived and fraudulent."[56]

The Soviet archival evidence talks of fabricating evidence to help "prove" that the Americans had engaged in germ warfare. The claims are acknowledged as a useful weapon against the Americans in the peace negotiations. The aim was to make America look bad in the eyes of the global community, and to provide cover for the spread of diseases by Chinese troops in North Korea. Many North Koreans and Chinese did die of disease in the harsh winter of 1951–1952 but not, it seems, from germs dropped by US pilots; many of the Chinese soldiers fighting in Korea were simply inadequately clothed, with their wellbeing callously disregarded by Mao.[57]

The broader context of the claims was that America and Japan were about to sign the 1952 Mutual Security Assistance Pact, which China and the Soviets opposed. Moreover, America had previously granted immunity at the end of WWII to the Japanese biological weapons units in exchange for their research and development.[58] Connecting the Americans with germ warfare was thus not just a means of discrediting America, but also of suggesting US–Japanese relations were fascistic and drew on unethical Japanese WWII research and activities.[59] For those wanting to believe the worst about America these conspiracies proved irresistible.

However, after Stalin's death, as in a number of other areas, the Soviet leadership re-examined their position on the germ warfare claims. On May 2, 1953 the Soviets sent the following message to Mao:

> For Mao Zedong
> The Soviet Government and the Central Committee of the CPSU were misled. The spread in the press of information about the use by the Americans of bacteriological weapons in Korea was based on false information. The accusations against the Americans were fictitious.
> To give recommendations:
> To cease publication in the press of materials accusing the Americans of using bacteriological weapons in Korea and China.[60]

Although the claims were first raised by the North Koreans, the Chinese were the most vocal and repetitive in stating them; their ability to get this story into the press and spread across the globe is described by one author as "a masterstroke, in the realm of international politics and psychology."[61]

This archival evidence paints Burchett's accusations against the Americans and his behaviour in a very poor light. Turning back to my anti-American categories from the beginning of this chapter, Burchett's reporting displays clear anti-American prejudice and it would seem fair to call him an iconic anti-American ideologue. Burchett clearly sided with the Communists in the Korean conflict, not only ignoring Chinese and North Korean abuses of the rights of POWs, but also actively involving himself in the creation of propaganda. Lietenberg, at the end of his article on the Soviet archival material, suggests that those making false claims about the use of a weapon of mass destruction should be punished in some international forum. Burchett's death in 1983 makes this impossible, but those who continue to celebrate his career as a great journalist and humanist must be strongly questioned. Gavin McCormack's effusive praise of Burchett as "a journalist inspired by an uncommon moral passion" and "an honest man who tried to tell the truth" seems hollow indeed.

The people and the soldiers on the non-American side of this conflict paid an awful toll and their stories are truly the unknown narrative of this conflict. Wilfred Burchett was one of the few journalists in the right place to cover this story from the other side. However, his overenthusiasm for the North Korean and Chinese regimes saw him squander this opportunity. Rather than producing an important record of reportage from the North Korean perspective, Burchett has left a propagandist's legacy that holds anti-Americanism at its core.

Conclusion

In this chapter, I have examined two Australian case studies to ascertain whether they truly show the marks of "anti-Americanism" or whether they can be viewed as simply valid criticism. In the case of Wilfred Burchett, it would seem charges of inaccuracy and anti-Americanism were most warranted. In the case of the ABC's *AM* journalists Linda Mottram and John Shovelan, the attempt to discredit their coverage of the Iraq War was excessive and politically indulgent. Indeed, it represented part of a concerted campaign by the Howard and Bush governments to paint the Iraq conflict in the best possible light. When one compares the fabrication and obvious bias of Burchett with the largely objective coverage of the ABC journalists, the incongruity of the two being placed together in the same category makes a very good case for a more critical and differentiated view of anti-Americanism. Ultimately, greater honesty and accountability may well be the best defence against anti-Americanism. Fighting a war and adhering to the basic principles of democracy is not going to be easy but, in the long term, transparency is the best weapon in the war of ideas and perceptions. Such transparency can only be achieved when a term such as anti-Americanism is given a real and clear definition. Therefore, as I stated earlier in this chapter, anti-Americanism is a serious claim, akin to prejudice. Scholars have an important role pointing out where reasonable criticism has falsely been called anti-Americanism for political point-scoring purposes.

Notes

1 John Pilger, "Preface," in *Burchett Reporting the Other Side of the World 1939–1983*, ed. Ben Kiernan (Melbourne: Quartet Books, 1986); Ben Kiernan, "Introduction," in Ibid.

2 Robert Manne, "Wilfred Burchett and the KGB," *The Monthly*, August 2013, <https://www.themonthly.com.au/issue/2013/august/1375315200/robert-manne/wilfred-burchett-and-kgb>.

3 Richard Alston, "Alston Seeks Urgent Investigation into AM's Iraq Coverage," May 28, 2003; Annabel Crabb, "Alston Threatens ABC with Censor," *Age*, May 29, 2003. <http://www.theage.com.au/articles/2003/05/28/1053801445726.html>. It is interesting that this bias was being discussed at the same time as the media coverage of the 60th anniversary of the worst aviation disaster on Australian soil – the crash of a US Air force bomber in 1943 killing 40 men (with one sole survivor). This event was censored by the Australian and US governments of the day; the result of this censorship is that this event is still not widely known about in Australia. More alarmingly, it is estimated that in 2003, 22 of the 40 American families who lost relatives in the disaster still did not even know that the crash had occurred, let alone that it had happened in Australia. ABC, "Anniversary of Australia's Worst Air Disaster," June 14, 2003, <http://www.abc.net.au/am/content/2003/s879788.htm>. Other prominent examples of less-than-truthful media coverage during war include the bombing of the Australian city of Darwin in 1942, which was largely kept a secret from the public, and the far from honest communiqués of Douglas MacArthur during WWII. See Tony Griffiths, *Beautiful Lies* (Kent Town: Wakefield Press, 2005), 4–5, for information on the Darwin bombings and Paul Ham, *Kokoda* (Sydney: Harper Collins, 2004) for details on MacArthur.

4 Richard Alston, "Alston Seeks Urgent Investigation into AM's Iraq Coverage," May 28, 2003.

5 The two journalists attacked most heavily by Minister Alston were Linda Mottram and John Shovelan, who denied their reporting was anti-American and defended their reports in the Green inquiry into Alston's allegations. I interviewed Mottram and Shovelan separately, and they both strongly denied they were anti-American.

6 For further details see Brendon O'Connor, "Perspectives on Australian Foreign Policy, 2003," *Australian Journal of International Affairs* 57, 1 (2010), 207–220. Also see this document which provides a list of initial and immediate post-war Australian military involvements in Iraq <http://www.defence.gov.au/FOI/Docs/Disclosures/049_1617_Documents.pdf>.

7 Valerie Lawson, "With One Voice, the World Says No," *Age*, February 17, 2003; Marcus Priest, "PM Not Swayed by Size of Peace Rallies," *Australian Financial Review*, February 17, 2003.

8 Simon Crean, "Address to the House of Representatives," Canberra, March 18, 2003.

9 Mark Latham, "Address to the House of Representatives," Canberra, February 5, 2003.

10 Maxine McKew, "Tom Schieffer United States Ambassador," *Bulletin*, February 12, 2003.

11 Murray Goot, "Public Opinion and the Democratic Deficit: Australia and the War Against Iraq," *Australian Humanities Review* (May 2003). <http://australianhumanitiesreview.org/2003/05/01/public-opinion-and-the-democratic-deficit-australia-and-the-war-against-iraq/>.

12 ABC Complaints Review Executive, "Determination on a Series of Complaints from Senator Richard Alston, Minister for Communications, Information Technology and the Arts," May 28, 2003.

13 Ibid., 99–100.

14 Ibid., 100.

15 Independent Complaints Review Panel, "Review of 68 Complaints made by the Minister for Communications, Information Technology and the Arts, Senator Richard Alston, Carried out at the Request of the Managing Director of the ABC," October 2003, 6.

16 Seymour Hersh, "Offense and Defense," *New Yorker*, April 7, 2003.

17 Details of the 12 statements the external Independent Complaints Review Panel felt displayed serious bias:

Complaint 6: (upheld by both reviews) John Shovelan claims that the president not watching the opening of the air offensive on television is an indication of just how sensitive he is to launching a massive bombing campaign in an area so heavily populated. The word "sensitive" is taken by both the CRE and the ICRP to be central to the complaint. While the CRE says that the reporter was only engaging in speculation the ICRP goes further and finds the word, in the context it was used, to be one man's (John Shovelan's) judgmental opinion.

Complaint 7: John Shovelan gives his opinion on whether the Joint Chiefs of Staff really meant to say that progress would have been swifter than if chemical weapons had of been used. The ICRP saw this statement as open to the interpretation that (a) the US had considered using chemical weapons, and (b) was concerned that an unguarded remark had revealed this to the general public. They state there was no evidence to support these allegations. The CRE read this completely differently, interpreting that the chemical weapons were being used by the Iraqis rather than the Americans.

Complaint 12 and 13: John Shovelan states that the guerrilla tactics of Hussein loyalists is "really unsettling the Pentagon."

After listening to a report from one of the US military, Linda Mottram states that they sound "unnerved". The ICRP could not find evidence to support the contention that the Pentagon was unsettled and on listening to the report could not detect any signs that the US military spokesperson was "unnerved".

Complaints 15 and 16: While the ICRP states that, on listening to the transcript, Linda Mottram's analysis of a Pentagon spokesperson "diving in" seems accurate, they could not find any support for her next claim that Major General McChrystal "did not seem very comfortable with these questions at all". They also upheld complaint 16 in which the Minister asserts that Mottram takes the supposed discomfort of this one spokesperson to raise doubts about the entire Administration with her quote "is any of that discomfort translating to the upper echelons". The ICRP argues that this is a totally speculative proposition.

Complaint 51: Mottram uses the word "apparent" to describe the Coalition's progress. The ICRP states "there is no justification to use the word 'apparent' at this late stage of the war especially by a presenter who has been following it closely and commenting on it daily."

Complaints 54 and 55: The ICRP states that Linda Mottram's comments on the deaths of three journalists were "open to the interpretation that the Coalition had a policy of deliberately targeting independent journalists, or at least of not taking care to ensure their safety. There was insufficient evidence to support these serious imputations."

Complaints 58: (upheld by both reviews) This complaint was upheld by the ABC and the ICRP who both agreed that John Shovelan's remarks "oh the civility of this US military. The daily Pentagon briefings begins with an illustration of its mercy and kindness" were excessive.

Complaints 59 and 60. The ICRP upheld that Shovelan's comments of "clean killing skills" in response to a Pentagon video showing the precision guidance of US bombs and his "And when the US military goes out of its way to avoid 'collateral damage', a wartime euphemism for killing civilians, it's sure to get top bill at the brief" showed in the words of the ICRP a "serious bias and lack of objectivity."

18 David Marr, "The Shape of the Argument," Overland Public Lecture, 2004, <http://www.safecom.org.au/marr-lecture.htm>.

19 Mark Day, "Allison Lifts ABC Strike-rate, but Loses Overall," *Australian*, October 11, 2003, 4.

20 John Pilger, "Preface," in ed. Ben Kiernan; Gavin McCormack, "Korea: Wilfred Burchett's Thirty Years' War," in ed. Ben Kiernan; Anne-Marie Brady, "The Curious Case of Two Australasian 'Traitors', or, New Zealand, Australia and the Cold War," *New Zealand Journal of History* 35, 1 (2001).

21 Burchett played a Zelig-like role in the Cold War (Zelig being the main character in a 1983 Woody Allen film who has an uncanny knack for being present at key moments in 20th century history; the film has been described as a thinking person's Forrest Gump). From the Hungarian show trials to claims that the US engaged in germ warfare during the Korean War; from the peace negotiations to end the wars in Korea and Vietnam (in the latter case meeting with Henry Kissinger to help open up channels of communication with Hanoi), to playing an instrumental role in organising the infamous Jane Fonda tour of Vietnam in 1972, Burchett played a role as a reporter and propagandist in a number of key events of the Cold War. See Rick Perlstein's excellent article on how Jane Fonda's trip to Hanoi in 1972 lives on in America as an iconic anti-American action committed by an American. Rick Perlstein, "Operation Barbarella," *London Review of Books*, November 17, 2005.

22 Robert Manne, *Agent of Influence: The Life and Times of Wilfred Burchett* (Toronto: The Mackenzie Institute, 1989), 8–9.

23 Ibid., 9.

24 Wilfred Burchett, *Memoirs of a Rebel Journalist – The Autobiography of Wilfred Burchett*, ed. George Burchett and Nick Shimmin (Sydney: University of New South Wales Press, 2005), 264–265.

25 Two more sophisticated takes on this topic are Geir Lundestad, "Empire by Invitation? The United States and Western Europe, 1945–1952," *Journal of Peace Research* 23, 3 (September, 1986), 263–277 and Christopher Layne's *Peace of Illusions* (Ithaca, NY: Cornell University Press, 2007).

26 Tariq Ali, *The Clash of Fundamentalisms* (New York: Verso, 2002).

27 Manne, *Agent of Influence*; Kevin Rowley, "Burchett and the Cold War in Europe," in ed. Ben Kiernan.

28 Michael Godley, "When the East Wind Prevailed in China," in ed. Ben Kiernan, 148.

29 PBS, "The Korean War," <http://www.pbs.org/wgbh/amex/bomb/peopleevents/pandeAMEX58.html>.

30 Robert Pape, *Bombing to Win* (Ithaca: Cornell University Press, 1996), 145.

31 Conrad Crane, *American Airpower Strategy in Korea, 1950–1953* (Lawrence: University of Kansas Press, 2000), 168.

32 Curtis LeMay interviewed in *Strategic Air Warfare*, eds. Richard Kohn and Joseph Harahan (Washington DC: Office of Air Force History, 1988), 86–89. LeMay's position seems to have been that the decision by the US government to minimise civilian casualties in the first year of the Korean War was a mistake, and that it would have been better to attack northern Korea more dramatically and brutally in 1950 with the aim of ending the war as a soon as possible.

33 See Jon Halliday and Bruce Cumings, *Korea: The Unknown War* (London: Viking, 1988), 88–90.

34 Korea had its own My Lai, or Abu Ghraib scandal that went unreported at the time. It was exposed 50 years later (in 2000) by Associated Press journalists in a Pulitzer Prize winning effort. The journalists uncovered that Korean refugees fleeing south during 1950–1951 were strafed by US pilots. Records indicate a particular event in July 1950 when about 400 refugees were killed by US warplanes and Army troops. See, <https://www.pulitzer.org/winners/sang-hun-choe-charles-j-hanley-and-martha-mendoza>. Overall the treatment of refugees (and POW) by the UN forces in Korea seems much better than the behaviour of the Chinese and North Koreans; however, such incidents of UN inhumanity were long covered up to suppress negative attitudes towards America in particular in South Korea. Such cover-ups and what is often seen as hypocrisy have ultimately fed a strong undercurrent of anti-American opinion.

35 Max Hastings, *The Korean War* (London: Michael Joseph, 1987), 419.

36 Jung Chang and Jon Halliday, *Mao* (New York: Knopf, 2005).

37 Harry Spiller, *American POWs in Korea* (Jefferson, North Carolina: McFarland and Company, 1998); Eugene Kinkead, *In Every War but One* (New York: Norton, 1959);

Philip Chinnery, *Korean Atrocity* (Annapolis: Naval Institute Press, 2000); Lewis Carlson, *Remembered Prisoners of a Forgotten War* (New York: St Martin's Press, 2002).

38 Manne, *Agent of Influence, 20*.
39 Ibid.
40 Robert Manne writes that the methods used in the North Korean POW camps included "brutal beatings; solitary confinement for months at a time, often in boxes of 5 foot by 2 or 3 foot, without adequate clothing, food or water; and a variety of more refined and shocking tortures." Ibid.
41 R. J. Rummel, *Statistics on Democide*, <http://www.hawaii.edu/powerkills/SOD.CHAP10.HTM>.
42 Milton Leitenberg, "Resolution of the Korean Biological Warfare Allegations," *Critical Studies in Microbiology* 24, 3 (1998), 170.
43 Burton Kaufman, *The Korean War*, 2nd ed., (New York: McGraw-Hill, 1997), 153–154.
44 Alexander Werth, *France 1940–1955* (New York: Henry Holt, 1956), 577–579.
45 Leitenberg, "Resolution of the Korean Biological Warfare Allegations," 190.
46 Ibid., 171
47 William White, *The Captives of Korea* (New York: Charles Scribner's Sons, 1957).
48 See Roland Perry, *The Exile – Burchett* (Melbourne: William Heinemann, 1988), 149, 150, 153.
49 Leitenberg, "Resolution of the Korean Biological Warfare Allegations," 172.
50 Perry, *The Exile*.
51 Burchett, *Memoirs of a Rebel Journalist*, 405; Wilfred Burchett, *The Monstrous War* (Melbourne: Joseph Waters, 1953), 311.
52 Burchett, *Monstrous War*, 313.
53 Wilfred Burchett, *Passport* (Melbourne: Thomas Nelson, 1969), 222.
54 Halliday and Cumings, *Korea*.
55 Milton Leitenberg, "Resolution of the Korean Biological Warfare Allegations"; Milton Leitenberg, "New Russian Evidence on the Korean War Biological Warfare Allegations," *Cold War International History Project* 11 (Winter 1998); Kathryn Weathersby, "Deceiving the Deceivers," *Cold War International History Project* 11 (Winter 1998); Chang and Halliday, *Mao*.
56 Leitenberg, "Resolution of the Korean War Biological Warfare Allegations," 169.
57 Chang and Halliday, *Mao*.
58 Leitenberg, "Resolution of the Korean War Biological Warfare Allegations," 173.
59 Ibid.
60 Weathersby, "Deceiving the Deceivers," 183.
61 Mark Ryan, *Chinese Attitudes towards Nuclear Weapons* (Armonk: M. E. Sharpe, 1989).

4

ANTI-AMERICANISM OR ANTI-BUSH?

During the 2000 US presidential election campaign George Walker Bush promised not to be the "ugly American" who would go around telling the world what to do. However, as president, he was viewed globally as exactly that. In this chapter I examine the principal stereotypes that formed around President Bush and how they often detracted from meaningful criticisms of his ill-conceived and faulty policies. I then examine the survey data which amply demonstrates Bush's international unpopularity during his presidency and ask whether this unpopularity principally reflects Bush's policy choices, or his much-maligned personal style. Finally, I examine the impact of Bush's global unpopularity on Americans. The ultimate test for this question was the 2004 presidential election and I conclude with a case study that examines the *Guardian* newspaper's campaign to convince voters in Ohio not to reelect Bush. The total failure of this campaign demonstrates just how counterproductive condescension of Americans and their presidents can be. I write none of this as a supporter of President Bush; in fact I have profound disagreements with his policies in Iraq and on global warming, taxation, public welfare, and the place of religion in public policy. However, this chapter is animated by a concern that many of Bush's critics preferred to take the easy path of character assassination and anti-Americanism rather than undertaking the hard work of specifying their disagreements and suggesting feasible alternatives. Bush's style made this anti-Americanism all too tempting to indulge in, but it is an indulgence that seems at times counterproductive, particularly in the case of Bush's reelection in 2004. Some critics may well argue that the attacks on Bush's character ultimately helped pave the way for the election of a very different type of president who was far more intelligent and worldly in 2008. This argument is hard to dismiss entirely as a strong sense of disillusionment with Bush did contribute to Obama's election in 2008. However, in 2016, the notion that condemning an American presidential candidate as an "ugly American" would dissuade American electors was once again shown to be a fantasy. The experiences with George W. Bush and anti-Americanism provide us insights into how to more effectively respond to the Trump presidency. Although playing the man and his foibles is tempting, it is not always effective. The following discussion of the attacks on the Bush persona convincingly illustrate this.

A Christian cowboy

How many ways can I hate thee? Being a born–again Texan conservative whose rhetorical style was seen by many as a combination of moralistic jingoism, cowboy fightin' words and mangled syntax, Bush evoked longstanding stereotypes of the American philistine and redneck. Add to this claims that his achievements are solely due to his daddy's connections and the image that comes to mind is of a politician born to rule with a silver foot in his mouth. As if this was not enough to attract the wrath of his opponents, Bush's disputed election victory, his dismissal of the Kyoto Protocol, his tax cuts overwhelmingly in favour of the rich and his policies in Iraq and Afghanistan all added fuel to their passionate hatred. Nevertheless the Republican base, which includes a very large number of Evangelical Christians, delivered Bush two terms in the White House.

From the outset of his first presidential race, George W. Bush proved an easy target for the world's desire to laugh at the powerful. This was based on the congruence of two different aspects of his public personality: his bumbling oral style, and the ease with which he could be associated with popular stereotypes about Americans. In terms of his oral style, there was soon a constant commentary on his verbal slipups. From his difficulties pronouncing foreign names and even remembering the names of foreign leaders to his malapropisms, the image of a man unable to "string two sentences together," as a British journalist put it, became widely entrenched. It was not much of a leap to take this inarticulate style and portray it as a symptom of stupidity. Such conclusions were aided and abetted by suspicions about Bush's Christianity and his Texan roots. For many abroad, Bush's religiosity was key to his undesirability as a leader. Contempt for Bush's religiosity in Europe reflects a secular intellectual culture where evangelical Christians are often poorly regarded and poorly understood.[1] Discussing evangelicals in a balanced manner is clearly difficult for many, with much commentary reminiscent of H. L. Mencken's claims during the Scopes "monkey trial" that evangelicals and fundamentalists were "rustic ignoramuses."[2] Such criticism tends to exaggerate the differences between evangelicals and non–evangelicals in today's America, and does little to help people understand the appeal and power of evangelical Christianity. Not surprisingly, in this context, Bush's Christianity was the source of a great deal of scorn, particularly within Europe where the American religious style has long been seen as vulgar and sanctimonious.[3] Bush's religiosity, like his Texan style, has been a lightning rod for many critics.

Bush likes to say: "I'm of Texas." The Lone Star state roots exemplified by this quote are an essential component in Bush's own mythology. In 1992, asked how he differed from his father, he replied: "He attended Greenwich Country Day [a private New England school] and I went to San Jacinto High School in Midland [a Texas public school]."[4] Asked in 2000 to describe the difference between Gore and himself, Bush again played the populist schooling card saying he went to San Jacinto whereas Gore went to St. Albans, an elite private school in the nation's capital.[5] Truth be told, Bush was born in New Haven Connecticut, and went to San Jacinto Junior High for only one year before attending an elite private school in Houston and then following in his father's path to Phillips Academy Andover – one of the most exclusive schools in America. Yet although the paths of father and son have much in common, Bush's style and persona is far more genuinely Texan than his father's; something that is widely acknowledged in the Bush biographies. Bill Minutaglio sees Bush's connections with Texas as so fundamental that he suggests that his Bush "biography is meant to serve, in some way, as an introduction to and exploration of the place and state of mind called Texas."[6]

The image of Texas and Texans abroad is often particularly negative; cowboy boots and hats are Bush's favoured gear in many cartoons, and shorthand for the viewer to be very worried about this man. Both the Texan and the cowboy stereotypes are well worn; Presidents Lyndon Johnson and Ronald Reagan were portrayed thousands of times as gun-slinging know-nothings. As Josef Joffe argues in *Überpower*, the image of the cowboy boots is a quintessential part of the lexicon of the ugly American within Europe. The fact that Texas is also the home of a dynamic independent music scene, the starting point for the organic supermarket chain Wholefoods, and the host of one of America's largest and strongest public universities, tends to be ignored internationally.

The strong dislike that the world generally held for Bush can be to some extent explained simply by his Republican roots. Much of the world (particularly Europe) is more sympathetic to the policies and style of the American Democratic Party and Democratic presidential aspirants than they are to Republicans, who generally start at a disadvantage outside of America. The press that covers US politics in newspapers in Europe reflects these preferences, although there are notable exceptions. Republicans are associated with policy positions generally unfashionable in Europe, such as support for the death penalty, evangelical social policy, and neoliberal economic policies. The party's opposition to environmental regulation and the welfare state more generally are also disadvantageous to its image in Europe. Although many Democrats may in fact not be profoundly different on these issues to Republicans, this is obscured by the style of those Democrat politicians known globally. Individuals such as Bill and Hillary Clinton, Al Gore and John Kerry are known to be well traveled and highly educated, and articulate enough to speak on a variety of global issues with some sophistication. These factors allow for the overlooking of certain policy *faux pas*, a case in point being Bill Clinton's strong support of the death penalty when he was Governor of Arkansas. For followers of US politics with an eye for detail, this differentiation between Democrats and Republicans seems common, with some going so far as to describe Europe as a "blue state."

The basis for the stereotypes of Bush as a cowboy and rabid Christian also come from a long tradition of stereotyping America based on its supposed "exceptionalism." For many people America is a confounding place, combining religious zealotry with the most libertine values on the planet. The long-time *Baltimore Sun* journalist Will Englund commented during the Bush era that European newspapers cover America like North Eastern American papers cover California. In other words, it is a weird place where bizarre events constantly occur ("only in California" is the regular refrain within America) and where life is more fantastic and less genuine; in sum it is a place not particularly desirable but for some unfathomable reason the inevitable future for us all. The lure of American exceptionalism and the cliché "only in America" is a recurrent explanation for the nation's behaviour across the planet. Foreign commentary on American presidential elections often takes this "only in America" tack, usually combining it with a strong air of condescension. This condescension by foreign media masks discomfort and fear. In the eyes of the world, America's unsophisticated culture allows its citizens to remain ignorant of the basic geography and politics of the rest of the world. Yet inexplicably it dominates the world like no other state, with all corners of the globe submitting to ever increasing levels of Americanisation.[7] This state of affairs, coupled with concerns about American power and cultural penetration, creates obvious anxieties and fears.

Cementing stereotypes

At times Bush seems perfectly cast for the caricatures of Texans, Americans and evangelical Christians he has evoked from media the world over. His syntax-mangling, "dead or alive" threats to America's enemies, talk of "evildoers," and his public expression of his evangelical Christian faith all reinforce the stereotypes. Commentary on Bush's lack of finesse and sophistication began with US comedians and news networks, and then spread overseas. Jon Stewart, Jay Leno, David Letterman, Michael Moore, and Jacob Weisberg led the way. A rash of American-made anti-Bush websites soon followed, along with Bush jokes, photos and quotes that were spread online. The most notable was Jacob Weisberg's "Bushisms" list on *Slate*.[8] Foreign media lapped it up, enjoying the chance to have some fun at America's expense, and to continue their long obsession with the odd and bizarre aspects of America in general. Of course Americans too enjoy observing the more bizarre aspects of their own country. The difference is that in America such oddities are saved for the end of the news bulletin, whereas abroad they are often the main event, at least in the popular imagination. The resulting image for many is a president who is widely seen as a cartoon character: in frame one he is Ronald Reagan the B-grade cowboy, in the next he is Bonzo the chimpanzee, and then the simpleton Alfred E. Neuman. Foreign cartoonists adopt these caricatures, cementing the enduring image of Bush as a dunce; only the most powerful can be portrayed in such a manner without fear of claims of national prejudice.

The international portrayal of Bush as an unsophisticated ignoramus can be traced back to the generally hostile coverage he received abroad during the 2000 campaign. Non-Americans were more likely to know he called Greeks "Grecians," than that he campaigned as a "compassionate conservative" who was against "nation-building" abroad. The cliffhanger nature of the 2000 election ensured it was followed intensely around the world. Some clearly enjoyed the predicament America found itself in, with the British tabloids predictably satirising the situation. The *Daily Mirror*'s post-election front page shows Bush and Gore sitting together on a park bench in matching Forrest Gump suits, neither understanding what had happened. For many abroad, and within America, the US democratic system failed the test in Florida when unelected judges rather than the voters made the decisive call. The real problem, however, for many foreigners was not so much the process, but the fact that the wrong person had won: the man associated with hereditary power, the Republican Party, born-again Christianity, Texas, and American big business.

However, the negative stereotypes drawn from Bush's blunders and supposed lack of intellectual sharpness extended well beyond the 2000 elections. The first presidential debate of the 2004 campaign saw the Australian media widely discuss the possibility of a secret transmitter under Bush's suit sending answers from a presumably more intelligent source. This innuendo ignores Bush's very effective performances in the 2000 presidential debates in which he probably won most of the debates by repeating simplistic but consistent ideas. The conspiracy theory also ignores the fact that of his six presidential debates, this first one in 2004 was his worst performance. When giving a crucial speech on immigration in May 2006, Bush was caught on live television practicing the speech, a mistake claimed to be the fault of CNN. This embarrassing mix-up, rather than the topic of the important speech or its reception, was the headline story in Australia. Bush's regular, but often trivial, verbal mistakes similarly became the main story for many, providing evidence for his label as ignoramus.

As I mentioned earlier, Bush is certainly not the first American president to enjoy foreign scorn. Before him there was Ronald Reagan, who was preceded by Lyndon Johnson.[9] Like Bush, Reagan too was the dumb gun-happy cowboy. Even Carter and Clinton suffered from early commentary that depicted them as Southern simpletons. Carter the nuclear engineer was more regularly referred to as a "peanut farmer" and Clinton the Rhodes Scholar was frequently portrayed as a Southern bubba. As with Bush, many of these images started life domestically in the US. In the case of Carter and Clinton, they originated in northeastern American commentary where Southerners are still often portrayed as intellectually inferior. However, in the US such negative commentary is balanced against more favourable and often more nuanced analysis, whereas abroad the predominant images are these negative stereotypes. With them the constant focus, it becomes much harder to offer a more balanced understanding.

What's Wrong with a Laugh?

Before I begin to sound entirely humourless, I acknowledge that the comic response to Bush was understandable given the intransigence of American politics. At times, if one did not laugh one would cry. Moreover, critical humour is a useful curative against the self-righteousness of politicians, and can help draw issues to the attention of those put off by conventional political debates and commentary. However, an over-reliance on the pantomime creates a situation where the play is mistaken for the reality and where depth is forsaken for cheap laughs. In Bush's case, critiques all too often slid into anti-American, anti-evangelical Christian and anti-Texan ridicule thereby undercutting valid criticisms levelled at the president and his record. As a result, preconceptions are reinforced and the reality behind the stereotypes escapes proper examination. For example, an over-reliance on stereotypes about Bush's evangelism overshadows debate on the reality that Bush's religious views were projected into his politics. On the evidence we have there seem good reasons to be concerned about this influence. For instance, the Schweizers quote a relative of Bush's who states that:

> George sees this [the war on terrorism] as a religious war. He doesn't have a pc view of the war. His view of this is that they are trying to kill the Christians. And we the Christians will strike back with more force and more ferocity than they will ever know.[10]

Bush's certainty about the transformative power of ideas clearly drew on his personal religiosity.[11] In his second inaugural address Bush claimed that "the ultimate goal" of US policy was "ending tyranny in our world,"[12] elsewhere he asserted the goal of his administration was to "rid the world of evil."[13] Such pronouncements draw on biblical language to make dramatic statements about America's mission in the world being ultimately to bring about paradigmatic change. Bush seems to believe wholeheartedly this change would be life-altering for people everywhere. This replicates his own experience of being born again as a Christian, a transformation that Bush underwent in 1985 when he sought guidance from the evangelist preacher Billy Graham, whom he credits for helping him giving up drinking alcohol altogether in 1986 and becoming a deeply religious person.[14] This personal journey gave Bush a certain inner confidence; before running for the presidency he confided to the Texan evangelist preacher James Robinson that "I feel like God wants me to run for President. I can't explain it, but I sense my country is going to need me. Something is going to happen… I know it won't be easy on me or my family, but God wants me to do it."[15] Bush's evangelistic outlook was not just personal – it extended to his view of the US role in the world: we see this in a number of Bush's speeches where he pronounces that there are certain God-given political rights that all humans want. For example, Bush stated in 2003 that: "Americans are a free people, who know that freedom is the right of every person and the future of every nation. The liberty we prize is not America's gift to the world, it is God's gift to humanity."[16] Similarly, at a rally in 2004 he claimed that: "I believe millions in the Middle East plead in silence for their liberty. I believe that, given a chance, they will embrace the most honorable form of government ever devised by man. I believe all these things, not because freedom is America's gift to the world, but because freedom is the Almighty God's gift to every man and woman in this world." Sounding like an evangelical preacher in his second inaugural, Bush proclaimed that: "We have confidence because freedom is the permanent hope of mankind, the hunger in dark places, the longing of the soul."[17] What are we to make of Bush's religious ideology and how it infused into the Bush Doctrine and the occupation of Afghanistan and Iraq? The political rights that Bush calls God's gifts to the world are the same rights that influential neoconservatives were promoting. The overlap is powerful in its reinforcing qualities, which seem to have insulated the Bush administration from facing up to the evidence of just how unsuccessful its policies in Afghanistan and Iraq were. Bush's own religious certitude, coupled with a belief system that was promoted by a particularly brash and self-righteous group of intellectuals and policy experts, was a deadly combination that propelled America into war in Iraq in 2003 with unrealistic expectations that the Americans would be treated as liberators. When they were not, Bush kept repeating claims that America was bringing freedom and democracy to the Iraqis as if repeatedly proclaiming these words would make them true. This heady mix of religious faith and overconfident ideology created America's greatest foreign policy disaster since the Vietnam War.

Domestically Bush's religious beliefs had a concrete impact on his administration's policies with two examples being the promotion of faith-based social policy, and the appointment of anti-abortion federal judges. Furthermore, the Bush administration's delegation to the 2002 UN Special Session on Children:

> objected to sex education for adolescents, tried to restrict information on sexually transmitted infections and contraception to heterosexual married couples, and fought to redefine "reproductive health services" to exclude abortion.[18]

They also objected to offering counselling to children in post-war situations, fearing that girls who had been raped could be offered abortions. These retrograde positions clearly stem from the religious values of Bush and his administration, values that are shared by many Republicans and many Americans. As backward as they are, such values need to be rebutted with serious arguments not condescension about the evangelical pulpit or the Texas ranch.

In part, the cartoon image is the result of the media circus that covers modern politics, with its fixation on personality and contrived conflicts, rather than on policies or in-depth analysis. It is also the continuation of what President Clinton called "the politics of personal destruction" or "politics by other means" as it was dubbed by political scientists Benjamin Ginsberg and Martin Shefter.[19] When it is not connected to substantive differences on decisions or policies it can lead to an unhealthy personalisation of much political debate, and even a tendency towards character assassination.

Another reason for the dominance of cliché over debate is the polarised nature of US commentary on Bush. Contempt for Bush's path to power and his policies make it difficult for many commentators to write objectively about his presidency, with many descending into thinly veiled abuse or clichés. Much of this is to be expected as part of the rough and tumble of partisan politics in America. However, the outside world, including academe, too often buys the cheap shots. Critics of Bush show an unsettling certainty in their assessment of his failings. This is despite the fact that Bush was in many ways a very private leader, with only limited quality information available on his decision-making and analytical abilities. Bush's verbal gaffes and mannerisms were taken to reveal the man's limitations, which I would contend is a dangerous assumption. The most notable insider account, Bob Woodward's two books *Bush at War* and *Plan of Attack* are in fact fairly neutral.[20] Others close to the action, such as former Secretary of Treasury Paul O'Neil, leave the impression of a president at times out of his depth, with Cheney playing a very dominant role.[21] However, the truth is that we need much more information if we are to make informed judgments about a president's decision-making skills. Furthermore, the biographical literature on Bush raises as many questions as answers around how Bush could have an undergraduate degree from Yale and an MBA from Harvard but be seen as a dunce. There is evidence that Bush was in fact a big reader,[22] but lacked a curiosity to read or think broadly on issues such as terrorism, global warming and Middle Eastern peace.[23]

This lack of broad thinking coupled with poor advice help to explain Bush's ill-conceived foreign policies; this is particularly true of his administration's handling of its Iraq policy. However, critiquing him and his administration with the constant image of the cowboy killer is little better than rendering all Muslims as fanatical terrorists; neither image promotes understanding of the details and the root causes of serious problems. Instead they simply confirm pre-existing prejudices. Once again policies need to be critiqued on the basis of their failings rather than guilt by association.

The data on Bush

The Pew Global Attitudes Project carried out the first significant global poll on Bush in August 2001, less than a year into his first term. It asked respondents in France, Germany, Italy and Great Britain whether they "approved or disapproved of the way George W. Bush is handling international policy." Most disapproved rather than approved by more than two to one. The Germans were the most critical with 65% disapproving, in stark contrast to the 86% who said they had approved of the way Clinton had handled foreign policy. Another question showed that respondents believed Bush was more ill-informed about Europe than previous presidents and that he would take little notice of European opinions. The hostility of the opinions is explored later in the survey, with reasons including Bush's decision not to support the Kyoto protocol, and his development of a missile defence system which would see America withdraw from the ABM treaty.[24]

This early survey shows that Bush was poorly regarded internationally from the beginning of his presidency. His early policy clash with European leaders on the increasingly urgent issue of global warming opened a schism that generally widened each year of his presidency. His stance on global warming throughout his presidency continued to reinforce the belief that he was more interested in protecting US business interests than the global environment. The name of this first Pew report on Global Attitudes summed up the mood with these four key European allies neatly: "Bush unpopular in Europe, seen as unilateralist." For many critics the word unilateralist became symbolic for what was wrong with Bush and his administration.

However, for a brief period following the tragic events of September 11, 2001 it seemed global public opinion on Bush could be turned around. In an April 2002 Pew survey Bush received a much more favourable assessment from French, Germans, British and Italians, just as his popularity within the US received a significant boost after favourable assessments of his handling of the initial American response. This survey also saw some of Bush's policies receive widespread approval among Europeans. Notably his decision to increase foreign aid is widely lauded with 90% in France approving (interestingly only 53% of Americans approved of this decision). Bush's decision to go to war in Afghanistan also received strong support with French approval of 64%. There were similar levels of approval in Germany, Italy and Great Britain. However, Bush's "Axis of Evil rhetoric" won widespread disapproval, particularly among the Germans (74% disapproved of what was in part a reference that linked the WWII past of Germany with Bush's current "evil" enemies).

The bad reception Bush generally received in first term surveys bears a strong resemblance to the extreme unpopularity of Ronald Reagan's presidency in Western Europe in the early 1980s. However, unlike Bush, Reagan made some permanent improvements to his popularity as his presidency went on by combining tough rhetoric and policies with a willingness to negotiate with the Soviets. The result of the Gorbachev–Reagan summits was a major de-escalation of the Cold War, and a subsequent serious thawing of European attitudes to both Reagan and the US.

Bush seemed to believe that, like Reagan, the future would prove his policies correct, thus nullifying current opinion poll results. This thinking was revealed in his response to a Spanish leader who commented that in Europe Bush was "nearly as unpopular as Ronald Reagan." Bush's reply was that "I'm keeping pretty good company." However Bush's decision to call for military action against Iraq and to go to war without French or German support ended any speculation that opinion in Europe on Bush after September 11 was permanently warming. He was to become more unpopular than ever until the end of his presidency.

In the Pew surveys following the Iraq invasion it is starkly apparent that the Bush administration's earlier claims that the invasion was part of its "global war on terror" fell on deaf ears. Opinion on the United States went into free fall. This was a predictable outcome in the Middle East. However, American popularity also took a pummeling among European allies. In 2002, 63% of French respondents and 61% of Germans had a favourable opinion of America but by March 2003 the figures were down to 31% and 25% respectively. Opinions in Turkey, Indonesia, and Pakistan were even more negative when surveyed in April–May 2003. In June 2003 an effort to ascertain Bush's role in this rise in antipathy toward America, Pew asked those with an unfavourable attitude toward the US a follow-up question: "What's the problem with the US? Mostly Bush? America in general? or Both?" The question was asked in 20 states as well as the Palestinian authority territory and the response was overwhelmingly "mostly Bush." In France and Germany, 74% gave this reply, in Indonesia 69%, in Nigeria 60%; only South Koreans went significantly against the trend with 72% choosing to blame "America in general."

More worrying in regard to combating terrorism are the ratings given to eight world figures by respondents from Muslim nations. In the same 2003 Pew survey, respondents in Indonesia, Jordan, Morocco, Pakistan, and the Palestinian authority territory rated Osama bin Laden as one of the top three favoured figures and all rated him ahead of Bush. This preference for bin Laden over Bush was reconfirmed in Pakistan, Jordan and Morocco in a March 2004 Pew survey where bin Laden received a "favourable" status of 65% in Pakistan, 55% in Jordan, and 45% in Morocco. Meanwhile in the same countries Bush only managed meager "favourable" ratings of 7%, 3% and 8% respectively. Bush's consistent ranking lower than Osama bin Laden revealed a worrying loss in the popularity stakes. Ultimately the war on terror is not just a campaign of military action or secret intelligence, but a fight for minds and hearts. For any doubters of the depth of Bush's unpopularity in the Muslim world these figures make for sober reading.

Was the animosity toward America notably recorded by the Pew surveys mostly due to Bush's style and rhetoric? Conversely are these matters of personality largely immaterial, with people's objections to the decision to go to war against Iraq being the more crucial issue? Separating out responses to Bush from opposition to the Iraq war is difficult as after all it was his decision to take America to war. Furthermore, the way the Bush administration, particularly Donald Rumsfeld, handled disagree- ment in the West over the decision to go to war in Iraq upset many people, making issues of substance and style also difficult to separate. It seems fair to say style is not an unsubstantial factor in the rise in anti-Americanism and it also seems reasonable to speculate that if a Clinton or even a Gore administration had gone to war in Iraq in 2003 this action would have engendered less anti-Americanism. Nonetheless, the Iraq War was a war of choice where no weapons of mass destruction were found, no significant links to al Qaeda were proved, and where the post-war reconstruction has been bloody and prolonged. This war would have been globally unpopular whoever the US president and however they sold the need for it.

The 2004 elections

The US presidential election of 2004 was very closely and seriously followed globally. Large majorities of non-Americans around the world hoped it would signal the end of the Bush presidency, and global media coverage and debate on the election often assumed American voters would be influenced by the international unpopularity of their president. Extensive polls conducted in June–August 2004 by Globescan showed that out of the 35 countries surveyed Kerry was favoured in all but four states: Nigeria, the Philippines, Poland, and Thailand. In most cases this approval of Kerry was overwhelming and this was particularly the case amongst America's allies: France, Germany, Italy, the UK and Japan. Germans were particularly convinced Bush was the wrong man to be president with 74% preferring Kerry to win, while only 10% preferred Bush.[25] In 2008 and 2012 Obama was similarly favoured in global surveys over Romney by a large margin. Trump was certainly not favoured in 2016 over Hillary Clinton, but global support for Trump although fairly unflattering in the teens tended to be higher than support for Bush Jnr or Romney.

Globescan conducted a similar ten-nation survey in September and October of 2004 for the *Guardian* and other newspapers in which once again Kerry was overwhelmingly favoured in most countries. The exceptions were Russia, where Bush was slightly more favoured than Kerry, and Israel (not included in the earlier survey) where Bush was overwhelmingly favoured.[26] A 2004 Globus survey produced similarly negative results for Bush with strong majorities in Canada, Australia, France, Germany, Italy, Spain and the UK voicing an unfavourable opinion of the incumbent. Once again the Germans led the way with 78% of respondents holding an unfavourable view of the US president.[27] John Kerry highlighted this global negativity in the presidential debates, saying that most foreigners and world leaders would like to see him elected president.[28]

While Ronald Reagan began his presidency as unpopular as Bush, his turnaround is a salient lesson in how a policy shift can bring about a change in attitude. As mentioned earlier, Reagan enjoyed a considerable thawing of transatlantic relations during his second term after the success of arms negotiations with the Soviets. In this case it would seem ultimately policies matter more than the individual. However, more recent history provides contrary evidence. Hillary Clinton voted in 2002 as a Senator for the *Authorization for Use of Military Force Against Iraq Resolution* to support the Bush administration invading Iraq if it deemed it necessary. This ill-conceived vote had less impact on foreign opinion of Hillary Clinton than it might have had, pointing to the importance of her persona over her policy record.

Do Americans care?

Whether because of his personality or policies, or a combination of both, Bush undoubtedly gained a reputation as one of America's most unpopular leaders globally. Does this have an impact on Americans? Furthermore, did the negative attitudes of non-Americans toward Bush have any impact on the US presidential elections? The Program on International Policy Attitudes commissioned a survey to ascertain whether the negative opinion of Bush shown clearly in other global survey results would affect the way Americans voted. They found that if Americans "received information that one or the other candidate was preferred by world public opinion, a small percentage of swing voters say that it would increase the likelihood they would vote for that candidate – twice as many as say it would decrease the likelihood." So the negativity could have made a marginal difference, but this of course presumes that Americans knew which candidate was more disliked. The same survey found that in fact many Americans did not appear to even know about Bush's global unpopularity with only a third of the respondents assuming the world preferred Kerry to Bush.[29]

Despite this analysis, negative global opinion may well have led not to a domestic backlash against Bush but to increased support for him instead. On a broad level Bush won the 2004 election because he was seen as the stronger candidate on issues of national security and in the battle against terrorism (a campaign he had convincingly defined in the minds of many Americans). With American nationalism and the battle against anti-American forces his strong suit, he was able to nullify the influence of foreign disapproval, even when it came from NATO allies such as France and Germany. These states could be written off as pre-9/11 dinosaurs who were not facing up to the threats of the 21st century, a claim made closer to home by Karl Rove when disparaging the Democratic Party. During the first presidential debate John Kerry suggested that American military actions abroad should meet a "global test where your countrymen, your people understand fully why you're doing what you're doing and you can prove to the world that you did it for legitimate reasons." The Bush campaign team promptly seized upon this, launching an advertisement called the "Global Test" that stated that Kerry would "seek permission from foreign governments before protecting America." Although they clearly distorted Kerry's position, Bush's campaign team seemed to be correct in their judgment that many Americans were not interested in receiving the approval of other states on issues of national security; war by committee was not the American way. Beyond the very broad evidence of Bush's national victory the following case study examines at a more specific level whether American voters care about foreign opinions on the leader of their country.

Operation Clark County

It started as "a quixotic idea dreamed up last month in a north London pub" wrote Ian Katz, feature editor at the *Guardian* newspaper and mastermind behind "Operation Clark County."[30] The idea was to reduce George W. Bush's vote in the November 2004 election by persuading American citizens in an important swing state not to vote for him. In introducing the "Operation" to its readers the *Guardian* suggested that: "British political life may now be at least as heavily influenced by White House policy as by the choices of UK voters."[31] The *Guardian* and many others described the 2004 presidential election as "the most important in living memory,"[32] and the British seemed very keen on the whole to see Bush removed from the presidency. This was certainly reflected in a *Guardian* poll, which showed that only 22% of Britons wanted to see the incumbent reelected to the White House. One can surmise that far fewer than 22% of regular left-leaning *Guardian* readers wanted a second Bush term. The *Guardian*'s Operation Clark County was thus a small part of a global campaign to unseat President Bush.

The left-liberal *Guardian* suggested that rather than feeling powerless, readers should send a letter to registered independents in an important swing state in the upcoming election. The *Guardian* chose Clark County, Ohio and set up a website where a reader could receive the name and address of a single Clark County voter who had registered themselves as an independent.[33] The idea was that the reader would write his or her own personal plea urging the individual voter to support John Kerry.

Although the Operation was somewhat tongue in cheek from its beginnings the *Guardian* realised the idea had the potential to misfire. To avoid this, the newspaper introduced the scheme to readers by continually stressing the need to be "diplomatic" when composing one's letter. Other words of advice included "keep in mind the real risk of alienating your reader by coming across as interfering or offensive"[34] and "please remember to be courteous and sensitive in what you say."[35] The *Guardian* claimed that Bush's constant referral to Tony Blair when discussing Iraq – something the British would be much more aware of than the average American – would give them as British "a certain leverage"[36] in the US. Realising their "modest proposal" to change the course of history had its weaknesses, they launched the Operation Clark County website.

The judicious tone set by the *Guardian's* introduction to the Operation was rather undermined by the sample letters "from three prominent Britons" posted on the website, and presumably already mailed to Ohio. All three were high-handed and rather condescending if the aim was to win over swing voters. John Le Carré's missive offered a tirade against Bush which although not unjustified tends to trade in assertions rather than offering evidence that would potentially turn voters against Bush. He gives no reason to vote for Kerry, except that he is not George W. Bush. Le Carré calls the Iraq war a "hare-brained adventure,"[37] which, with the advantages of hindsight, is fairly justified. However, given that Clark County is the site of a large Air National Guard base, such a claim and the letter in general had a high probability of offending its reader.

While the next prominent Briton, Antonia Fraser, offered some praise of American history, she also called for a vote against "Bush and his gang" and their "savage militaristic foreign policy of pre-emptive killing."[38] Lastly Professor Richard Dawkins, a renowned British public educator on scientific and evolutionary matters, opened his letter with these condescending words "Don't be ashamed of your president: the majority of you didn't vote for him. If Bush is finally elected properly, that will be the time for Americans traveling abroad to simulate a Canadian accent."[39] Dawkins calls the pre-9/11 Bush "an amiable idiot" and Colin Powell "spineless." He claims the attack on Iraq was long planned and the World Trade Center attacks provided the perfect excuse. He criticises Bush for adopting "the Tony Martin school of foreign policy [Martin was a householder who shot dead a burglar who had broken into his house in 1999]." Dawkins' lack of effort and skill at connecting with Clark County voters helps us understand what happened in response to such missives.

In a matter of a few days, over 14,000 *Guardian* readers across the UK and soon around the globe had received the names and addresses of independent Clark County voters. Fortunately the pleas dispatched by rank and file *Guardian* readers were much more even-handed and sensible than those sent by their three illustrious examples. Often these readers had genuine connections with the US and expressed this in a heart-felt manner.[40] The scheme quickly attracted attention from Britons and other world citizens, reflecting an obvious global interest in shaping the outcome of the 2004 US presidential election. "Operation Clark County" became a brief blimp in media coverage of the campaign, with CNN and other news companies descending on the *Guardian* offices in London. However, the scheme's lack of success became apparent as soon as the *Guardian* website began posting responses from Clark County and elsewhere in America. Arranged under the telling headline of "Dear Limey assholes," the responses ranged from "Real Americans aren't interested in your pansy-ass, tea-sipping opinions" to regular references to 1776 and Britons as yellow-toothed snobs. Even the more positive responses seemed double edged, with one response stating that "your invitation to your readership and rationale for offering it are provocative at least, and laudable at best."[41] The general tone of responses was that the rest of the world should mind its own business. Even anti-Bush Americans promoted this position because they thought the campaign would backfire. The *Guardian*'s own hope that the idea of overseas citizens telling Ohioans how to vote would not be inflammatory may reflect the alcohol-fueled origins of this quixotic idea. Al Gore won Clark County in 2000 by a margin of 324 votes with Nader receiving 1,347 votes. In 2004 Bush won the county by 1,620 votes. More noteworthy is the fact that, of the 15 Ohio counties won by Gore, Clark County was the only one lost by Kerry. It was one of only 34 out of 3,142 American counties that switched from Democrat in 2000 to Republican in 2004.[42] It is difficult to precisely judge how much influence the *Guardian* letter writing campaign had, but it certainly failed to help Kerry preserve the Democratic majority won by his predecessor. Some may feel Americans have become particularly inoculated against outside criticisms since September 11, 2001, but a similar campaign launched by concerned Americans to unseat Tony Blair would surely also have backfired. Citizens from any country rarely appreciate outside criticism of their own government, no matter how well intentioned.

In defending the scheme, the *Guardian* editor suggests that "somewhere along the line, though, the good-humored spirit of the enterprise got lost in translation."[43] The tendency to satirise and laugh at politicians is alive and well in Britain, and long may it be. This desire to laugh at the powerful is a desire partially fulfilled by many around the world when they watch presidents like George W. Bush and Donald Trump on the nightly news. Nonetheless humour has its limitations. If you are going to write a personal letter calling someone's president an "idiot" or suggesting they pretend to be Canadian when traveling abroad this may not be seen as particularly clever or amusing. A Pew poll after the 2004 election showed Bush's win had worsened the attitudes of most foreigners to the US, a feeling expressed bluntly by the front page of the *Daily Mirror* on November 4 which stated: "How can

59,054,087 people be so DUMB?" However, the same Pew survey showed the US relief efforts for the 2004 Indian Ocean Tsunami had engendered favourable responses across the globe to how people viewed America,[44] reminding us that humane policies can make a difference.

There are those who believe that the Democrats "were robbed" again in 2004. Claims of electoral malfeasance generally centre on Ohio and the behaviour of the aggressively partisan Republican Ohioan Secretary of State Kenneth Blackwell. In the weeks leading up to the 2004 presidential election the *Guardian* and other newspapers did an excellent job of reporting on Blackwell's efforts to reduce the number of Democrats on the electoral rolls and to make the voting process as tedious and as lengthy as possible in Democrat strongholds.[45] Blackwell called upon an obscure electoral law that supposedly allows self-appointed challengers to question anyone in the voting queue. Blackwell's preferred tactic was to bus in young Republicans to target polling booths and question anyone who looked like non-citizens or sufferers of an intellectual disability. This particular tactic, which aims to have voters either declared ineligible or intimidate them so much that they do not vote at all, was successfully used in the South earlier in America's history to prevent blacks from voting. In this case, it was prohibited at the eleventh hour by a state judge. Blackwell's efforts and the types of electoral administration seen in action in Florida in 2000 have led many to ask whether America can be called a democracy at all. This style of electoral politics is an example of the excesses of one form of democracy, namely the tyranny of majoritarianism. It can happen when elected politicians rather than impartial administrators get to decide how future elections are conducted and administered. Partisan gerrymandering is also a significant problem in the US because of the excesses of majoritarianism. Blackwell's actions in Ohio seemed not to have been crucial in the 2004 election as Bush won the state by 118,775 votes. Robert Kennedy Jr, one of the 11 progeny of Ethel and Robert F. Kennedy, challenged this view in *Rolling Stone* magazine. His claim that the election was stolen raises some important concerns about Ohioan officials, electronic voting, and exit polling;[46] but in the end he exaggerates the case for fraud and fails to deal with contradictory evidence.[47]

Conclusion

Throughout this chapter I have made the case for criticising presidents on the basis of detailed evidence and by focusing on their policies, rather than on their personalities. I have argued for resisting cheap shots and instead made the case that scholars should put their efforts into spelling out the negative consequences of bad policy decisions. Taking this highroad was difficult to do with Bush because of the combination of his error-ridden speaking style and limited knowledge of foreign affairs that was coupled with what many saw as a particularly arrogant swagger. With president Trump the challenge of playing the ball (his policies) not the man is doubly difficult. Trump has been rightly criticised for his sexism and his racism. Nonetheless, the fixation on Trump's braggadocious persona was not a particularly effective way of challenging him electorally and has not stopped his administration from making many unfortunate policy decisions. Furthermore, calling some Trump voters "deplorables" as Hillary Clinton did, is not very politically savvy, even if Trump does attract vocal support from people on the far right with deplorable attitudes on issues such as race and immigration.[48]

Despite the significant global outrage at Trump and his supporters – best highlighted by the PEW surveys[49] and more viscerally by the enormous anti-Trump protest in London in July 2018[50] – anti-Americanism is less apparent under President Trump than it was under President George W. Bush. There are a range of reasons for this. Firstly, Trump does not personify America to foreigners in the way that George W. Bush did. Although Trump is a populist, it is more his policies and speeches that are populist than the man himself. Trump is famous for showing off his wealth and suggesting it makes him highly desirable to women and a role model for young entrepreneurs. In the 1980s and 1990s Trump flaunted his wealth to build a profile in the New York tabloids as a property tycoon and "ladies' man". In 2004 NBC launched *The Apprentice* where Trump rewarded the successful participants by inviting them to his lavish New York apartment and to his golf clubs. Trump may claim to speak for the "average American" but he is widely understood to be proud of his wealth and supposed elite status. In response to revelations about Michael Cohen (Trump's personal lawyer) paying Stormy Daniels $130,000 hush money, Trump tweeted: "These agreements are very common among celebrities and people of wealth."[51] In contrast, George W. Bush liked to suggest he was just a regular guy who happened to be born into a famous family. Bush's down-home self-presentation was largely accepted by foreigners who tended to see him as representative of all that was wrong with America and Americans, such as its moralistic religiosity, insularity and lack of interest in foreign affairs, gun culture and fast food, and righteous sense of violent vengeance. To many, Bush's cowboy boots on the desk and Texan drawl said it all.[52]

The notion that the president is the personification of the nation has not been anywhere near as apparent with Trump. The other reason that Bush was seen to represent American attitudes was that his highly controversial victory in 2000 was quickly forgotten by foreigners following the events of 9/11, which led to his popularity skyrocketing. In September 2001 Bush received the highest approval of any president since surveys were initiated in the 1940s. The Gallup survey had his public approval at 90%[53] and an ABC News poll the same month had his approval peaking at 92%.[54] Trump's approval rating in the Gallup surveys has never been higher than 45%.[55] The other factor that made anti-Americanism more apparent during the Bush presidency than during the Trump era to date, was a sense that most Americans supported the Bush administration's decision to invade Iraq in 2003. This rallying around the flag during the Bush era where unity was demanded and often achieved, stands in marked contrast to the Trump era where it is obvious to non-Americans that many Americans were very unhappy that Trump was elected. The Women's March in Washington DC the day after Trump's inauguration which attracted half a million protestors received a lot of global coverage and inspired similar (although smaller) Women's Marches across the world. Whereas during the Bush Presidency the anti-Iraq War marches of the weekend of February 14–16, 2003 were much bigger outside of the US than within America. In London and Madrid over a million people turned out to protest against Bush's proposed war, and more than 100,000 protestors participated in demonstrations in Berlin, Sydney, Athens, Barcelona, Seville and Paris. Meanwhile, the largest US march was in New York City where around 100,000 turned out to oppose the war – a number similar to that in the much less populous cities of Lisbon and Dublin.

Another reason that anti-Americanism is less apparent today than during the Bush presidency is non-Americans began to take much greater interest in American presidential elections at a granular level in 2008 with the rise of Barack Obama and his victory over Hillary Clinton in the primaries and subsequent defeat of John McCain in the main event. The primaries and the general election have been covered since 2008 in many nations outside of the US with constant information and commentary in the local newspapers and other media services. As a result, following American presidential elections became habitualised like following the FIFA World Cup or the Olympics.[56] The rules governing the primaries and the Electoral College became more widely understood. In my view, this closer following of US elections has reduced anti-Americanism because it has exposed non-Americans to the difference of opinion in the US and how many Americans oppose the winning candidate. As a result, it is widely understood how divided America is between Trump supporters and those Americans that not only oppose Trump but despise him. The other factor that has reduced anti-Americanism since the Bush era was the presidency of Barack Obama. As the Pew surveys show, Obama was very popular outside of the US where his time in the Oval Office was watched with much interest and hope.[57] The most obvious example of this was Obama being awarded the Nobel Prize for Peace in 2009. Obama's prominence and global popularity led to Americans and America being thought of differently. As noted earlier in this book, Obama liked to present himself as the quintessential 21st century American: with a white mother and a black father, with longstanding and recent immigrant ties to America, and a pragmatic willingness to compromise on political matters.[58] The fact Trump and the birther movement slandered Obama for supposedly not being born in America, and even for being a closet Muslim, generally made him more popular abroad. Obama was seen as an ideal antidote to the globally unpopular Republican Party.

Non-Americans were largely impressed by this persona and the new America Obama described. As a result, America once again became hip around the world. In my hometown of Sydney, American-styled dive bars and pricey "Southern food" restaurants opened after an absence of such ventures during the Bush presidency. Obama's urbane and worldly personality challenged the stereotype of all Americans being warmongering, insular, and nativist and even the election of Trump has not entirely washed this new understanding of America out of the collective consciousness of non-Americans. For all of the reasons listed in this conclusion, it seems fair to conclude that the Bush presidency is likely to be the global high point for the type of prejudiced anti-Americanism discussed in this book. In the years since Bush left the Oval Office a more nuanced view of America and Americans has been more predominant.

Notes

1 Alan Wolfe, *The Transformation of American Religion* (New York: Free Press, 2003).
2 Mencken's descriptive rant went on to include the further two definitions of "anthropoid rabble," and "gaping primitives of the upland valleys." H. L. Mencken, "Coverage of the Scopes Trial," <https://archive.org/stream/CoverageOfTheScopesTrialByH.l.Mencken/ScopesTrialMencken.txt>, 1925.
3 Simon Schama, "The Unloved American," *The New Yorker*, March 3, 2003.
4 Molly Ivins and Lou Dubose, *Shrub: The Short but Happy Political Life of George W. Bush* (New York: Random House, 2000).
5 Nicholas Lemann, *Sons: George W. Bush and Al Gore* (Redmond: Slate eBooks, 2000).
6 Bill Minutaglio, *First Son* (New York: Three Rivers Press, 2001), ix.
7 For sophisticated reflections on this topic see Peter Conrad's *Americanisation of Everywhere* (London: Thames and Hudson Limited, 2014).
8 Jacob Weisberg, "W.'s Greatest Hits: The Top 25 Bushisms of All Time," *Slate*, January 12, 2009, <http://www.slate.com/articles/news_and_politics/bushisms/2009/01/ws_greatest_hits.html>.
9 Thomas Alan Schwartz, *Lyndon Johnson and Europe* (Cambridge, MA: Harvard University Press, 2003).
10 Peter Schweizer and Rochelle Schweizer, *The Bushes: Portrait of a Dynasty* (New York: DoubleDay, 2004), 517.
11 Robert Jervis, *American Foreign Policy in a New Era* (New York: Routledge, 2005), 83. Robert Jervis, "Understanding the Bush Doctrine," *Political Science Quarterly* 118, 3 (2003), 379; Brendon O'Connor, "Back to the Future, Again," *Australian Journal of Politics & History* 47, 4 (2002); Brendon O'Connor, "Beyond the Cartoon," *Political Studies Review* 3, 2 (2005).
12 George W. Bush, "President Sworn-In to Second Term," the Second Inaugural Speech from the Office of the Press Secretary in *The White House Archives*, January 20, 2005: <http://georgewbush-whitehouse.archives.gov/news/releases/2005/01/20050120-1.html>.
13 George W. Bush, "Remarks at the National Day of Prayer & Remembrance Service," Speech in *White House Archive*, 14 September 2001, <https://georgewbush-whitehouse.archives.gov/news/releases/2001/09/20010914-2.html>; Bush similarly claimed, "My administration has a job to do and we're going to do it. We will rid the world of the evildoers," in Manuel Perez-Rivas, "Bush Vows to Rid the World of 'Evil-doers,'" *CNN*, 16 September 2001, <http://edition.cnn.com/2001/US/09/16/gen.bush.terrorism/>.
14 O'Connor, "Beyond the Cartoon."
15 Paul Harris, "Bush Says God Chose Him to Lead his Nation," *The Guardian*, November 2, 2003, <https://www.theguardian.com/world/2003/nov/02/usa.religion>.
16 George W. Bush, "President Delivers 'State of the Union,'" in *The White House Archives*, January 28, 2003: <http://whitehouse.georgewbush.org/news/2003/012803-SOTU.asp>.
17 George W. Bush, "President Sworn-In to Second Term," the Second Inaugural Speech from the Office of the Press Secretary in *The White House Archives*, January 20, 2005: <http://georgewbush-whitehouse.archives.gov/news/releases/2005/01/20050120-1.html>.
18 Molly Ivins and Lou Dubose, *Bushwhacked: Life in George W. Bush's America* (New York: Random House, 2003), 260.
19 Benjamin Ginsberg and Martin Shefter, *Politics By Other Means* (New York: Norton, 2002).
20 I am not entirely convinced that Woodward's account of the Bush administration is without some scripting; it seems Cheney's role is underplayed by Woodward, and Cheney always seems to be saying that of course Bush is in command. For more details on this critique see Brendon O'Connor, "Bush-Bashing: The Hated and the Haters," *Griffith Review* (Spring 2004).
21 Ron Suskind, *The Price of Loyalty* (New York: Simon & Schuster, 2004).
22 Richard Cohen, "George W. Bush as an Avid Reader,' *The Washington Post*, December 30, 2008, <http://www.washingtonpost.com/wp-dyn/content/article/2008/12/29/AR2008122901896.html>.

23 For an overview of this literature see O'Connor, "Beyond the Cartoon."

24 This first set of statistics are from: Pew Research Center for the People and the Press, "Bush Unpopular in Europe, Seen as Unilateralist." Released August 15, 2001.

25 Globescan, *Global Pubic Opinion on the US Presidential Election and US Foreign Policy*, "Questionaire", 2004, 2–3. In the same survey respondents were asked if George W. Bush's foreign policy had made them feel better or worse about the US. The results were overwhelmingly the latter. Once again the Germans held the strongest opinions with 83% saying it made them feel worse about the US. Strangely in Venezuela, a supposed hotbed of anti-Americanism, the numbers were evenly divided between better and worse, reminding us of the vagaries of public opinion surveys (see Globescan, *Global Pubic Opinion on the US Presidential Election and US Foreign Policy*, 4–5).

26 Globescan for *Guardian* and other newspapers, September–October, 2004 cited in Philip Everts, "Images of the U.S. – Three Theories of Anti-Americanism," Workshop on Anti-Americanism in Comparative Historical Perspective, European Consortium for Political Research, Nicosia, Cyprus, April 25–30, 2006, 37.

27 Globus, International Affairs Poll by IPSOS Public Affairs for the Associated Press, November 19–27, 2004, cited in Everts, "Images of the U.S.,"42.

28 Keith Richburg, "Kerry is Widely Favoured Abroad" *Washington Post*, September 29, 2004, A14. Kerry's claim was something few foreign leaders publicly commented on although it seems accurate, given the data. The Australian Prime Minister John Howard was one of the few world leaders to publicly state on the record that he hoped for a Bush victory.

29 Program on International Policy Attitudes, "Americans Think Negative Global Attitudes toward US are a Problem," September 8, 2004.

30 Ian Katz, "The Last Post," *Guardian*, October 21, 2004.

31 Ibid.

32 Oliver Burkeman, "My Fellow Non-Americans…," *Guardian*, October 13, 2004.

33 When you sign up to vote in America you have the choice of registering as a Republican, a Democrat or as an independent.

34 Oliver Burkeman, "My fellow non-Americans…," *Guardian*, October 13, 2004.

35 "Operation Clark County," *Guardian*, <https://www.theguardian.com/world/2004/oct/18/uselections2004.usa2>.

36 Oliver Burkeman, "My fellow non-Americans…," *Guardian*, October 13, 2004.

37 John Le Carré, "Dear Clark County Voter, Give us back the America we Loved. Yours Sincerely, John Le Carré," *Guardian*, October 13, 2004. <https://www.theguardian.com/world/2004/oct/13/uselections2004.usa13>

38 Antonia Fraser, "Dear Clark County voter, Give us back the America we loved. Yours sincerely, John Le Carré," *Guardian*, October 13, 2004.

39 Richard Dawkins, "Dear Clark County voter, Give us back the America we loved. Yours sincerely, John Le Carré," *Guardian*, October 13, 2004.

40 "America, Let us Love you Again…," *Guardian*, October 18, 2004.

41 "Dear Limey Assholes," *Guardian*, October 18, 2004.

42 Peronet Despeignes, "Brits' Campaign Backfires in Ohio," *USA Today*, November 4, 2004; Andy Bowers, "Dear Limey Assholes…," *Slate*, November 4, 2004. <https://slate.com/news-and-politics/2004/11/a-crazy-british-plot-to-help-kerry.html>.

43 Ian Katz, "The Last Post," *Guardian*, October 21, 2004.

44 Pew Global Attitudes Project, "US Image Up Slightly, But Still Negative," June 23, 2005.

45 Brendon O'Connor, "Politician, Reform Thyself," *Financial Review*, October 29, 2004.

46 Robert F. Kennedy Jr., "Was the 2004 Election Stolen?" *Rolling Stone*, June 1, 2006.

47 For a rebuttal of Kennedy's claims see Farhad Manjoo's "Was the 2004 Election Stolen? No," *Salon*, June 3, 2006.

48 Philipp Oehmke, "The Alt-Right Movement Behind Trump's Presidency," July 14, 2017, *Spiegel*, <http://www.spiegel.de/international/world/the-alt-right-movement-behind-trump-s-presidency-a-1155901.html>; Sarah Posner, "Meet the Alt-Right 'Spokesman' Who's Thrilled with Trump's Rise," *Rolling Stone*, October 18, 2016: <https://www.rollingstone.com/politics/politics-features/meet-the-alt-right-spokesma

n-whos-thrilled-with-trumps-rise-129588/>; Tina Nguyen, "The Far Right Rejoiced as Trump Says Immigrants are Destroying European 'Culture,'" *Vanity Fair*, July 13, 2018: <https://www.vanityfair.com/news/2018/07/donald-trump-culture-wars-britain>; Dana Milbank, "Yes, Half of Trump Supporters are Racist,' *The Washington Post*, September 12, 2016: <https://www.washingtonpost.com/opinions/clinton-wasnt-wrong-about-the-deplorables-among-trumps-supporters/2016/09/12/93720264-7932-11e6-beac-57a4a412e93a_story.html?noredirect=on&utm_term=.516c78d3d3dc>.

49 Richard Wike, "9 Charts on How the World Sees President Trump," *Pew Research Center*, July 17, 2017, <http://www.pewresearch.org/fact-tank/2017/07/17/9-charts-on-how-the-world-sees-trump/>.

50 ITV Report, "Tens of Thousands March in London Against Donald Trump," *ITV*, July 13, 2018, <http://www.itv.com/news/2018-07-13/tens-of-thousands-march-in-london-against-donald-trump/>.

51 Trump tweet, 846pm May 3, 2018.

52 Oliver Stone, *W* (2008), <https://www.imdb.com/title/tt1175491/>.

53 Gallup, "Presidential Approval Ratings – George W. Bush," *Gallup:* <https://news.gallup.com/poll/116500/presidential-approval-ratings-george-bush.aspx>.

54 Gary Langer, "Poll: Bush Approval Rating 92 Percent," *ABC News*, October 10, 2001, <https://abcnews.go.com/Politics/story?id=120971&page=1>.

55 "Trump Job Approval," <https://news.gallup.com/poll/203207/trump-job-approval-weekly.aspx?version=print>.

56 Brendon O'Connor, "Buying into American Dreams: Following US Presidential Elections, Exceptionalism, and Global Power," in G. Banita and S. Pöhlmann eds., *Electoral Cultures* (Heidelberg: Winter University Press, 2014).

57 Richard Wike, "7 Charts on How the World Views President Obama," *Pew Research Center*, June 24, 2015, <http://www.pewresearch.org/fact-tank/2015/06/24/7-charts-on-how-the-world-views-president-obama/>.

58 Obama's two memoirs emphasise these points. Barack Obama, *Dreams from My Father: A Story of Race and Inheritance* (New York, NY: Times Books, 1995) and Barack Obama, *The Audacity of Hope: Thoughts on Reclaiming the American Dream* (New York, NY: Three Rivers Press, 2006).

5

WHAT IS AMERICAN EXCEPTIONALISM?

A key component of American nationalist ideology

In the hands of American politicians, American exceptionalism is generally expressed as a belief that America is superior to other nations: a providential nation that is the "greatest" on earth with an exceptional role to play. Believing that your nation is superior, not just materially but in terms of its history, values, destiny or a way of life, is clearly specious. Nonetheless, American exceptionalist grandiloquence saturates American politics. During his presidency, Barack Obama frequently engaged in such rhetoric.[1]

> We honor the strivers, the dreamers, the risk-takers, the entrepreneurs who have always been the driving force behind our great free enterprise system, the greatest engine of growth and prosperity that the world's ever known...But we keep our eyes fixed on that distant horizon knowing that providence is with us and that we are surely blessed to be citizens of the greatest nation on earth.
>
> *(President Obama, Democratic Party Convention Speech, 2012)*[2]

> Terrible things happen across the globe, and it is beyond our means to right every wrong. But when, with modest effort and risk, we can stop children from being gassed to death, and thereby make our own children safer over the long run, I believe we should act. That's what makes America different. That's what makes us exceptional. With humility, but with resolve, let us never lose sight of that essential truth.
>
> *(President Obama, Syria Speech, 2013)*[3]

In the hands of political scientists,[4] American exceptionalism tends to be defined as viewing America as different or unique.[5] For example when the term has been used in the *American Political Science Review* in the 21st century, it has implied

America's significant difference when compared to other nations.[6] The dominance of this approach in the study of American exceptionalism by political scientists can be traced to the long legacy of Seymour Martin Lipset. I argue that viewing exceptionalism as difference should be rejected because exceptional difference cannot be convincingly measured in comparative terms – the standards are too arbitrary and often paper over an ideological predisposition. A more sensible and useful approach is to recognise American exceptionalism as a key ideological component of American nationalism. Following the scholarship of Michael Freeden I take an expansive view of ideologies, which sees them as complex, popular, often malleable, and ever present in politics.[7] This view rejects the simplistic understanding of ideologies as principally dogmas or as totalising systems of thought. I also reject the dichotomy that Marx and Mannheim[8] drew between truth and ideology, the latter of which they depict as falsehood. Like Freeden, I start with an understanding of ideologies as belief systems. I also borrow from critical theorists the understanding of ideologies as structural, cultural, and emotional. Integrating these two approaches I have developed the below three-tiered model for ideological analysis (Figure 5.1). The top and overarching level is the macro level where we find the hegemonic values and beliefs of American political culture. At this level we are dealing with a broad and perhaps vague sets of ideas, but they are no less important for that. American exceptionalism as shown in the diagram is a key element of American nationalism at the macro level. These macro ideas constitute America's civic nationalism and also invest this nationalism with a sense of moral superiority. Although the political culture changes, and is contested from within, these hegemonic values persist over relatively long periods of time and change very slowly. These values and myths are consciously and subconsciously at the core of American nationalism. This conception of ideology borrows from the Frankfurt School and Clifford Geertz. The model will be applied in the second

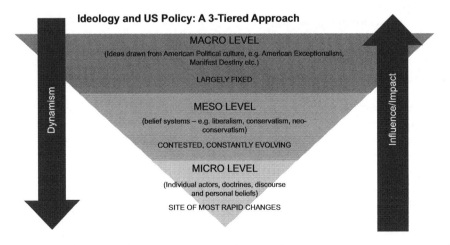

FIGURE 5.1 Ideology and US policy: a 3-tiered approach

part of the chapter; in the first part of the chapter I point to the failings of the dominant political science approach to exceptionalism. As I present it, based on analysis of American political speeches and commentary, the ideology of American exceptionalism has three main pillars – the exceptionalism of birth, the exceptionalism of opportunity, and the exceptionalism of role – which are not entirely fixed but rather adapt to suit the times or interests of particular parties or politicians. Often used in combination, they are: a belief in America's founding as unique and as a blueprint for greatness; a belief in America as a land of unrivalled opportunity; and a belief in America's ability as a nation to achieve great things in our world.

This ideological analysis not only questions the tendency to see American exceptionalism as difference but also aims to address a significant silence amongst 21st century political scientists regarding a term that ignited a raging public debate during the Obama presidency. Work by a blogger at the *Atlantic* shows the discrepancy in the usage of the term over time: it appeared in national publications only 457 times between 1980 and 2000, and 2,558 times in the following decade, but from 2010 to March 2012 usage skyrocketed with the term appearing in print and online over 4,000 times.[9] This near silence from political scientists is even more perplexing when you consider that for much of the 20th century they had almost exclusive use of the term. Yet in the last 20 years in the pages of the *American Political Science Review* the term has largely been confined to book reviews: it rates a passing mention in seven articles, not even garnering a paragraph's worth of discussion.[10] It is worth noting that claims of American exceptionalism were not only central to Obama's convention speech in 2012, but also in the 2012 campaign books of Mitt Romney and Newt Gingrich. Sarah Palin, who was touted as a possible candidate, made it paramount to her claims in *America by Heart*. In 2015, Dick and Liz Cheney's *Exceptional* argues that the concept is the essence of America. Marco Rubio never seems to tire of talking about the magic of American exceptionalism.

This poverty of intellectual engagement by political scientists is unfortunate because the current political understanding and use of the term has three particularly negative consequences on American politics and society. Firstly, the ideology of American exceptionalism helps ossify the constitution and the system of government, thus preventing sensible reform.[11] Secondly, this ideology leads to exaggerations about the ease of economic and social mobility and the openness of opportunity for all in America. Thirdly, the ideology sees America's role in the world as inviting hubris in terms of America being a model for others to follow or as a nation that has the capacity to intervene to bend the arc of history towards justice and democracy. Given the negative influence of American exceptionalism in American public discourse, there is a necessity for a more sophisticated understanding of the term by political scientists. It would be too much to expect to be able to entirely erase the currently hyperbolic use, but rather than wishing the term away from public discourse, as both Stephen Walt and James Ceaser suggest,[12] political scientists can try the more productive approach of creating a more sophisticated discourse. Attempting to expunge terms from political discourse is an all too common response from academics when once specialist and nuanced concepts enter the public arena to be used in cruder and more strident ways by politicians and commentators.[13] My argument here, and in general, is that academics should seek to contest the meaning of these terms and therefore be part of the world of living words, rather than court irrelevance by rejecting popular use. To contribute to these debates this chapter concludes by not dismissing American exceptionalism as a myth, but by identifying it as a key element of American nationalist ideology that needs to be better challenged. Before delineating the character of this ideology this chapter examines the origins of the term and the crucial role that Seymour Martin Lipset played in shaping academic debates about American exceptionalism.

Other disciplines have tended to be more nuanced and sophisticated than political science in their understanding of American exceptionalism. Historians have rightly questioned the insularity of exceptionalist analysis with transnational histories picking empirical holes in exceptionalist claims.[14] Meanwhile the discipline of American Studies has tended to treat American exceptionalism as a powerful and dangerous myth.[15] While a political science approach starts behind the pack in terms of sophistication and insights, I would argue that ultimately the approach offered here, with its focus on the conceptual nature of American exceptionalism as an ideology, is preferable to treating it as a myth or offering a contextualist or transnational historical approach to American exceptionalism.[16] Although it often feels personally satisfying to call ideas one opposes myths, this is not the best way to understand and combat the power of this idea. Meanwhile transnational interpretations, for all their insights, too often pore over the same comparative terrain as mistaken political scientists. Although these transnational works often effectively debunk claims of exceptionalism,[17] this analysis underplays the fact that American exceptionalism is principally an ideological and emotional term. As a result, historians – like political scientists – focus on the empirical details of supposed American exceptionalism and end up paying too little attention to the ongoing power and influence of American exceptionalism which is largely immune to such academic myth-busting.

The origins of the term American exceptionalism

The origins of the term American exceptionalism are generally traced to either Alexis de Tocqueville or Joseph Stalin. In both cases we can see tension between American exceptionalism being viewed as an ideology or a term in comparative political analysis. The claims that Tocqueville first used the term are much pronounced but are a misinterpretation of his overall argument and a misrepresentation of particular quotes. The supposedly hard evidence that Tocqueville is the progenitor of the term is usually given as this passage from Volume II of *Democracy in America* where Tocqueville writes:

The position of the Americans is therefore quite exceptional, and it may be believed that no democratic people will ever be placed in a similar one. Their strictly Puritanical origin — their exclusively commercial habits — even the country they inhabit, which seems to divert their minds from the pursuit of science, literature, and the arts — the proximity of Europe, which allows them to neglect these pursuits without relapsing into barbarism — a thousand special causes, of which I have only been able to point out the most important — have singularly concurred to fix the mind of the American upon purely practical objects. His passions, his wants, his education, and everything about him seem to unite in drawing the native of the United States earthward: his religion alone bids him turn, from time to time, a transient and distracted glance to heaven. Let us cease then to view all democratic nations under the mask of the American people, and let us attempt to survey them at length with their own proper features.[18]

This sounds like a declaration of American exceptionalism as we know it until you take the effort to read the preceding paragraph or more importantly the entire book. In the paragraph immediately before the above excerpt Tocqueville writes: "I cannot consent to separate America from Europe, in spite of the ocean which intervenes. I consider the people of the United States as that portion of the English people which is commissioned to explore the wilds of the New World."[19] In short, Tocqueville argues that America is not exceptional; but their circumstances at that point in time were exceptional giving them a head start to a broader democratic process. At a philosophical level this reveals the fine balance between universalistic and particularistic arguments in *Democracy in America*. First, and ultimately foremost, Tocqueville saw the American democratic experience as a precursor to a likely broader democratic experience for humankind (well at least European humankind to begin with), therefore the American democrat was a stand in for what democratic man was likely to be into the future. Tocqueville goes to pains to emphasise this as his main argument by authoring in 1848 a new preface to *Democracy in America* written after a period of further reflection, in which he writes:

However sudden and momentous be the events which have just taken place so swiftly, the author of this book can claim that they have not taken him by surprise. *This work was written fifteen years ago with a mind constantly preoccupied by a single thought: the thought of the approaching irresistible and universal spread of democracy through the world.* [20]

Secondly, although democracy is in Tocqueville's view a universalist set of ideas,[21] he is also very attuned in his study to pointing out the particularities of the American experience. Given the influence of Guizot[22] and Montesquieu[23] on his thinking about political culture this is not surprising. Furthermore, like Louis Hartz in the mid-20th century, Tocqueville is also drawn to the notion of fragment cultures: the theory that particular types of religious and political immigrants created a particular political culture that had noteworthy regional and national tendencies. This eye for the particularities of the American experience led Tocqueville to emphasise two features of American political culture that are important to those who make exceptionalist claims about the US: namely that the Puritan immigrants in the New England townships created an enviable political model and that the American frontier created broad opportunities.[24] Once again these did not mean America was superior or alone in its march towards greater equality of conditions and democracy; they simply gave America certain advantages at important points in time, which in Tocqueville's view hastened the democratic processes in the US.

In contrast to my reading of Tocqueville, which draws heavily on the work of Alan Ryan and other leading Tocqueville scholars,[25] is the view adopted by many politicians, commentators and some academics that Tocqueville provides enough commentary on the distinct and special nature of the US to make him the godfather of American exceptionalism. One of many examples comes from Charles Dunn, the emeritus chair of the United States J. William Fulbright Scholarship Board, who opened his edited book *American Exceptionalism* (2013) with the statement: "Perhaps no one ever better expressed the case for American Exceptionalism than Alexis de Tocqueville, who argued that America has no equal."[26] Here Dunn makes the central ideological connection between American exceptionalism and American superiority, a connection that had been long implicit in American political speeches before 2009 from which point on the actual word started being used explicitly and widely by politicians. The notion, and now the specific term, has been attractive to American politicians because it speaks of a glorious past and future, as it affirms America's specialness and providence. Not surprisingly Tocqueville has long been drawn upon to buttress such therapeutic speech-making:

> To this day, most Americans who have heard of Tocqueville think of him as the country's cheerleader, plain and simple. Eisenhower, Reagan and Clinton all made speeches quoting, and attributing to Tocqueville, a poetic passage that described American pulpits 'flaming with righteousness', and concluded: 'America is great because she is good.' Tocqueville never wrote it. He would never have written something this fulsome.[27]

As this quote from David Bell rightly emphasises, Tocqueville was in fact deeply ambivalent about the United States. In the chapter where he calls America "quite exceptional" he also notes the "unfavourable" conditions of fine arts and literature in America. In *Democracy in America* he abrades, criticises, and admonishes Americans for their "annoying" patriotism, their need for constant praise, their lack of poetry and understanding of the poetic, their tendencies toward conformity and sameness, their lack of intellectual or artistic brilliance, and their tendency toward a "tyranny of the majority". Every positive Tocqueville has to say about America is tempered by a negative comment close at hand.

Tocqueville should not be seen as the godfather of American exceptionalism but rather as the developer of an approach to the study of American political culture that emphasised certain particularities, merits and pitfalls of the American experience with the aim of charting the contingent and crooked path to democratisation around the world. This is ultimately the opposite of the exceptionalist mindset because it describes America as the new normal. One objection here might be that American exceptionalism, in its Wilsonian expression,[28] has universalist tendencies. In other words it believes that what America has today with respect to democracy and human rights, the world will have tomorrow and, if absolutely necessary this state will be achieved with the help of American intervention. In Wilson's words America could help "make the world safe for democracy"; in George W. Bush's words, when talking about the Iraq war, "Freedom is not our gift to the world it is God's gift to humanity." This is a key pillar of the ideology of American exceptionalism, but it is not Tocqueville's view of what drove the democratic project, which he located in emerging social orders within states, that would demand greater equality of conditions. His vision of democracy was largely sociological and bottom-up; not something that would spread as an elite export project, rather it emerged from a human desire for recognition, a desire that is not exceptionally American, at all.

The misuse of Tocqueville was aided and abetted by Seymour Martin Lipset who took up throughout his career the Tocquevillian challenge of interpreting American political culture via the political sociological tradition to conclude that America is exceptional. However, he misinterpreted Tocqueville to write: "In his great book, Tocqueville is the first to refer to the United States as exceptional – that is, qualitatively different from all other countries. He is, therefore, the initiator of the writings on American exceptionalism."[29] Methodologically Lipset followed Tocqueville offering an historical sociology of America led by the belief that American society (although complex) had a core character to it that could be studied and enunciated.[30] Like Tocqueville, Lipset adopted a broad analysis that he called "macroscopic," but he added a further dimension by taking on a much more obviously comparative approach than Tocqueville. As a noted polymath, Lipset was interested in key Tocquevillian questions like "why democracy in America?", "why such religiosity?", "why such high rates of volunteerism?" – questions which Lipset, unlike Tocqueville, tended towards with the supposition: because America is exceptional. However, Lipset was also interested throughout his career (in keeping with his own early socialism) with the question of why "no socialism in America?" This last question brings us to Joseph Stalin and the regularly accepted academic understanding of the first notable use of the term "American exceptionalism."[31]

Marx and Engels were struck by the strength of American capitalism, which led them to fluctuate between seeing America as an exception to the rule of the global spread of the laws of communism or as an example of how hyper-capitalism would help bring on a workers' revolution.[32] However, by the 20th century it was hard to see America as fertile ground for communist foment. Reflecting on this, Werner Sombart published *Why Is There No Socialism in the United States?* in 1905. This book and question significantly influenced Lipset who himself has authored a book, chapters and articles asking this same question. The answer to this question offered by Sombart and by many others since, was that there was an American exception to the laws of communism. American communists in the early 20th century were not likely to accept this, but faced with the monumental challenge of bringing about a revolution in America some were drawn to see the road to socialism as likely to be slower in the US, and it was the debate over this that led to the coining of the term American exceptionalism, according to a number of experts.

It is widely claimed that the etymology of "American exceptionalism" comes from an English translation in 1929 of comments made by Joseph Stalin towards the leader of the Communist Party of America Jay Lovestone and his Lovestoneites in a push to expel them from the Party. Lovestone and his faction were sympathetic to Nikolai Bukharin and a more gradual and moderate path to socialism in the US given the grip of capitalism on American society. With Bukharin's removal from the Comintern, as well as his loss of the editorship of *Pravda* and eventual dismissal from the Politburo in 1929, Lovestone's leadership thus came under threat. In this move against the "rightists" Stalin described Lovestone's views on the American path to socialism as "the heresy of American exceptionalism". Lovestone was in 1929 dismissed from the Party and replaced by his long-time pro-Stalinist rival William Foster. This fascinating, but somewhat obscure passage of American history, along with the way the term American exceptionalism came into usage in American communist circles,[33] might suggest that American exceptionalism has meant different things in different periods of time and thus a "contextualist" or "history of ideas" approach is the best way to understand the term.[34] As much as I have enormous regard for the contextualising scholarship of Quentin Skinner, J. G. A. Pocock, John Gray and Ian Tyrrell – all historians and philosophers who deserve serious attention – there are limitations to contextualism. It can be possibly too wary of drawing connections across time periods and can potentially hold us back in the task of building new theories. This focus on creating new theories and conceptual understandings is one of the advantages that the best political science has over the work of historians.[35] The relevance of the argument here is that American exceptionalism across time, from its origins to its current usage, is an ideological term, often employed in ideological battles. Ideology is the key issue because if we look at *Democracy in America* what is crucial is the interpretation of Tocqueville as a highly complimentary believer in the genius of American democratic society. This view is decidedly selective and tells us far more about various users and interpreters of Tocqueville's work than it does about the complex and highly contingent argument made in the text itself. Seeing Stalin's contribution as ideological with talk of "heresy" from Comintern doctrine is of course not difficult, but the complicating factor is that Stalin is ultimately saying America is no different: it will bend to Marxist-Leninist laws, and sooner rather than later. The Lovestoneites were arguing that America was different. Just how different compared to other nations is the question I will now turn to.

Seymour Martin Lipset and comparative American exceptionalism

The "why no socialism in the US" question points to an obvious problem with seeing American exceptionalism as comparatively different. So many nations have failed to conform to Marx's predictions of revolution that it is the Soviet Union rather than the United States that is better seen as the exception to the rule. Even if one uses the lower bar of socialist policies, the US is generally more anti-statist than other OECD nations, but there are so many contradictions within American anti-poverty programs and attempts to address inequality that sweeping claims of exceptionalism obscure as much as they reveal.[36] This points to a central problem for comparative exceptionalism, namely, how do you set a standard for difference: different from all others? Different on how many social dimensions? Different across how many policy areas? Different for what duration? And if all nations end up being different in certain ways, what adds up to a single nation being exceptionally different? Then there is the challenge of how you conduct this analysis free of nationalism and national biases. Seymour Martin Lipset, President of both the American Political Science Association and the American Sociological Association, tried throughout his career to answer these questions, concluding that America is exceptional in positive and negative ways. However, I will argue that Lipset's patriotism and deductive starting point undermined his quest. Lipset profoundly shaped the academic discourse on American exceptionalism with his three books on the topic: *First New Nation* (1963), *Continental Divide* (1990), and *American Exceptionalism* (1996).

Lipset interpreted Tocqueville, Sombart, and others as having concluded that America is "qualitatively different"[37]; from this starting point he argued that through quantitative and historical analysis, which was often comparative in nature, these differences could be spelled out. Lipset does not totally ignore ideology. Rather, he under-theorises it and provides an academic defence of the ideology of American exceptionalism which is ultimately unconvincing. In his later works Lipset edges towards a deeper understanding of ideology with a customary nod to Hofstadter's quote that "it had been our fate as a nation not to have ideologies but to be one."[38] Ultimately, however, he never quite shakes his association with the "end of ideology" crowd who had presented ideology in the 1950s and 1960s as almost exclusively a Marxist category. The end-of-ideologists claimed that, in contrast to Marxists, the proper job of scholars was to set themselves aside from political controversies and offer thorough, careful, and sober analysis which provided social scientific insights into major debates. Such technical analysis was what they believed post-ideological societies like America most needed. This was the founding principle behind the establishment of the neoconservative journal *The Public Interest* in 1965, which Lipset was intellectually associated with. Claims by Daniel Bell, Irving Kristol and Lipset in the 1950s and 1960s that scholars should be guided by evidence were made with a certain lack of self-awareness.[39] The end of ideology advocates drew on evidence-based social science to interrogate Great Society welfare programs. However, these same scholars often did not challenge preconceptions and engage in empirical research without assumptions when analysing American exceptionalism; instead its existence tended to be assumed. For all his sophistication, Lipset is ultimately unable to sit outside of his own experience and see American exceptionalism as an ideology and not, as he presents it, the result of America's supposedly unique tussle between egalitarianism and individualism. In Lipset's view, expressed in *First New Nation* (1963), America is exceptional because of its particular commitment in its core values to both egalitarianism and personal achievement.[40] Much later in *American Exceptionalism* (1996) Lipset expands these core values to include: "liberty, egalitarianism, individualism, populism, and laissez-faire."[41] The problem with outlining an ideology of "Americanism" with key political cultural aspects is that Lipset sets out to prove that this is an exceptionalist set of national values that produces exceptional outcomes. Lipset's underlying premise is that American exceptionalism on balance is a positive component of the ideology of Americanism, or what I would call American nationalism. Through comparative analysis he seeks to show this exceptionalism is empirically accurate. In contrast, my approach is to offer a critique of this ideology; I argue that no evidence can substantiate these claims, and that the reality instead is that American exceptionalism is a powerful prevailing perception.

For all Lipset's knowledge of methodological debates and his research into broad comparative questions he ends up offering unconvincing deductive research. His starting point is that America has an exceptional political culture and he then marshals comparative examples to confirm this belief; this being particularly the case in *American Exceptionalism* (1996). His work presents comparative statistics on the percentage of young adults engaged in higher education, crime and incarceration rates, litigiousness, patriotism, and church attendance. This is not the type of inductive evidence-led research which shows how different America is from other nations, which *The Public Interest* and Lipset once advocated. As I will argue below this is the blinkered approach of a patriot scholar. Furthermore, even on Lipset's own terms the comparative evidence he presents across his three exceptionalism books is not especially convincing and can often be rebutted with counter-evidence. For example, in *First New Nation* (1963) he makes much of American college and university attendance being significantly higher than in other OECD nations. However, by the 21st century American patterns of higher education attendance no longer outstrip those of other wealthy nations as they generally did in the decades immediately following WWII. America's supposedly exceptionalist mantle has also slipped when it comes to university graduation levels with a 2012 OECD study placing America 14th in terms of 25 to 34-year olds with a degree. The United States was in second place when Lipset wrote *American Exceptionalism* in the mid-1990s with other nations obviously catching up,[42] making it once somewhat exceptional – hardly a significant finding. Similarly national church attendance rates look very high compared to most of Europe *except* for Malta, Poland, Northern Ireland, Georgia, and Turkey. And when you analyse religiosity based on a state-by-state basis America looks even less of an outlier.[43] With patriotism too, the national pride expressed in surveys by Americans is no more than that of Australians.[44] Lipset's data is ultimately unconvincing as proof of American exceptionalism. Political scientists have better words for the differences he identifies, such as outlier and laggard.

The problem with the term "exceptionalism" is that it quickly leads to chauvinistic claims about American greatness, or conversely anti-Americanism about societal inferiority. Lipset for all of this reading and erudition is guilty of being unable to healthily separate in his research an American patriotism, and this brings us back to the lack of neutrality of the term American exceptionalism. One reviewer described Lipset's *American Exceptionalism* "as the sociology of a patriot." In his memoir *Steady Work*, Lipset reflecting on this review writes: "By this he meant that I think the United States is a great and effective country. I do." Lipset says he believes this, despite America's many faults. In his memoir and in his large corpus of scholarship one gets the sense that Lipset tends to equate his own immigrant success story to his nation's success. Seeing Lipset in this autobiographical way, as a successful son of working class Russian Jewish immigrants, is lent weight by how often Lipset researched and wrote about topics close to his father's work experiences and his own work experiences within universities.[45] Ian Tyrrell has written convincingly about the challenges of overcoming nationalism when historians write about the nation they live in or have grown up in. Lipset's comparative political science provides a good example of someone too close at times to his nation for the good of the analysis. Thus his notion of exceptionalism is overlaid with excessively positive connotations and a desire to stretch his empirical findings to confirm this exceptionalism; for balance, some negative exceptions are put in the mix, but the negative never overtakes the positive.

Could it be otherwise? Could a neutral political science of American exceptionalism be written? I think not, and an attempt would be even more difficult now, because the term cannot be rescued from its popular 21st century usage. Particularly since 2009 when President Obama was asked if he believed in "American exceptionalism," the term has been constantly used as a hyperbolic marker of one's level of love of country by American politicians and commentators. The term has lost whatever nuance it might have had. It would be unfair to blame this all on Lipset; however, Lipset's *American Exceptionalism* undoubtedly helped popularise the term, and as I have argued, for all of its caveats, the book was a defence of the position that sees America as superior to other nations in certain dimensions. Therefore, Lipset's legacy makes American exceptionalism, as a comparative political science term, too tainted to be worth trying to rescue. What is the alternative? At a general level, the study of American exceptionalism needs to be more explicitly linked to the study of American nationalism. Anatol Lieven provides a skilful example of this in *America Right or Wrong* where he illustrates how American exceptionalism is used to justify American foreign interventions. This approach rightly views American exceptionalism as an ideology employed to make various aggrandising statements about the nature of the US and its role in the world.

From the founders to the 2012 election

The political speeches made by Republican and Democrat politicians claim America's exceptionalism is based not on America having the largest GDP in the world, the highest rate of military expenditure or more immigrants than other nations, but rather on intangible claims about the special nature of America's past, present and future.[46] Political scientists following Lipset have generally ignored this rhetoric and focused instead on material measures that rarely rate a mention with these advocates of exceptionalism. To avoid missing the essence of how exceptionalism is conceived of, and used, in American politics I will argue that the most practical and useful option is to see American exceptionalism as an ideology (i.e. as a belief system). Here, my use of the term ideology follows the work of Freeden,[47] who compiles the following definition:

> A political ideology is a set of ideas, beliefs, opinions, and values that:
>
> 1.   exhibit a recurring pattern
> 2.   are held by significant groups
> 3.   compete over providing and controlling plans for public policy
> 4.   do so with the aim of justifying, contesting or changing the social and political arrangements and processes of a political community.[48]

The existence of recurring patterns is crucial to Freeden's understanding of ideologies because the more familiar we are with a set of claims, the more powerful and alluring these arguments can become, enhancing the likelihood of their shaping politics and policies.

As I proposed at this chapter's beginning, the three main pillars of American exceptionalism are the exceptionalism of birth, the exceptionalism of opportunity, and the exceptionalism of role. Pillar one is present in most exceptionalist rhetoric. In this view, America had a unique founding that has been at the heart and soul of its culture and politics ever since. The narrative here is that America was founded by pilgrims seeking religious freedom. They created a "city upon a hill" and their offspring fought the British for their political freedom. They went on to codify their liberty in the sacred documents of the Declaration of Independence and the Constitution, thus establishing a freedom- and liberty-loving nation and the world's first constitutional democracy. This foundation story is enhanced by a sense that America was founded by great men, the likes of whom have rarely been seen since. Freedom, egalitarianism, democracy, or other values can be given particular emphasis depending on the teller of the tale; similarly, the story can be given a more secular or religious bent according to the narrator's propensity. Regardless, the common thread is that these grand beginnings set America on a path to greatness and, in many retellings, superiority. In terms of the nation's "exceptional" history, it is hard to deny either the grandness of American history (especially as presented by Hollywood) or America's great success in a relatively short period of time. And yet, as scholars such as Tyrrell and Hodgson show,[49] an "exceptionalist" mindset is a blinkered and nationalistic way of examining history. With nations always borrowing ideas and people from each other, transnationalism can be just as fruitful as nationalism when developing historical understandings of events.[50] Colonial and revolutionary America was populated by settlers who of course had strong ties with Europe and were often inspired by ideas originating in Europe.[51] These deep ties are often forgotten in contemporary American politics, which regularly presents America and Europe as two vastly different civilisations, with the European approach regarded by American conservatives as innately faulty and undesirable.[52]

The second pillar of the exceptionalist ideology is America as the land of opportunity. At the centre of this conception is the shifting notion of the "frontier," where opportunity lay for those willing to take it. In the 19th century, the risk-takers were Europeans fleeing the fixed class systems and slums of their homelands. The premise is the same today: anyone can make it good in America if they are prepared to work hard. This outlook was used to justify continental expansion even by Thomas Jefferson, who otherwise worried about America becoming just another imperial colonial power. Jefferson specifically justified the Louisiana Purchase as an opportunity for individual farmers to help create an expanded "agrarian paradise" or what others call an "empire of liberty".[53] The frontier story was of course a major part of America's self-identity in the 19th century as the nation pushed across the continent, but conquering its geographical limits did not spell the end of America's frontier story. It simply migrated into other areas: overseas markets and territories, spheres of influence, military bases on foreign soil, space exploration, global media dominance, and technological advancement. In 1945 Vannevar Bush wrote the influential *Science: The Endless Frontier* which helped establish the National Science Foundation and sums up a post-territorial notion of the frontier as being based on research, technology and human imagination all of which America was seen to have a special gift for. The "New Frontier" was the title chosen by John F. Kennedy in 1960 for his presidential agenda, and his administration with its emphasis on economic growth, technological advancement, military strength, and space exploration provided an excellent example of frontierism in action; it continues to be a dominant theme in American exceptionalism today.

The third pillar is a belief that America can achieve great things in our world. In other words, it is not just the American people who are exceptional, but America as a nation as well. In the twentieth century, this outlook was animated by a tremendous growth in American power. The catch cry of this pillar is that America can achieve things that other nations cannot. Expressing this outlook in 2009, US General David McKiernan, the then chief US commander in Afghanistan, declared that the failed history of the British and of the Soviet Union in Afghanistan should not be seen as a predictor of America's future in the country. "There's always an inclination to relate what we're doing now with previous nations," he said in a press conference, and then added, "I think that's a very unhealthy comparison".[54] This third pillar has two strands: both see America's role in the world as a model and as an example for others, but they draw different conclusions about the exporting of American ideals. The first strand advocates avoiding foreign entanglements for a variety of reasons, from costs and debt to the concern that intervention abroad may well undermine the American Constitution. The ultimate fear here is that such involvement will make America the same as other rapacious great powers and thus no longer an exemplar.[55] The second strand of thinking sees America as having a special mission to spread its values throughout the world.[56] The presidencies of Woodrow Wilson and George W. Bush are oft-cited examples of the latter outlook.[57]

Both sides of American politics embrace these three pillars, using the ideology of American exceptionalism in a therapeutic manner to reassure Americans of their nation's bright future and its enduring status as the best place in the world to live. Not surprisingly there is partisan contestation over which party believes more whole-heartedly in American exceptionalism. The Republicans in recent decades have generally been more strident in their celebration of America's history as overwhelmingly glorious, believing more fully that opportunity for all still abounds – often in the face of evidence to the contrary – and believing with little doubt in America as a role model for other nations with little to apologise for regarding its past or recent interventions in the affairs of other nations. This strident nationalism makes it challenging for the Democrats to compete for ownership of the ideology of American exceptionalism. Yet having been on the receiving end in electoral politics of claims of anti-Americanism – both historically in the Vietnam period,[58] and more recently with the swift boat veterans campaign against John Kerry – they are unwilling to cede the nationalist high ground to the Republicans. As a result the Democrats are constantly developing their own claims as the true party of American exceptionalism: that they are the party of immigrants, the party of real economic opportunity and – drawing on their Wilsonian tradition – the party of humanitarian intervention that will best serve the global community. Consciously creating a modern-day version of Abraham Lincoln's "log cabin to White House" story, Obama as a rising politician crafted his own "Altgeld Gardens public housing advocate to the White House" narrative.[59] In terms reminiscent of Bruce Springsteen, Obama has framed addressing inequality and creating greater economic opportunity in America as patriotic causes. In foreign relations Obama has often mixed prudent caution with exceptionalist rhetoric, a classic example of this is his 2013 Syrian speech quoted in the opening to this chapter. These exceptionalist embellishments can be found sprinkled amongst Obama's speeches but are particularly noticeable in his State of the Union addresses from 2009 onwards and in his 2012 Democratic Party Convention speech. Arguably these flourishes served the functional purpose of pushing back against Republican criticisms of Obama's patriotism and commitment to the ideology of American exceptionalism. Obama's opponents frequently claimed that *they* were the true defenders of the exceptionalist creed, that Obama was not fully committed to it, and that he, in fact, sought to undermine it. Although generally not explicitly stated, Obama's skin colour, name, upbringing in Indonesia, and Kenyan lineage on his father's side were all used by conservatives as evidence to show that Obama was not totally committed to the idea of American exceptionalism. Sarah Palin voiced this line of criticism towards Obama and his supporters during a campaign speech in 2008, when she referred to small-town America as the "real America" and referred to the "pro-American areas of this great nation".[60]

Obama felt this censure from conservatives most strongly in 2009 after his response to a question about exceptionalism caused significant criticism. At a press conference in Strasbourg, Obama was asked by Ed Luce from the *Financial Times* whether he subscribed, as many of his predecessors had, "to the school of American exceptionalism that sees America as uniquely qualified to lead the world." Obama replied: "I believe in American exceptionalism, just as I suspect that the Brits believe in British exceptionalism and the Greeks believe in Greek exceptionalism. I'm enormously proud of my country and its role and history in the world".[61] To many this would seem a sensible political response, but given the exaggerated nature of partisan politics in the US, Obama's comparison of American exceptionalism to exceptionalism elsewhere unleashed a torrent of conservative condemnation, which argued that Obama did not fully subscribe to the American exceptionalist tradition.[62] In many ways this contrived panic over Obama's remarks was the latest iteration of the culture wars that have been central to American electoral politics since the 1960s. In her book *America by Heart*, Palin quotes Obama's Strasbourg speech and concludes that Obama's comment implied that "he doesn't believe in American exceptionalism at all. He seems to think it is just a kind of irrational prejudice in favor of our way of life".[63] American exceptionalism's connection to a particular understanding of American history and foreign relations means that it can only tolerate limited criticism. Furthermore, exceptionalist ideology makes it hard for Americans to look at policies or governments elsewhere in the world with the idea of learning from them. In line with Freeden's definition of an ideology as aiming to justify, decontest, or change the social and political arrangements and processes of a political community, the constant attack by conservatives on Obama's definition of exceptionalism shows a keen contest for ownership of the term.

The contrivances of the conservative critique of Obama are obvious if we look at Obama's own statements, in Strasbourg and elsewhere, where he champions an understanding of American exceptionalism that is indeed very similar to that of his conservative critics. In response to Luce's question he also stated: "we have a core set of values that are enshrined in our Constitution, in our body of law, in our democratic practices, in our belief in free speech and equality that, though imperfect, are exceptional".[64] He then went on to talk about the important role America played in WWII and in the post-WWII reconstruction of Europe, and about how America still has a lot to offer the world. These are the very values and actions that Palin highlights in her chapter on American exceptionalism.[65] This ideology is clearly broadly held by both parties. Obama was attacked by conservatives because, along with believing in America's exceptionalism, he at times admitted that America has erred in the past, for example with Iran in the 1950s, and suggested that America could learn from other nations. These very mild and cautious comments were misrepresented by conservatives as an "apology tour".[66] Romney's 2012 campaign book was entitled *No Apology*, suggesting that America never does anything wrong in the world. Romney writes that Obama's foreign policy departed from the American tradition established in the post-WWII era:

Never before in American history has its president gone before so many foreign audiences to apologize for so many American misdeeds, both real and imagined. It is his way of signalling to foreign countries and foreign leaders that their dislike for America is something he understands and that is, at least in part, understandable. There are anti-American fires burning all across the globe; President Obama's words are like kindling to them.[67]

Romney is contemptuous of Obama's supposed apologies and he calls for the fulsome trumpeting of American exceptionalism and greatness. However, this is largely pantomime; what is revealing for our purposes here about this debate over exceptionalism, and the degree of Obama's actual commitment to a traditional conception of exceptionalism, is the endless capacity of Americans to talk about (and talk up) their national mythologies and identity. The ideology of American exceptionalism is glaringly obvious in each new presidential election with its cycle of reflection and accusation creating a soap-opera like narrative with familiar tropes, conflicts and patterns. Rubio's and Cruz's speeches declaring their candidacies for the Republican Party nomination in 2016 are good examples of this.

What does this ideological analysis tell us about American nationalism and the study of political culture? Firstly, treating American exceptionalism as a synonym for America being different or an exception to the rule is not particularly useful. Claims of difference have in the past been used as markers for America's superiority over other nations. When we confront a word with an "ism" at the end of it, we are being signalled that this is not a neutral term. The "ism" tells us that generalising and, in fact, essentialising arguments about the true nature of the United States are likely to occur when using the term American exceptionalism. The sensible alternative to treating the term as descriptive is to view it up front as an ideological term that suggests a positive understanding of America's differences and the role of America in the world. In political science this fairly straightforward conclusion has generally been avoided because of the long shadow cast by Seymour Martin Lipset's legacy in understanding America's supposed peculiarities and particularities. As insightful as his overall corpus of work is, it is wrong to think, as Lipset does, that American exceptionalism can be delineated and detailed through careful historical and comparative analysis. Objectively the term is a misnomer: it exists as a rhetorical point of view, but not as a reality. Lastly, it is a dangerous rhetorical position that ossifies the American constitution from reform, exaggerates the extent to which America is a land of opportunity, and leads to America believing it has an ability, unique among nations, to solve international problems.

Notes

1 Obama's State of the Union addresses and his 2012 convention speeches are saturated with exceptionalist language. See Ben Mathis-Lilley and Chris Wade, "Watch Barack Obama Talk About How America is the Greatest Country on Earth in 13 Different Speeches," *Slate*, February 20, 2015, <http://www.slate.com/blogs/the_slatest/ 2015/02/20/barack_obama_loves_america_and_thinks_it_s_great_video_evidence_contra dicts.html>; Glenn Kessler, "Giuliani's False Claims About Obama's Speeches," *The*

Washington Post, February 22, 2015, <https://www.washingtonpost.com/news/fa ct-checker/wp/2015/02/22/giulianis-false-claims-about-obamas-speeches/>. For an alternative viewpoint, see Steve Contorno, "Rudy Giuliani: Barack Obama Said American Exceptionalism No Better Than Other Countries," *Tampa Bay Times*, February 23, 2015, <http://www.politifact.com/punditfact/statements/2015/feb/23/rudy-giuliani/ rudy-giuliani-barack-obama-said-american-exception/>; Richard Lowry and Ramesh Ponnuru, "An Exceptional Debate: The Obama Administration's Assault on American Identity," *National Review Online*, March, 2010, <https://www.nationalreview.com/ nrd/articles/339276/exceptional-debate>. See also Mitt Romney, "Remarks at the 2012 Republican National Convention," August 30, 2012, transcript, *The Washington Post*, <https://www.washingtonpost.com/politics/rnc-2012-mitt-romney-speech-to- gop-convention-excerpts/2012/08/30/7d575ee6-f2ec-11e1-a612-3cfc842a6d89_story. html>; Marco Rubio, "Keynote Speech at 2010 CPAC Conference," February 18, 2010, transcript, *The Washington Post*, <http://voices.washingtonpost.com/44/2010/ 02/marco-rubios-cpac-speech-the-t.html>; Sarah Palin, "Speech at 'Showdown in Searchlight' Tea Party Express Rally," March 27, 2010; Newt Gingrich, "Speech at American Solutions Event," October 21, 2010; "Samantha Power's Nomination Hearing," July 17, 2013, transcript and video, UN Watch, <http://blog.unwatch.org/index. php/2013/07/19/samantha-powers-nomination-hearing-video-transcript/>.

2 Barack Obama, "Remarks at the 2012 Democratic National Convention," September 6, 2012, transcript, National Public Radio, <http://www.npr.org/2012/09/06/ 160713941/transcript-president-obamas-convention-speech>.

3 Barack Obama, "Remarks by the President in Address to the Nation on Syria," September 10, 2013, transcript, The White House, <https://www.whitehouse.gov/the-press-of fice/2013/09/10/remarks-president-address-nation-syria>. This claim was immediately and strongly criticised as hubristic by Vladimir Putin, see "A Plea for Caution from Russia," *New York Times*, September 11, 2013, <http://www.nytimes.com/2013/09/12/ opinion/putin-plea-for-caution-from-russia-on-syria.html?_r=1>. He asserted that:

> I would rather disagree with a case he made on American exceptionalism, stating that the United States' policy is "what makes America different. It's what makes us exceptional." It is extremely dangerous to encourage people to see themselves as exceptional, whatever the motivation. There are big countries and small countries, rich and poor, those with long democratic traditions and those still finding their way to democracy. Their policies differ, too. We are all different, but when we ask for the Lord's blessings, we must not forget that God created us equal.

4 Seyla Benhabib, "Claiming Rights Across Borders: International Human Rights and Democratic Sovereignty," *American Political Science Review* 103 (2009), 691–704; Eileen McDonagh, "Political Citizenship and Democratization: The Gender Paradox," *American Political Science Review* 96 (2002), 535–552; Benjamin R. Barber, "The Politics of Political Science: 'Value-Free' Theory and the Wolin-Strauss Dust-Up of 1963," *American Political Science Review* 100 (2006), 539–545; Andrew Reynolds, "Representation and Rights: The Impact of LGBT Legislators in Comparative Perspective," *American Political Science Review* 107 (2013), 259–274; David Kettler, "The Political Theory Question in Political Science, 1956–1967," *American Political Science Review* 100 (2006), 531–537, Noam Lupu and Jonas Pontusson, "The Structure of Inequality and the Politics of Redistribution," *American Political Science Review* 106 (2011), 316–336, Aurelian Craiutu and Jeremy Jennings, "The Third 'Democracy': Tocqueville's Views of America After 1840," *American Political Science Review* 98 (2004), 391–404.

5 Martin Seymour Lipset, *The First New Nation: The United States in Historical and Comparative Perspective* (London: Heinemann, 1964); Martin Seymour Lipset, *American Exceptionalism: A Double Edged Sword* (New York: W.W. Norton & Co., 1996); McDonagh, "Political Citizenship and Democratization"; Reynolds, "Representation and Rights"; Lupu and Pontusson, "The Structure of Inequality and the Politics of

Redistribution". An exception to the general trend of dismissing exceptionalism or seeing it as a synonym for difference is offered by David H. McKay, who writes:

> A final characteristic of American ideology is its uniqueness. No other country subscribes to a similar set of values and beliefs. Americans are also convinced of the superiority of their way of doing things. Exceptionalism, therefore, has always been expressed in moralistic terms. US democracy, institutions and constitutional arrangements are believed to be inherently superior to those of other countries because they are the conscious creation of the people – not of some distant and arbitrary state".
>
> (David H. McKay, Politics and Power in the USA (London: Penguin, 1994), 26)

6 Benhabib, "Claiming Rights Across Borders"; McDonagh, "Political Citizenship and Democratization"; Barber, "The Politics of Political Science"; Reynolds, "Representation and Rights"; Kettler, "The Political Theory Question in Political Science, 1956–1967"; Lupu and Pontusson, "The Structure of Inequality and the Politics of Redistribution"; Craiutu and Jennings, "The Third 'Democracy'".
7 Michael Freeden, *Ideologies and Political Theory: A Conceptual Framework* (Oxford: Clarendon Press, 1996); Michael Freeden, *Ideology: A Very Short Introduction* (Oxford: Clarendon Press, 2003).
8 Karl Mannheim, *Ideology and Utopia* (London: Routledge, 1936).
9 Richard Gamble, "American Exceptionalisms," *The American Conservative*, September 4, 2012, <http://www.theamericanconservative.com/articles/american-exceptionalisms/>.
10 Benhabib, "Claiming Rights Across Borders"; McDonagh, "Political Citizenship and Democratization"; Barber, "The Politics of Political Science"; Reynolds, "Representation and Rights"; Kettler, "The Political Theory Question in Political Science, 1956–1967"; Lupu and Pontusson, "The Structure of Inequality and the Politics of Redistribution"; Craiutu and Jennings, "The Third 'Democracy'".
11 Desmond King, Robert Lieberman, Gretchen Ritter, and Lawrence Whitehead, (eds.) *Democratization in America: A Comparative Historical Analysis* (Baltimore: Johns Hopkins University Press, 2009). Lawrence Jacobs and Desmond King (eds.) *The Unsustainable American State* (Oxford: Oxford University Press, 2009).
12 For two compelling but ultimately flawed pieces see: James Ceaser, "The Origins and Character of American Exceptionalism," in *American Exceptionalism: The Origins, History and Future of the Nation's Greatest Strength*, ed. Charles W. Dunn (Lanham: Rowman and Littlefield, 2013); Stephen Walt, "The Myth of American Exceptionalism," *Foreign Policy*, October 11, 2011, <http://foreignpolicy.com/2011/10/11/the-myth-of-america n-exceptionalism/>.
13 Other examples of this are anti-Americanism, terrorism, and genocide.
14 Ian Tyrrell, "American Exceptionalism in an Age of International History," *American Historical Review* 96 (1991), 1031–1055.
15 Donald Pease, *The New American Exceptionalism* (Minneapolis: University of Minnesota Press, 2009).
16 Duncan S.A. Bell, "Political Theory and the Functions of Intellectual History: A Response to Emmanuel Navon," *Review of International Studies* 29 (2003), 151–160, Duncan S.A. Bell, "What is Liberalism?" *Political Theory* 42 (2014), 682–715.
17 Ian Tyrrell, *Transnational Nation: United States History in Global Perspective since 1789* (Basingstoke: Palgrave MacMillan, 2007); Thomas Bender, *A Nation among Nations: America's Place in World History* (New York: Hill and Wang, 2006).
18 Alexis de Tocqueville, *Democracy in America*, trans. Henry Reeve (1899), 36–37, <http://xroads.virginia.edu/~HYPER/DETOC/toc_indx.html>. I use the Reeve translation for this quote because this is the one used by Wikipedia to mistakenly claim Tocqueville as the progenitor of American exceptionalism and therefore the quote students tend to misuse.
19 Tocqueville, *Democracy in America*, 36.

20 Alexis de Tocqueville, *Democracy in America*, trans. George Lawrence, ed. J.P. Mayer (New York: Double Day and Co. 1969), xiii.

21 One should not ignore that there are clearly racist limits to how far Tocqueville considers the "universal" spread of democracy to be.

22 Tocqueville had been attending François Guizot's lectures on "The History of Civilization in Europe" during the previous three years. Guizot's influence is manifest throughout *Democracy in America*. Indeed, a criticism of *Democracy in America* at the time was that its author had read too much Guizot before he had seen America." Alan Ryan, "'Visions of Politics.' Review of *Tocqueville Between Two Worlds: The Making of a Political and Theoretical Life*, by Sheldon S. Wolin," *The New York Review of Books*, June 27, 2002, <http://www.nybooks.com/articles/2002/06/27/visions-of-politics/>.

23 "Like Montesquieu, Tocqueville emphasized the centrality of *moeurs*, the congeries of beliefs and values and the 'habits of the heart' that provide the cultural soil in which political institutions can grow." Ryan, "Visions of Politics". See also: "Among his predecessors, he was closest to Montesquieu, while rejecting Montesquieu's geographical determinism." Robert O. Paxton, "'The Divided Liberal.' Review of *Tocqueville: A Biography* by André Jardin, translated by Lydia Davis, with Robert Hemenway, and *Tocqueville and the Two Democracies* by Jean-Claude Lamberti, translated by Arthur Goldhammer," *New York Review of Books*, March 2, 1989, <http://www.nybooks.com/articles/1989/03/02/the-divided-liberal/>.

24 Daniel J. Boorstin is one of the most noted promoters of this idea that from an exceptional land America emerged an exceptional nation. His analysis is a form of environmental determinism. Daniel J. Boorstin, *The Genius of American Politics* (Chicago: University of Chicago Press, 1953).

25 Alan Ryan, *On Tocqueville: Democracy and America* (New York: Liveright, 2014); Seyla Benhabib, "Democracy and Difference: Reflections on the Metapolitics of Lyotard and Derrida," *Journal of Political Philosophy* 2 (1994), 1–23; David A. Bell, "'Come and see for yourself.' Review of *Tocqueville: The Aristocratic Sources of Liberty*, by Lucien Jaume, translated by Arthur Goldhammer," *London Review of Books*, July 18, 2013, <http://www.lrb.co.uk/v35/n14/david-a-bell/come-and-see-for-yourself>; Paxton, "The Divided Liberal"; Francois Furet, "'The Passions of Tocqueville.' Translated by Devid Bellos. Review of *Alexis de Tocqueville: Selected Letters on Politics and Society*, edited by Roger Boesche, translated by James Toupin and Roger Boesche," *New York Review of Books*, June 27, 1985, <http://www.nybooks.com/articles/1985/06/27/the-passions-of-tocqueville/>; John Gray, "'The Dangers of Democracy.' Review of *The Confidence Trap: A History of Democracy in Crisis from World War I to the Present* by David Runciman," *The New York Review of Books*, March 20, 2014, <http://www.nybooks.com/articles/2014/03/20/dangers-of-democracy/>; H.S. Commager, "Introduction," in Alexis de Tocqueville, *Democracy in America*, trans. Henry Reeve (Oxford: Oxford University Press, 1947); James Wood, "Tocqueville in America: The Grand Journey, Retraced and Reimagined," *The New Yorker*, May 17, 2010, <http://www.newyorker.com/magazine/2010/05/17/tocqueville-in-america>; Alan Ryan, "'Tocqueville in Saginaw.' Review of *Tocqueville: A Biography*, by André Jardin, translated by Lydia Davis and Robert Hemenway," *London Review of Books*, March 2, 1989, <http://www.lrb.co.uk/v11/n05/alan-ryan/tocqueville-in-saginaw>; Ryan, "Visions of Politics", 82; Gary Wills, "Did Tocqueville 'Get' America?" *New York Review of Books*, April 29, 2004, <http://www.nybooks.com/articles/2004/04/29/did-tocqueville-get-america/>.

26 Charles W. Dunn ed., *American Exceptionalism: The Origins, History and Future of the Nation's Greatest Strength* (Lanham: Rowman and Littlefield, 2013), 1. To justify this claim Dunn misrepresents this quote from *Democracy in America*: "The position of the Americans is therefore exceptional, and it may be believed that no democratic people will ever be placed in a similar one."

27 Bell, "Come and see for yourself".

28 Walter Russell Mead, *Special Providence: American Foreign Policy and How it Changed the World* (New York: Routledge, 2002); Anatol Lieven, *America Right or Wrong: An Anatomy of American Nationalism* (New York: Oxford University Press, 2012).

29 Lipset, *American Exceptionalism*, 18.
30 The study of political culture practiced by Tocqueville and Lipset is largely overtaken in the late 20th century by more quantitative approaches and what Lipset calls in *First New Nation* more microscopic focused political science. One of the few recent political science books in this more macroscopic, principally qualitative tradition, is Howard Wiadra, *Political Culture, Political Science, and Identity Politics* (Surrey: Ashgate, 2014). This book has much to recommend it; however, when discussing Tocqueville and American exceptionalism it slips into the usual misinterpretations and clichés. While Wiadra rightly emphasises that Tocqueville (like Lipset) was interested in delineating the key attributes of American political culture, he then moves from this analysis to offer more nationalist flourishes that undermine his scholarship. Wiadra writes:

> De Tocqueville was interested in all aspects of America but particularly in our unique political culture. He especially emphasized the aspects of free speech, egalitarianism, religiosity, and a lack of rigid class consciousness – all aspects of American political culture – that he found in America. And in doing so, de Tocqueville probably came closer than just about anyone in describing what is particular, unique, and glorious about America. In today's time, we would say that de Tocqueville is an analyst of and an advocate for American exceptionalism.
>
> *(Wiadra, Political Culture, 23)*

31 Donald Pease, "Exceptionalism," in *American Exceptionalism Keywords in American Studies*, ed. Bruce Burgett and Glenn Hendler (New York: New York University Press, 2007), 108–112.
32 Eric Foner, "Why Is There No Socialism in the United States?" *History Workshop* 17 (1984), 57–80.
33 In June 1930, during the national convention of the Communist Party USA in New York, it was declared that, "The storm of the economic crisis in the United States blew down the house of cards of American exceptionalism and the whole system of opportunistic theories and illusions that had been built upon American capitalist 'prosperity'". Bernard Johnpoll, *A Documentary History of the Communist Party of the United States*, vol. II (Connecticut: Greenwood Press, 1994), 196.
34 Bell, "Political Theory and the Functions of Intellectual History"; Bell, "What is Liberalism?"
35 This is not to deny that the books of historians are generally more engaging and informative than those authored by political scientists.
36 The story of America as an anti-Statist outlier is complicated by the nature of the American welfare system with its government health-care provisions at the state government level; city taxes on the very wealthy; the Great Society experiments such as Head Start and CAPs; government funded community workers; public schooling; Social Security; Medicaid and Medicare; government employment programs and subsidised child-care; the existence of property tax. All of these programs could be better and more inequitable. However, it is not the case that they are all the stingiest or most limited in the OECD. See Jacob S. Hacker, *The Divided Welfare State: The Battle over Public and Private Social Benefits in the United States* (New York: Cambridge University Press, 2002). John Schwarz, *America's Hidden Success: A Reassessment of Twenty Years of Public Policy from Kennedy to Reagan*, Revised Edition (New York: W. W. Norton, 1988).
37 Lipset, *American Exceptionalism*, 13.
38 This quote is often used somewhat out of context: Hofstadter's argument is about the America of the 18th and 19th century rather than of the 20th century. Arguably his claim is timeless, but needs to be discussed more by those employing Hofstadter to make what is an arresting point. The full quote is:

> In earlier days, after all, it had been our fate as a nation not to have ideologies but to be one. As European antagonisms withered and lost their meanings on American

soil in the eighteenth and nineteenth centuries, the new nation came to be conceived of not as sharing the ideologies which had grown out of these antagonisms but as offering an alternative to them, as demonstrating that a gift for compromise and plain dealing, preference for hard work and common sense, were better and more practical than commitments to broad and divisive abstractions.

(Richard Hofstadter, Anti-Intellectualism in American Life *(New York: Knopf, 1952))*

39 Lipset was ultimately too sophisticated a scholar and instinctive a social democrat to persist with this *Public Interest* moment. Nonetheless his work is affected by this narrow understanding of ideology.
40 Lipset, *The First New Nation.*
41 Lipset, *American Exceptionalism,* 19.
42 (OECD) Organisation for Economic Co-operation and Development. *United States – Education at a Glance: OECD Indicators 201* (Paris: OECD, 2012).
43 Jason D. Berggren and Nicol C. Rae, "George W. Bush, Religion and Anti-Americanism," in *Anti-Americanism: History, Causes and Themes, Volume 1: Causes and Sources,* ed. Brendon O'Connor (Connecticut: Greenwood World Publishing, 2007).
44 "Survey: What the World Thinks of America," (BBC) British Broadcasting Corporation, 2003, <http://news.bbc.co.uk/2/shared/spl/hi/programmes/wtwta/poll/html/>.
45 Everett Carll Ladd Jr. and Martin Seymour Lipset, *The Divided Academy: Professors and Politics* (New York: McGraw-Hill, 1975); Martin Seymour Lipset, Martin A. Trow and James Samuel Coleman, *Union Democracy: The Internal Politics of the International Typographical Union* (New York: Free Press, 1956); Martin Seymour Lipset and Sheldon S. Wolin, *The Berkeley Student Revolt: Facts and Interpretations* (New York: Anchor Books, 1965); Martin Seymour Lipset, *Student Politics* (New York: Basic Books, 1967).
46 Obama, "Remarks at the 2012 Democratic National Convention"; Romney, "Remarks at the 2012 Republican National Convention"; Rubio, "Keynote Speech at 2010 CPAC Conference"; Palin, "Speech at 'Showdown in Searchlight'"; Gingrich, "Speech at American Solutions Event"; Power, "United Nations Confirming Hearing".
47 Freeden, *Ideology*; Freeden, *Ideologies and Political Theory.*
48 Freeden, *Ideology,* 32.
49 Tyrrell, "American Exceptionalism in an Age of International History"; Godfrey Hodgson, *The Myth of American Exceptionalism* (New York: Yale University Press, 2009).
50 Tyrrell, *Transnational Nation.*
51 Hodgson, *The Myth of American Exceptionalism*; Eliga Gould, *Among the Powers of the Earth: The American Revolution and the Making of a New World Empire* (Cambridge: Harvard University Press, 2012).
52 For example, Romney claimed during the 2012 campaign:

> Under the pressure of a crisis, people turn to what they really believe. With our economy in crisis, the President and his fellow liberals turned to Europe for their answers. Like the Europeans, they grew the government, they racked up bigger deficits, they took over healthcare, they pushed cap and trade, they stalled production of our oil and gas and coal, they fought to impose unions on America's workers, and they created over a hundred new agencies and commissions and hundreds of thousands of pages of new regulations. Theirs is a European-style solution to an American problem. It does not work there and it will never work here! The right answer is not to believe in European solutions. The right answer is to believe in America—to believe in free enterprise, capitalism, limited government, federalism—and to believe in the constitution, as it was written and intended by the founders.
>
> *(Mitt Romney, "Remarks at the 2011 Conservative Political Action Conference," February 10, 2011, transcript, <http://www.washingtontimes.com/blog/watercooler/2011/feb/11/mitt-romney-2011-cpac-speech/>")*

53 Robert Tucker and David Hendrickson, *Empire of Liberty* (New York: Oxford University Press, 1992); Peter Onuf ed., *Jeffersonian Legacies* (Charlottesville: University of Virginia Press, 1993).

54 Elisabeth Bumiller, "General Sees Long Term for Afghanistan Buildup," *The New York Times*, February 19, 2009, <http://www.nytimes.com/2009/02/19/world/asia/19iht-afghan.1.20299585.html>. On this theme see Andrew J. Bacevich, *The Limits of Power: The End of American Exceptionalism* (New York: Holt Paperbacks, 2009).

55 Jason A. Edwards, "Debating America's Role in the World: Representative Ron Paul's Exceptionalist Jeremiad," *American Behavioural Scientist* 55 (2011), 253–269; Mead, *Special Providence*.

56 Mead, *Special Providence*.

57 Lieven, *America Right or Wrong*; Bacevich, *The Limits of Power*; Peter Beinart, *The Icarus Syndrome: A History of American Hubris* (New York: Harper Collins, 2010).

58 E. J. Dionne, *Why Americans Hate Politics* (New York: Simon & Schuster, 1991).

59 Barack Obama, *Dreams From My Father: A Story of Race and Inheritance* (New York: Random House, 1995).

60 Sarah Palin, *America By Heart: Reflections on Family, Faith and Flag* (New York: Harper Collins, 2010), 63.

61 Lowry and Ponnuru, "An Exceptional Debate".

62 Lowry and Ponnuru "An Exceptional Debate"; Jonah Goldberg, "The Bashing of American Exceptionalism," *Los Angeles Times*, November 9, 2010, <http://articles.latimes.com/2010/nov/09/opinion/la-oe-goldberg-exceptionalism-20101109>; Charles Krauthammer, "Decline is a Choice: The New Liberalism and the End of American Ascendancy," *The Weekly Standard*, October 19, 2009, <http://www.weeklystandard.com/decline-is-a-choice/article/270813>; Palin, *America By Heart*; Newt Gingrich, *A Nation Like No Other: Why American Exceptionalism Matters* (Washington: Regnery, 2011); Mitt Romney, *No Apology: The Case for American Greatness* (New York: St. Martin's Press, 2010).

63 Palin, *America By Heart*.

64 Andrew Malcolm, "Full Text of Barack Obama's Strasbourg Town Hall with Questions," *Los Angeles Times*, April 3, 2009, <http://latimesblogs.latimes.com/washington/2009/04/full-text-of-barack-obama-in-strasbourg-town-hall.html>.

65 Palin, *America By Heart*, 61–90.

66 Romney, *No Apology*, 25.

67 Romney, *No Apology*, 25.

6

DON'T KNOW MUCH ABOUT GEOGRAPHY

American insularity, decline, and anti-Americanism

The spectre of decline has long haunted America. This long-misplaced narrative[1] is now, with the rise of China, becoming a reality, at least in relative terms.[2] The most commonplace explanations for America's relative decline and China's rise are divergent economic growth rates and the loss of American resources, lives and standing as a result of the invasions and occupations of Afghanistan and Iraq. However, for other analysts the diminishing of America's power globally has strong domestic roots: George Packer blames inequality,[3] Fareed Zakaria the political system,[4] and Ed Luce falling educational standards amongst an array of other domestic problems.[5] The president of the influential Council on Foreign Relations Richard Haass brought all of these concerns together succinctly in his book *Foreign Policy Begins at Home*.[6] Another discernible, although underdeveloped, jeremiad zeros in on the American people with the idea that Americans never effectively adjusted to the post-Cold War world of globalisation but instead took a "holiday from history".[7] In other words, it is argued that the American people are particularly uninterested in international affairs and in the age of globalisation this has become America's Achilles' heel.[8] It is this last thesis that this chapter will interrogate by expanding our understanding of how domestic factors influence US foreign policy-making. The chapter will specifically examine the impact of public ignorance and insularity on the quality of US decision-making. In the last two decades or so state-centric approaches to international relations have rightly been challenged by work that places a greater emphasis on how public opinion, identity, and culture shape foreign policy.[9] These bourgeoning areas of scholarship have so far included only a small number of studies on the impact of ignorance.[10] This chapter will first examine popular understandings of American ignorance. It is commonplace for non-Americans to believe Americans are particularly ignorant about the rest of the world. The ignorant American is a widely recognised stereotype in conversations and comedy about Americans. The second section of the chapter will ask whether this stereotype is fair. The scholarly evidence on this question is limited but not at all flattering regarding American knowledge. The third section of the chapter will argue that the "ugly American" stereotype is facile and exaggerated. Unfortunately one of the few books to examine this stereotype, Loch Johnson's *Seven Sins of American Foreign Policy*, is rather careless with the evidence on American ignorance.[11] The last section of the chapter will examine why the "ugly American" stereotype is powerful but often exaggerated, leading to anti-Americanism.

Popular discussions of American ignorance

Many people from around the world have their favourite anecdote about the American who was surprised to find that New Zealanders spoke such good English or who thought that Australia was a country in Europe.[12] A standard routine for comedy teams is to travel to the US to conduct interviews in the American street to highlight American ignorance about global affairs and geography. Sacha Baron Cohen has made a not-so-small fortune highlighting American ignorance, most famously in his movie *Borat*, which stars a character from a country that few Americans apparently realise exists: Kazakhstan. Anecdotes and vox populi powerfully shape and perpetuate the widespread perception that Americans are both ignorant about, and uninterested in, the rest of the world. Perceptions of American ignorance are made doubly powerful by the feeling that these supposed flaws are not just the failings of the masses, but of American leaders and elites also. The anecdotal evidence here is just as plentiful. One of the most embarrassing examples is a US Congressman in the 1980s who told a committee investigating America's lack of proficiency in foreign languages compared to that of the Soviets: "If English was good enough for Jesus Christ, it's good enough for me."[13] More recently, Hillary Clinton presented the Russian foreign minister with a large red button that read "Reset" in English, but had been mistranslated by the US State Department to read "overload" in Russian (just what the Russians needed – a gift that reminds them of Chernobyl!).

Rather than being viewed as errors, these mistakes are often seen as indicative of America's disregard for the rest of the world. Presidents also provide plenty of material. It is claimed that after visiting Latin America on a presidential trip, Reagan said that he had not realised they were all different countries down there.[14] At a state dinner in Brazil in 1982, Reagan toasted the people of Bolivia, and then explained away the mistake by saying he was off to Bolivia next, much to the bewilderment of the Colombian government, whom he was scheduled to meet with the next day.[15] This reminds one of James Reston's quip that "Americans are willing to do anything for Latin America except read about it." George W. Bush was of course legendary for his verbal and mental slip-ups. While campaigning to be the US president in 1999, he referred to Greeks as "Grecians", East Timorese as "East Timorians", and Kosovars as "Kosovians". It is claimed that while president in 2001, Bush according to *Der Spiegel* asked the Brazilian President Fernando

Cardoso "Do you have blacks, too?"[16] (Brazil has roughly 15 million black people and 89 million people of mixed black and white ethnicity.)[17] The Bush White House forcefully denied that Bush asked this question, which may make the story apocryphal and therefore a case of casting the president as another ignorant American, alternatively as was often the case with Bush his spoken words might not have entirely expressed what he meant to say.[18]

The anecdotal evidence to prove Americans are more ignorant about the rest of the world, than say Canadians or Germans, seems endless. While this insularity and ignorance is often asserted, however, little serious systematic evidence has ever been collected and analysed to justify this claim in order to verify whether or not the anecdotes of American unworldliness are *representative*. As a result, anecdotes rule, and we non-Americans get to feel a little superior to those powerful (but ignorant) Americans. This in part accounts for why a totally incoherent response from 2007's Miss Teen South Carolina to the question: "Recent polls have shown a fifth of Americans cannot locate the US on a world map, why do you think this is?" has been viewed roughly 67 million times on YouTube[19] (and the version with subtitles another 12 million times).[20] Her muddled response seemingly provides further evidence that Americans are indeed hopeless when it comes to worldly knowledge. Nonetheless, finding ignorant (or to be kind, nervous) people in a nation of 325 million people is not that difficult.

As we consider the evidence, it only seems fair to ask whether these stories about American ignorance are insightful at all, or whether they are more correctly examples of anti-American prejudice. In other words, do stories about Americans and geography rely on dubious stereotypes – are they the equivalent of other national stereotypes? Or are Americans truly more ignorant about the rest of the world – and given the global influence of the United States, should this not be highlighted and rightly criticised? This second question raises two important issues. Firstly, do we have enough evidence to say with confidence that Americans are more ignorant? Secondly, if they are more ignorant, is it clear that this would have a negative impact on American behaviour in world affairs (for instance, might not ignorance lead to isolationism on certain issues that is highly desirable or does it more regularly lead to blundering unilateralism)?[21] It has been claimed many times over that American insularity accounts for the high levels of fossil fuel consumption in America and the American government's failure to ratify the Kyoto Protocol. Failed American policies in Vietnam in the 1960s and 1970s and in Iraq this century have regularly been blamed on America's particular ignorance and insensitivity regarding foreign cultures. These claims are plausible but difficult to prove.

Evidence that I have collected does suggest a clear weakness in America's knowledge and general engagement with the outside world compared to most other developed nations. However, it is questionable to assume that this *relative* ignorance among the American people is indicative of ignorance within government policy; this belief conflates government behaviour with the attitudes of the populace. In most other countries, foreign policy making is considered an elite pursuit executed by highly educated foreign service experts; in the case of America, however, foreign policy is often criticised for being both too reflective of the ignorance of the people while at the same time being directed by a cabal of elites. This seemingly contradictory critique sees America as having an approach to foreign policy that might be dubbed "populist imperialism". Unsurprisingly, the presidencies of George W. Bush, Ronald Reagan and Donald Trump have done much to fuel these negative opinions.

While many peoples around the world are happy to dismiss their own politicians as unrepresentative chameleons, they often assume that the American president is truly representative of America and Americans. This view is the product of a number of converging forces. It reflects that Americans and non-Americans alike take the words of the Gettysburg Address, with its famous claim that American government is "of the people, by the people, for the people", rather seriously. This view of America mixes populism with symbolism: the president is both the man of the people and emblematic of American society and its values. The author of the Address, Abraham Lincoln, is of course also famous for his personal journey from a humble log cabin to the White House. The heavy emphasis on personal biography in American politics and the tendency of presidential candidates to link their personal narrative with national mythology account for much of the tendency to see American leaders as "of the people". It also reflects an electoral system with a direct vote for its head of state, rather than for local candidates and political parties, as in the Westminster system. There is thus a tendency in America to view election results as a reflection of the political and social mood of the nation at large. As a result of this phenomenon, George W. Bush's narrow victories were said to be representative of a "right nation" (and even symbolic of a transatlantic divide). On the other hand, Barack Obama's election victory over John McCain was reported in many places around the world as America overcoming its racist past (by the same token, if Obama had lost, even by a narrow margin, America would have been declared by many to be a racist nation). Such sweeping analyses are not without some insights, but they often overstate the case for certain trends. It is always worth remembering how many Americans do not bother to vote, how important a small number of "battleground" states are in deciding who wins the electoral college vote (and thus the presidency), and how the media often overstates and over-amplifies the passions of the people on many so-called controversial political topics in America. Aristotle's claim that "man is a political animal" seems overstated not just in the American case, but in the case of most modern democracies. However, nations do have political cultures which are shaped by the values, history, and myths of societies. America's political culture is clearly more populist than that of many other developed nations, so the challenge is not to overstate or understate the importance of populism in shaping American politics and foreign policy.

Cordell Hull, America's longest serving Secretary of State, once claimed that "The Government of the United States is never far ahead of the American public; nor is it very far behind."[22] This populist tradition is partly reality and partly mythology, used by politicians and recycled endlessly in analyses of America. For example, Stephen Brooks writes, "When Ronald Reagan was asked the secret of his popularity he did not hesitate to attribute this to the fact that when many Americans looked at him they saw themselves. It is hard to imagine a François Mitterrand or Jacques Chirac saying the same!"[23] Americans and non-Americans buy these claims too readily, suggesting a degree of gullibility, both American and French leaders are elites that are removed from the people they serve. That is a reality of being a national leader of millions of people. Nonetheless, the oft-stated importance of being a spokesperson for the "people", or more significantly, "bringing the people with you", often leads to particularly stark (and undiplomatic) language being used when American politicians argue for foreign interventions. When President Truman sought to convince the American public to support his containment policies and fund post-WWII reconstruction in Europe, Senator Vandenberg famously advised Truman: "scare the hell out of them, Harry."[24] In this classic statement, George Kennan provides an endorsement of the view that Americans are not especially interested in foreign policy, and thus need to be aroused with strong language. However, once aroused, the government may not be in control of where the passions of the people will take things:

> But I sometimes wonder whether in this respect a democracy [read: America] is not uncomfortably similar to one of those prehistoric monsters with a body as long as this room and a brain the size of a pin: he lies there in his comfortably primeval mud and pays little attention to his environment; he is slow to wrath – in fact, you practically have to whack his tail off to make him aware that his interests are being disturbed; but once he grasps this, he lays about him with such blind determination that he not only destroys his adversary but largely wrecks his native habitat. You wonder whether it would not have been wiser for him to have taken a little more interest in what was going on at an earlier date and to have seen whether he could not have prevented some of these situations from arising instead of proceeding from an undiscriminating indifference to a holy wrath equally undiscriminating.[25]

Joseph McCarthy obviously practiced the most extreme version of this approach, and scared a generation of US politicians into being more bellicose than situations called for (Johnson's policies and rhetoric in Vietnam being the most obvious examples of this). Then there was George W. Bush's "war on terror" language, with its talk of "evil-doers", the "axis of evil"[26] and "good versus evil."[27] In fact, President Bush used the phrase "evil-doers" 24 times in the eight months after the September 11, 2001 terrorist attacks.[28] This language is often called simplistic or Manichean. If we believe that the American people are insular and care little about the outside world, then it would seem necessary to scare them into fighting foreign threats and to exaggerate the nature of those threats.[29] In a country where people often talk in creedal terms about their nation's mission or place in the world, it is not surprising that outsiders and internal critics often reverse this national mythologising to talk about the flaws in the American character and how they infect US politics and foreign policy. In a similar fashion, Senator J. William Fulbright in his

1966 classic *The Arrogance of Power* comments on how the dreams and ignorance of the American people have impacted on American foreign policy:

> We have not harmed people because we wished to; on the contrary, more often than not we have wanted to help people and, in some very important respects, we have helped them. Americans have brought medicine and education, manufactures and modern techniques to many places in the world; but they have also brought themselves and the condescending attitudes of a people whose very success breeds disdain for other cultures. Bringing power without understanding...[30]

However, to justify such sweeping and generally derisive arguments about American ignorance and the political manipulation of that ignorance, much evidence is required. It is precisely what the evidence about America is, and how the impact of this evidence is perceived, that I am most interested in.

Harder evidence

I have attempted to gather the best available evidence on whether Americans are really more ignorant about the rest of the world than people elsewhere. I have collected a range of data that points to high levels of American insularity: these include statistics on comparative geographic and current affairs knowledge, on foreign language study and proficiency, on passport ownership and foreign travel, on study abroad, on the intake of foreign news, and on the travel of presidential candidates. I have interviewed officials at the State Department about foreign language skills, and recruitment and training, while gathering statistics on foreign language training in general. During the Cold War, there were continuous calls for Americans to be more proficient in the languages of the countries they were involved in and to know more about local languages and cultures. The classic telling of this story appeared in the book and the film *The Ugly American* (1958). At the back of the book there is a "factual epilogue", where the authors Lederer and Burdick state:

> ...in France, Italy, Germany, Belgium, the Netherlands, Norway, and Turkey, our ambassadors cannot speak the native tongue ... In the whole of the Arabic world – nine nations – only two ambassadors have language qualifications. In Japan, Korea, Burma, Thailand, Vietnam, Indonesia, and elsewhere, our ambassadors must speak and be spoken to through interpreters. In the entire Communist world, only our ambassadors to Moscow can speak the native language ... On the other hand, an estimated nine out of ten Russians speak, read, and write the language before they arrive on station. It is a prior requirement. The entire functioning staff of the Russian embassies in Asia is Russian, and all the Russians – the officials, stenographic help, telephone operators, chauffeurs, servants – speak and write the language of the host country.[31]

This almost certainly exaggerates the language skills of the Russians; however, it hits on a perennial concern about the US foreign service and American society in general: that there is a lack of cultural sensitivity. This is part of a conventional wisdom that views the nations of Europe as more sophisticated and, quite frankly, better in their foreign diplomacy than the US. James Reston, writing in the *New York Times* in 1958, claimed: "fifty percent of the entire Foreign Service officer corps do not have a speaking knowledge of any foreign language. Seventy percent of the new men coming in the Foreign Service are in the same state".[32] With regard to American involvement in Iraq this century, the lack of language proficiency and regional knowledge has been highlighted time and again. One of the most damning accounts is Rajiv Chandrasekaran's *Imperial Life in the Emerald City*, which gives an alarming view into life in the "Green Zone" in Baghdad. The book is littered with examples large and small of a general insensitivity and disregard for the locals and their culture. There are numerous occasions in the book where Americans display not just an inability to use Arabic but demonstrated no interest in even attempting to learn the language.[33] These deficiencies undoubtedly hindered US policy making in Iraq. For example, it is claimed that of the 1,000 US Embassy staff in Baghdad, only 33 spoke Arabic, of whom only 6 were fluent. In 2005 the State Department had 8 native-level Arabic speakers. The total bi-lingual staff at the CIA is estimated to be around 13%.

On the issue of regional knowledge within the Middle East, a set of simple questions asked to senior officials by the *Congressional Quarterly* journalist Jeff Stein in 2006 is revealing. He asked the Chief of the FBI's National Security Branch, the Chair and Vice Chairman of the House of Representatives Subcommittee on Intelligence, and many other senior officials and politicians if they knew the difference between the Sunni and the Shia in the Middle East. Most did not or guessed incorrectly.[34] These examples fit the stereotype.

At other times evidence runs contrary to stereotype. For example, the widely believed myth that hardly any US Senators have a passport is incorrect. So broadly had this belief entered into the collective mind that Caspar Weinberger, the former Secretary of Defence during the Reagan administration (hardly an anti-American speaker), gave an address to the World Affairs Council in Los Angeles in 1999 where he claimed that more than 50 per cent of US Congresspersons did not have a passport. Other sources, including an introductory textbook on international politics, claim that 80 per cent of Congresspersons do not own a passport.[35] Closer to the truth was a 2000 *New York Times* study, which reported that 93 per cent of Congresspersons owned passports.[36] It is hard to imagine this percentage decreasing now that passports are required to travel to Canada, and more personal identification is required in American life than ever before as a reaction to the terrorist attacks of September 11, 2001.

This topic brings together a heady mix of myths and damning realities. For example, a 2002 National Geographic study showed Americans to be the least capable of the young people tested in 9 nations to correctly answer what the population of the US was (the most popular answer by Americans was between 1–2 billion people); and Americans were the least likely to be able to locate the United States on a world map.

Of the 9 nations surveyed – a sample of 18–24 year olds were asked a series of questions – Mexicans were the weakest, followed by Americans; Germans and Swedes were by far the most knowledgeable. In the 2002 survey, only 14% of Americans surveyed could locate Israel on a map of the Middle East; 13% could identify Iraq, and the same percentage could identify Iran. Later, in a 2006 study by National Geographic, 25% of Americans were able to identify Israel, 37% Iraq and 26% Iran, proving Ambrose Bierce unfortunately right when he quipped "War is God's way of teaching Americans geography." However, Americans were the least knowledgeable on where the Taliban and al Qaeda were located, even after a war had been launched in Afghanistan. As for America's key ally Britain, only 36% of Americans could locate it on a map of Europe.

Why do Americans show this clear weakness in geography? It is not as though American education is the worst when compared to the other nations in the National Geographic survey. America has some of the best college students and universities in the world (Shanghai's Jiao Tong University's rankings and the London *Times* rankings attest to the strength of the US higher education system). At the high school level, American students rank mid-table in terms of literacy and numeracy in the highly regarded PISA rankings of educational attainment among OECD nations. One might then assume that Americans would score in middling fashion on geography tests; but this is not the case. The reasons for this weak showing in geographic knowledge are generally thought to be these: a lack of school study of geography; less likeliness among Americans to travel overseas compared to citizens of other nations; less time watching or reading foreign news; and less likeliness to study a foreign language. Conversely, according to the study, young Germans and Swedes – who scored highest – spend much more time following international affairs in the media, are more likely to have travelled outside of their own country, and are much more likely to speak a foreign language. Add to this America's size, importance in the world, domination of global media, and grip on the global public's imagination, and America's insularity begins to make some sense. One simple example of this is the way US elections are followed in incredible detail around the globe. Australians, Brits, and Germans follow US elections intently, but Americans barely follow foreign elections at all. The coverage of foreign elections in the American media is minuscule as shown by a survey of the coverage of a number of international elections in two American newspapers the *New York Times* and *USA Today*. [37] For the 2013 Australian and German elections *The Times* had 20 articles on each election while *USA Today* featured 8 on the Australian election and 13 on the Germany election. For the 2012 French election *The Times* had 30 articles and *USA Today* 8. As for the 2011 election in America's nearest northern neighbor Canada, *The Times* only had 14 articles in total.[38] Conversely the British *Guardian* had about 250 articles and the *Australian* newspaper had about 300 articles on the 2012 US elections.[39] These figures are representative of the generally unreciprocated interest foreigners show in American elections. A survey of television coverage would surely reveal more extreme asymmetries in coverage.

The academic literature on ignorance

That Americans are ignorant and insular has been a long-held conviction and stereotype in both academia and the public sphere worldwide. The best comparative evidence we have suggests it is true, which raises two more important questions: why are Americans particularly ill-informed about the rest of the world and how does this impact on US foreign policy? One of the challenges is how to measure ignorance, particularly in the cases of those who reject expert opinion or scientific finding. To avoid initially getting bogged down in such debates, the starting point for how I will measure knowledge will be simple factual questions about global geography and current affairs, for example, asking whether respondents can name the Secretary General of the UN. As Philip Converse argues, pop quizzes on current affairs may seem trivial, but this knowledge is "diagnostic of more profound differences in the amount and accuracy of contextual information voters bring to their judgments."[40] Furthermore, the small body of high quality academic articles written so far relies upon such quizzes to pronounce Americans particularly ignorant on foreign affairs compared to people in other industrialised countries. In the 1990s the leader in this academic field was Stephen Bennett who wrote two thorough and thoughtful articles on ignorance,[41] which drew particularly on two surveys conducted for the Times Mirror Center for the People and the Press.[42] Table 6.1 summarises the results in 1996.[43]

The best survey data also suggested that rank ignorance existed more commonly in the US than in other industrialised societies.[44] These scholars all asked why this ignorance was particularly strong in the US and concluded that Americans were let down by their media and education system, both of which did not focus significantly on global affairs.[45]

In a 2009 study by Iyengar et al., the authors compare the knowledge of Americans with that of the Swiss. Americans perform poorly in absolute and relative terms. The authors conclude that: "what little evidence there is suggests that Americans tend to know less than Europeans about international affairs."[46] In fact,

TABLE 6.1 Knowledge of foreign affairs

	Canada	Britain	US	Germany	France
Know Boris Yeltsin is president of Russia	59.3	64.8	52.9	94.2	60.2
Know North Korea may pull out of Nuclear Treaty	12.2	11.1	23.4	47.8	7.0
Know Boutros Boutros Ghali's job	26.0	22.6	14.8	60.5	31.3
Know Serbs surrounded Sarajevo	42.2	48.1	31.7	77.3	54.9
Know Israel made peace with Palestine	50.0	59.6	44.5	78.6	59.6

they have evidence that even Americans with a college degree were weaker on global current affairs questions than Swiss who had failed to complete high school; a disappointing outcome given the greater focus on global affairs and foreign relations over the last couple of decades in American higher educations. Tables 6.2a and 6.2b give a snapshot of these knowledge disparities:

TABLE 6.2A Hard news items

	Switzerland	United States
Knew name of Prime Minister of Britain	82.2	50.7
Knew name of President of Mexico (United States)/ France (Switzerland)	85.0	46.4
Knew name of Secretary General of United Nations	76.1	17.8
Named two countries with troops in Iraq	70.7	20.2
Knew the issue addressed in the Kyoto Protocol	56.7	18.9

TABLE 6.2B Soft news items

	Switzerland	United States
Knew name of winner of the Tour de France in 2005	72.3	60.8
Knew country to host 2008 Olympic Summer games	29.6	14.2
Knew crime Michael Jackson's accused of	91.0	77.1
Knew Tom Cruise's religious organization	46.5	50.3

Source: Iyengar, Shanto, K.S.Hahn, and H. Bonfadelli (2009), "Dark Areas of Ignorance: Revisited Comparing International Affairs Knowledge in Switzerland and the United States", *Communication Research*, 36(3), 341–358.

When researching for this chapter I came across these examples of American ignorance about foreign affairs:

- In 1964 a quarter of Americans had never heard of the Vietnam War and 54 per cent had never heard of Mao Zedong.[47]
- During the 1980s most Americans were unaware of who the Contras were, with one poll finding that 30 per cent of the respondents identified Norway as the country where the Contras were fighting instead of Nicaragua.[48]
- A 1988 survey identified that "one in three Americans could not name a single member of NATO" and remarkably "16 per cent thought the Soviet Union was a member of the Western Alliance."[49]
- Even after the 9/11 Commission had said there were no weapons of mass destruction in Iraq, a majority of Americans still believed there were. Only a third of Americans understood that much of the world opposed the invasion

of Iraq. Another third thought that the invasion had full global support while a third perceived the rest of the world to be neutral.[50]

• "In the spring of 2004 there was extensive coverage of the 9/11 Commission's finding that there was no evidence Saddam supported al Qaeda. Yet in August of the same year, according to a PIPA poll, 50 percent of Americans still insisted that Saddam had given 'substantial' support to al Qaeda. (A full two years later, in 2006, a Zogby International poll indicated that 46 percent of Americans continued to believe that 'there is a link between Saddam Hussein and the 9/11 terrorist attacks'. The illusion that Saddam was behind 9/11 had real-world consequences. A poll for Investor's Business Daily and Christian Science Monitor cited by the PIPA researchers found that 80 percent of those who backed the Iraq War in 2003 said that a key reason for their support was their belief that Saddam had ties to al Qaeda".[51]

The most comprehensive surveys of comparative geographic knowledge conducted by National Geographic in 1989, 2002, and 2006 have Americans consistently near the bottom of national rankings.[52] This evidence begins to substantiate the common perception that Americans are particularly ignorant about international relations.

Ignorance or anti-Americanism?

It would be extremely useful to know far more about how much the average American knows (compared to Europeans or Australasians) about world events, the leaders of various countries, and global geography from the end of the Second World War (the beginning of many large scale social science studies) until the present. However, this subject has not been studied in any great depth by social scientists to date, making the existing data patchy. One important reason for this paucity of data is that people tend not to test information on topics where the answers are thought to be obvious (and seldom challenged). An example demonstrating the scarcity of these data sets can be found in an article by Loch Johnson and Kiki Caruson published in 2003 in *PS*, an official publication of the American Political Science Association (in other words, an esteemed professional source that should be concerned with getting its facts straight). Johnson and Caruson claim that the United States "is the only nation in the world where scholars can earn a doctorate without demonstrating competence in any foreign language."[53] They also suggest that American high school students have the worst knowledge of world geography of students in any Western nation. On hearing these two "facts", many would nod their heads sagely, and lament what they perceive to be the continued insularity and ignorance of the American nation. I happened to have a personal interest in the first fact, and after reading it, I wrote to one of the article's authors, Loch Johnson, to invite him to write a piece for a four volume series on anti-Americanism I was editing, and to let him know that America's mono-linguistic tendencies were not as unique as he had claimed. After all, you do not need any proficiency whatsoever in another language to complete a PhD in Australia, New

Zealand or the United Kingdom. Apparently, my email was not heeded, as Johnson's more recent book, *Seven Sins of American Foreign Policy* (2007), repeats the same error about PhDs and language proficiency. Why he chose not to correct the error I am not sure, but such exaggerations suggest the power of certain myths. Johnson's book, which is certainly not without its merits, also claims that American high school students have the worst knowledge of world geography of any Western nation. He does present some damning statistics, such as the claim that "50 percent of high school students in Hartford, Connecticut, could not name three countries in Africa".[54] However, most of the statistics are from the 1980s. One would think that less dated statistics could be found on such an "important" subject that allegedly carries such negative consequences.

The above examples (the errant Weinberger claim and the unflattering National Geographic findings) clearly encapsulate the problem that this chapter confronts: namely that myths, exaggerations, and damning realities have become mixed up. The data I have collected will hopefully become the starting place for further studies and prompt the collection of more detailed statistics. However, such data ultimately only tell part of the story of strong perceptions of American ignorance around the world.

Such perceptions are nothing new: from as early as the 1830s this has been a fairly constant refrain, a time well before statistics and data were collected on many important topics.[55] The New World, and then the United States of America, has been contrasted with Old World Europe in a dichotomised fashion since its discovery. The New World was seen positively as a golden land – an Eden – compared to the corrupt and decrepit Old World; seen negatively, it was a humid and barren wasteland compared to the civilised beauty of Old World estates and long cultivated pastures of plenty (the Old World was a Wordsworthian paradise, whereas the New World was the deformed hell of Hieronymus Bosch). The positive accounts tended to focus on humanity's chance to start afresh in the New World, and appealed particularly to those fleeing religious persecution who established towns with names such as Eden, New Haven and New Jerusalem in colonial America. The negative critiques began with American nature and animals (e.g. that dogs did not bark in America or that animals and vegetables there were shrunken and deformed), but receded as they became empirically more and more difficult to sustain.[56] But the demise of the environmental critique soon gave way to negative cultural critique.

In the 1820s and 1830s a view of America as uncouth, while simultaneously brash and boastful was cemented as a dominant stereotype about Americans. This was not just the opinion of notoriously harsh critics of America (such as Frances Trollope and Charles Dickens), but the opinion of scores of European travel writers – I have looked at over 200 books written in the early 19th century by travellers and commentators, many of which attest to this. From these accounts, one can see the stereotype of the ignorant American being developed; and by their distribution, this stereotype was exported around the world. Strongly negative assertions about America were already circulating in the late 18th century (Talleyrand's "32 religions and just one dish" comes immediately to mind), but assessments of America became more consistently negative in the early 19th century. It was from this body of literature and commentary that the enduring negative tropes of Americans emerged. According to these works, Americans were culturally uncouth – altogether unsophisticated in matters of literature, the arts and world affairs. The style of writing during this period was sweeping and grand, leading to a bold summary of American traits that modern commentators might well baulk at. Some writers were more circumspect and nuanced, but it was the more brash statements about America that were remembered and regularly retold. This tendency to use extreme examples is certainly entertaining to the reader, but it unfortunately also serves to sensationalise and misrepresent nations and their people. In my view, 19th century travel writing was crucial in shaping perceptions about American society and about American ignorance and insularity.

It is important to acknowledge, however, that most of the important commentators had a combination of negative and positive things to say about America; but it was the period from the 1820s through to the 1850s (which has been deemed by Malcolm Bradbury as the most negative in transatlantic commentary) that was possibly the most important in shaping perceptions. This was the case because the populaces of Europe of this time period were clearly fascinated by America and eager to learn more about it (this accounts for the impressive sales figures for books about America in Europe, particularly for critical books). The popularity of Frances Trollope's *Domestic Manners of the Americans*, which went through numerous re-printings in the 19th century and was translated into a number of languages, is one of the many examples of this quest for information. Oscar Wilde noted in a moment of moderation that it was the barbaric America of Buffalo Bill that Europeans wanted to see or hear about, not the more refined America of New England theatre or American liberal arts colleges.

These stereotypes about Americans from the 1830s and 1840s have stuck,[57] creating a stock of characters and stories that Europeans and others instinctively call upon when they hear the word "American". These images have been enhanced and complicated by other historical events and developments, but the basic stereotypes were formed and cemented in the 1830s. They have been repeated ever since, with the repeaters simply updating older anecdotal characters with more modern, relevant ones. Many of the negative comments about President George W. Bush (that he was a know-nothing, inarticulate, unsophisticated hick, for example) had been said about Americans in the 1830s and 1840s. There was nothing new about these insults, and it was this familiarity that imparted some of their rhetorical appeal and bite.

In summary, the prevailing view of Americans as insular is best understood as a perception that developed throughout the nineteenth century rather than being a recent phenomenon. This perception was developed and then cemented in the European imagination about America in the 1830s and 1840s and has been recycled ever since. Part of the frustration here is with Americans for not reciprocating the interest non-Americans take in them. It is a totalising prejudice. Classic examples of anti-Americanism are statements such as "all Americans are fat," "Americans are ignorant," and "American foreign policies are evil." These examples, among others, are all normal markers of prejudice: a lack of differentiation, bias, fixation on the worst actions and events, exaggeration, prejudgment, one-sidedness, and a lack of context.

So how do we avoid falling into prejudices about American ignorance? My answer here is to use the tools of academic historians and social scientists to test anecdotal claims that Americans are less interested in and knowledgeable about the world than people in other developed countries. Using social science, I have collected the relevant data available to measure ignorance and insularity. The data analysed thus far suggests a comparative weakness in the global geographic and international affairs knowledge of Americans. The foreign language proficiency of Americans is also comparatively weak. However, while the data is useful to get to a more precise understanding of American ignorance, it is important to note that hard evidence is only peripheral to most discussions about American ignorance. To understand the powerful perception that Americans are without doubt more ignorant than anyone else we of course need to take an historical approach. I have collected around 200 diaries of travellers from the late 18th and 19th century, who, time and time again, complain about and comment on American uncouthness, ignorance and arrogance. These three negative characterisations of Americans have been oft-repeated throughout the last 200 years. These sentiments were expressed toward the populist President Andrew Jackson in the 19th century just as they have been expressed toward President George W. Bush and President Trump this century. Whether such leaders reflect the ignorance of the American people has been a topic of considerable attention. The stereotype has been that both leaders were propelled to victory by a wave of voting by poorly informed working class whites. This narrative often underplayed the large proportion of votes that Trump and Bush received from middle class and wealthy whites (in other words regular Republican voters). As Nancy Isenberg has argued in *White Trash*, blaming less educated whites for the election of Republican presidents, trades on long-standing anti-working-class prejudices.[58] However, minus the language of "blaming", it is an argument that should not be entirely dismissed. The evidence suggests that non-college educated whites swung in overwhelming numbers away from the Democratic Party in 2016 and voted instead for Trump. This voting behaviour is deemed pivotal to Trump winning the key states of Ohio, Pennsylvania, Michigan, and Wisconsin.[59] For non-Americans it is very tempting to blame these voters for being ignorant and gullible, to see them as the latest iteration of the ignorant American. Furthermore, to see this ignorance as responsible for putting the planet in peril as global warming worsens[60] while the plight of many millions of political, economic, and ecological refugees is not just ignored, but denigrated. The reality of why the US and much of the rest of the world is not addressing these calamitous problems is more complex. Nonetheless, ignorance about these problems is a significant impediment to why they are not more sensibly and more humanely addressed.

Notes

1 Paul Kennedy, *The Rise and Fall of the Great Powers* (London: Unwin Hyman, 1987); Eric Edelman, "*Understanding America's Contested Primacy*," Center for Strategic and Budgetary Assessments, 2010, <http://www.csbaonline.org/publications/2010/10/understanding-americas-contested-primacy/>; James Fallows "How America Can Rise Again." *Atlantic Monthly*, January/February 2010, <https://www.theatlantic.com/magazine/archive/2010/01/how-america-can-rise-again/307839/>.

2 Michael Cox, "Is the United States in Decline—Again? An Essay," *International Affairs* 83, 4 (2007), 643–653; Gideon Rachman, G. "Think Again: American Decline," *Foreign Policy* 184 (2011), 59–63; Stephen Walt, "The End of the American Era," *The National Interest*, October 2011; Charles Kupchan, "Second Mates," *National Journal*, March 15, 2012; Michael Beckley, "China's Century?" *International Security* 36, 3 (Winter 2011/12), 41–78.

3 George Packer, "Broken Contract: Inequality and American Decline," *Foreign Affairs* 90, 6 (2011), 21–30.

4 Fareed Zakaria, "Can America be Fixed? The New Crisis of Democracy," *Foreign Affairs* 92, 1 (2013), 22–33.

5 Edward Luce, *Time to Start Thinking: America and the Spectre of Decline* (London: Little, Brown, 2012).

6 Richard N. Haass, *Foreign Policy Begins at Home: The Case for Putting America's House in Order* (New York: Basic Books, 2013).

7 George Will, "The End of Our Holiday From History," *The Washington Post*, September 12, 2001 <https://www.washingtonpost.com/archive/opinions/2001/09/12/the-end-o f-our-holiday-from-history/9da607fd-8fdc-4f33-b7c9-e6cda00453bb/?utm_term=.62137a 81b949>.

8 Michael Hunt develops this argument when he contends that: "U.S. foreign-policy ideology has also proven disabling by cutting Americans off from an understanding of, not to mention sympathy for, cultures distant from our own. The sense of national superiority central to that ideology has given rise to stereotypes that diminish other people by exaggerating the seemingly negative aspects of their lives and by constricting the perceived range of their skills, accomplishments, and emotions. By denigrating other cultures as backward or malleable, these stereotypes raise in Americans false expectations that it is an easy enterprise to induce and direct political change and economic development." (Michael Hunt, *US Foreign Policy and Ideology* (Yale, 1987) 176)

9 David Campbell, *Writing Security: United States Foreign Policy and the Politics of Identity*. Revised edition (Minneapolis: University of Minnesota Press, 1998); Walter Russell Mead, *Special Providence: American Foreign Policy and How it Changed the World* (New York: Routledge, 2002); Ole Holsti, *Public Opinion and American Foreign Policy* (Ann Arbor: University of Michigan Press, 1996); Ted Hopf, *Reconstructing the Cold War: The Early Years, 1945–1958* (New York: Oxford University Press 2012); James M. McCormick, ed. *The Domestic Sources of American Foreign Policy: Insights and Evidence*. Sixth edition (Lanham: Rowman & Littlefield Publishers, 2012).

10 Stephen Brooks, *As Others See Us: the Causes and Consequences of Foreign Perceptions of America* (New York: Broadview Press 2006); Loch K. Johnson, *Seven Sins of American Foreign Policy* (New York: Pearson Longman, 2007).

11 Johnson, *Seven Sins of American Foreign Policy*.

12 Along with the significant reservoir of negative stories about American ignorance (and Americans in general), there are of course many positive stories. My favourite – which shows Americans to have both a sense of humour (one frequent claim is that they missed out on the humour gene) and a knowledge of geography – is this one: "Rumor has it that Anthony Hopkins was once in conversation with a New York taxi driver. "Where do you come from?" asked the driver. "Wales," said Hopkins. "What do you mean?" asked the driver. "Wales – which is it? Diana's feller, the big fish or them singing bastards?"" John Davies, "Wales and America", *North American Journal of Welsh Studies* 1, 1 (Winter 2001), 11.

13 Bill Bryson, *Mother Tongue* (New York: Avon Books, 1990) 195.

14 *Toledo Blade*, "Reagan Considering Trip to the Far East," December 6, 1982, 1.

15 Lou Cannon, *President Reagan* (New York: Simon & Schuster, 1991) 462.

16 *Der Spiegel*, "Do You Have Blacks in Brazil?" May 29, 2002, <http://web.archive.org/web/20021119114842/http://www.gwbush.com/copies/trans.html>.

17 CIA World Factbook, "Brazil," <https://www.cia.gov/library/publications/the-world-factbook/geos/br.html>. "After seeing the astonishment on the face of the Brazilian president at Bush's question, it was Condoleezza Rice, national security advisor,

who managed to salvage the situation by telling her own boss that Brazil probably had more blacks than the USA and that it is also probably the country with the most blacks outside of Africa. The black population of Brazil is a legacy of the fact that Brazil had far more slaves from Africa than anywhere else in the New World – up to eight times as many as were in the United States." *Der Spiegel*, "Gibt es Schwarze in Brasilien?" May 19, 2002, *Der Spiegel* <http://www.spiegel.de/panorama/bushs-allgemeinbildung-gib t-es-schwarze-in-brasilien-a-196865.html>.

18 David Milkkelson, "Bush on Blacks in Brazil," *Snopes*, June 6, 2002, <https://www. snopes.com/fact-check/black-tuesday/>

19 "Miss Teen USA 2007 – South Carolina Answers a Question" (August 24, 2007), [video file]. Retrieved from: <http://www.youtube.com/watch?v=lj3iNxZ8Dww>.

20 'Miss Teen USA South Carolina 2007 with Subtitles" (August 26, 2007) [video file]. Retrieved from <https://www.youtube.com/watch?v=WALIARHHLII>. Is Miss Teen South Carolina any more representative of the "average" American than the child geniuses who appear in the American National Geography Bee conducted amongst school children in America every year? A summary of the 2007 competition – "National Geographic Geography Bee" (September 18, 2006), [video file] retrieved from <http://www.youtube.com/watch?v=51VpD-TU2gw> – has a small number of hits compared with the gaffe by the Miss Teen entrant, bringing to mind Oscar Wilde's observation that "English people are far more interested in American barbarism than they are in American civilization." Oscar Wilde, "The American Invasion," *Virtual Library*, <http://www.farid-hajji.net/books/en/Wilde_Oscar/spp-chap07.html>.

21 On unilateralism, John Halstead writes: "The trouble is that unilateralism feeds on ignorance, and ignorance breeds bad policy. Less heed is paid to the views and interests of allies, and multilateral forms of consultation and cooperation may be bypassed. In the process, diplomatic methods may be subordinated to military measures, and political and economic leadership may be made hostage to the emphasis on military strength. Too easily, a vicious circle can be created in which freedom of action is bought at the expense of international cooperation, without which the policies undertaken cannot, in fact, succeed." (John G. H. Halstead, "From the North: A Canadian View" in *As Others See Us: United States Diplomacy Viewed from Abroad*, Margery Boichel Thompson (ed.) (Washington, D.C.: Institute for the Study of Diplomacy, 1989), 34–35)

22 William Lederer and Eugene Burdick, *The Ugly American* (London: Transworld Publishers, 1958), 287.

23 Stephen Brooks, *America through Foreign Eyes* (Don Mills, Ont.: Oxford University Press, 2002), 22.

24 George F. Kennan, *American Diplomacy, 1900–1950* (New York, Mentor Book/New American Library, 1951), 58–59. Walter Russell Mead argues that democracies are slower to go to war, but once at war a democracy may well be more brutal in its search for total victory than a non-democratic society would be. Mead, *Special Providence*.

25 Kennan, *American Diplomacy, 1900–1950.*

26 George W. Bush, "State of the Union Address," in *The White House Archives*, January 29, 2002, <https://georgewbush-whitehouse.archives.gov/news/releases/2002/01/20020129-11.html>.

27 In an October 11, 2001 press conference, George W. Bush posed a question to himself about why there was so much hatred in some Islamic countries towards America. His answer was: "I'm amazed that there's such misunderstanding of what our country is about, that people would hate us. I am – like most Americans, I just can't believe it because I know how *good* we are." George W. Bush, "Bush on State of War', *Washington Post,* October 11, 2002, <http://www.washingtonpost.com/wp-srv/nation/specials/attacked/transcripts/bush_text101101.html>.

28 *Source Watch*, "Evil-doers', <http://www.sourcewatch.org/index.php?title=Evil-doers>.

29 This would also enhance the powers of the presidency (creating what Schlesinger called the Imperial Presidency). Recent books by Andrew Bacevich (*The Limits of Power* (Melbourne, Black Inc., 2008)), Peter Beinart (*The Icarus Syndrome* (New York, Harper

Collins, 2010)), and John Mueller (*Overblown* (New York: Free Press, 2006)) all argue that the exaggeration of threats is a central theme of US foreign policy, from the Cold War containment doctrine (outlined most muscularly in NC68) through to the "war on terror".

30 J. William Fulbright, *The Arrogance of Power* (New York: Vintage Books, 1966), 12.

31 William J. Lederer and Eugene Burdick, *The Ugly American* (London: Corgi Books, 1958), 274–276.

32 James Reston in Lederer and Burdick, *The Ugly American*, 275.

33 Rajiv Chandrasekaran, *Imperial Life in the Emerald City* (New York: Vintage Books, 2007), 179–180, 183, 185, 242, 314.

34 Jeff Stein, "Can You Tell a Sunni From a Shiite?" *New York Times*, October 17, 2006, <http://www.nytimes.com/2006/10/17/opinion/17stein.html>. Jeff Stein, "Democrats New Intelligence Chairman Needs a Crash Course on al Qaeda," *CQ.com*, December 8, 2006, <http://www.freerepublic.com/focus/f-news/1751042/posts>.

35 Keith Suter, *50 Things You Want to Know About World Issues But Were too Afraid to Ask* (Sydney: Random House, 2009), 35.

36 Eric Schmitt and Elizabeth Becker, "Insular Congress Appears to Be Myth," *New York Times*, November 4, 2000.

37 The three highest circulation newspapers in the US are the *Wall Street Journal*, the *New York Times* and *USA Today* roughly in this order depending on how circulation is counted.

38 Admittedly the 2011 Canadian election was a snap poll after the budget was rejected by the House of Commons and the House went on to pass a non-confidence motion against the incumbent government. These circumstances meant that there was just over a month of official campaigning.

39 Evidence gathered from *Factiva* news database.

40 Philip E. Converse, "Assessing the Capacity of Mass Electorates," *Annual Review of Political Science* 3, 1 (2000), 331–353, 333.

41 Stephen E. Bennett, "'Know Nothings' Revisited Again," *Political Behaviour* 18, 3 (1996), 219–233; Stephen E. Bennett, Richard Flickinger, John Baker, Staci Rhine and Linda Bennett, "Citizens' Knowledge of Foreign Affairs," *The Harvard International Journal of Press/Politics* 1, 2 (1996). 10–29.

42 Andrew Kohut, Robert Toth and Carol Bowman, "Mixed Message about Press Freedom on Both Sides of Atlantic," *Times Mirror Center for the People and the Press News Release*, March 16, 1994.

43 Bennett, et al. "Citizens' Knowledge of Foreign Affairs," 15.

44 Shanto Iyengar, Kyo Hahn, Heinz Bonfadelli and Mirko Marr, "Dark Areas of Ignorance Revisited: Comparing International Affairs Knowledge in Switzerland and the United States," *Communication Research* 36, 3 (2009), 341–358.

45 Bennett, "Know Nothings Revisited Again"; Bennett, et al. "Citizens' Knowledge of Foreign Affairs,"; Iyengar, et al. "Dark Areas of Ignorance Revisited.

46 Iyengar, et al. "Dark Areas of Ignorance Revisited|.

47 Jerel Rosati and James Scott, *The Politics of United States Foreign Policy*, Sixth edition (Boston: Wadsworth, Cengage Learning, 2014), 345.

48 Mead, *Special Providence*.

49 Rosati and Scott, *The Politics of United States Foreign Policy*.

50 Bret Schulte, "The Ignorant American Voter," *USA Today*, June 3, 2008, <http://www.usnews.com/news/national/articles/2008/06/03/the-ignorant-american-voter>.

51 Rick Shenkman, *Just How Stupid Are We?: Facing the Truth about the American Voter* (New York: Basic Books, 2008).

52 National Geographic Education Foundation, "National Geographic – Roper 1988 Global Geographic Literacy Survey" (Washington, D.C.: Roper ASW, 1988); National Geographic Education Foundation, "National Geographic – Roper 2002 Global Geographic Literacy Survey" (Washington, D.C.: Roper ASW, 2002); National Geographic Education Foundation, "National Geographic – Roper Public Affairs 2006 Geographic Literacy Study" (Washington, D.C.: Roper ASW, 2006).

53 Loch Johnson and Kiki Caruson, "The Seven Sins of American Foreign Policy," *PS*, January 2003, 5.
54 Johnson, *Seven Sins of American Foreign Policy*, 56.
55 That is not to say statistics do not exist entirely. We have fascinating data on the establishment of public libraries and on book borrowing in 19th century America. This information leads Howard Munford Jones to conclude that the level of book reading in New England and Virginia was probably not that different to England in the early 19th century. However, the level of book borrowing was much less, as might be expected, in the frontier states of the mid-west (Howard Mumford Jones, *America and French Culture, 1750–1848* (Chapel Hill: The University of North Carolina Press, 1927)). However, measuring how much Americans knew about all sorts of important topics throughout the 19th century generally never occurred (elections thus remain the best insight into mass opinion in this period).
56 Antonello Gerbi, *The Dispute of the New World; The History of a Polemic, 1750–1900* (Pittsburgh: University of Pittsburgh Press, 1973).
57 Philippe Roger argues in his history of French anti-Americanism that the narrative begins earlier: "It did not start with the Vietnam War or with the cold war – or even in the 1930s, which was its peak. Nearly all the ingredients were there more than a century ago: its narrative structures had largely been formed, its argumentation polished up, and its rhetoric broken in as early as the 1890's" (Philippe Roger, *The American Enemy* (Chicago: Chicago University Press, 2005, p.xi). My problem with Roger's position is that the narrative does not take hold of the broader public imagination on America until later; perhaps he is correct about elite opinion, but I would claim that it takes longer for negative stereotypes of Americans as uncouth and unsophisticated to have widespread popular currency. Roger's view mirrors mine when he argues that "The statue of the American Enemy raised by the French, however, is a work in progress: each successive generation tinkers at it, tightening its bolts. But its pedestal is well established. And its foundations – the Enlightenment's strange hostility to the New World, which I will examine in the prologue—are over two hundred years old" (p. xi). Also, he rightly argues: "A discourse of this kind works through repetition. Its strength is in its stubbornness. Its peaks can of course be charted (by opinion polls, for instance), but its most important element is elsewhere: in a long, drawn-out stratification of images, legends, jokes, anecdotes, beliefs, and affects. Shedding light on all of these elements takes more than just opinion polls (which, rather than plumbing the depths, offer a snapshot of a given moment): you have to root around, dig up old deposits, excavate the matter, clear out the veins, and follow the seams." (pp. xi–xii)
58 Nancy Isenberg, *White Trash: The 400-Year Untold History of Class in America* (New York: Penguin, 2016).
59 John Sides, Michael Tesler and Lynn Vavreck, *Identity Crisis* (Princeton: Princeton University Press, 2018).
60 Elizabeth Kolbert, "What Is Donald Trump's Response to the U.N.'s Dire Climate Report?" *New Yorker*, October 22, 2018, <https://www.newyorker.com/magazine/2018/10/22/what-is-donald-trumps-response-to-the-uns-dire-climate-report>.

7

THE TRUMP FACTOR

The ugly American, popular culture, and populism

If non-Americans could have voted in 2016 for what is often called "the leader of the free world," Hillary Clinton would easily have been elected President. Late in 2016 Gallup surveyed world opinion and not surprisingly found that support around the world for Donald Trump was extremely weak, apart from in Russia. Trump support was polled at 15 per cent in Australia, 8 per cent in Germany, 5 per cent in Mexico, 4 per cent in Spain, and 3 per cent in Jordan, Japan and South Korea.[1] Some of this had to do with what Trump flagged as his possible foreign policies: the Japanese and South Koreans were described as key allies one day, and then told to look after themselves more the next day, possibly, by pursuing nuclear arsenals. Mexicans were told that they were going to pay for that "tremendous wall" along their roughly 3,200-kilometre border with the United States, which would cost approximately US$12 billion to build. This boast was unlikely to win Mexicans over to Trump. However, while there was widespread disapproval of Trump's nationalist, protectionist and racist policies during the 2016 campaign, it was Trump's persona that most repelled non-Americans. Trump continues to be strongly disliked across the world because he is the archetypal "ugly American": obnoxious, uncouth, boastful, materialistic, and duplicitous. Understanding this reaction forces us to consider longstanding stereotypes about Americans, how Trump's behaviour reinforces these stereotypes and how the stereotypes shape the discourse used to condemn Trump. Donald Trump is one of those types of Americans that foreigners have instantly strong opinions about. When George W. Bush ran for the presidency, and when Sarah Palin was chosen by Senator John McCain as his presidential running-mate, there was a mountain of criticism around the globe about their ignorance and parochialism. People everywhere seemed to be saying – based on very little information but with a certain astuteness – "I know this kind of American and I do not like them." This reaction occurs because there is a long-standing stock of negative stereotypes about the "ugly American" that go back to the early 19th century, which are instantly available to animate one's feelings. Future research on Trump and anti-Americanism has rich material with which to explore these stereotypes and ask: "what insights do they provide?" Below I will sketch what this research might examine.

Trump as the ugly American

In Chapter 2 of this book I outlined how European travel writers in the 1820s and 1830s crafted a caricature of the American people that has been oft-repeated ever since. This portrait of the American people highlighted six stereotypes, which have had a remarkably consistent and persistent shelf life, having been recycled for nearly two centuries. At times these stereotypes have been moderated by new developments and at times they have been animated by fresh events. The 19th century stereotypes were these: that American manners were extremely deficient; that Americans were often anti-intellectual, uncultured, and ignorant; that Americans lived ultimately bland lives; that Americans were particularly prone to boastful and annoying patriotism; that Americans were money obsessed and financially untrustworthy; and finally, that Americans were hypocrites. Trump, for many, is the embodiment of these negative national stereotypes: he is widely seen as the ultimate ugly American.

In terms of manners, Trump is the schoolyard bully as CEO. Trump's bad manners could generously be viewed as anti-elitist populism challenging the failing status quo. But many outside the US view them as the crude rantings of a narcissist. Bad manners are a key element of Trump's shtick.[2] He breaks with US political decorum repeatedly and with relish. Trump's default self, that he has become used to delivering in an unfiltered manner, is self-righteous, egotistical and boorish, and this is apparently what some people find genuine about him. In the era of endless selfies, commonplace lying about one's age, obsession with celebrity and reality television, we probably should not be surprised that this "look at me, no matter how nasty I am" type of person is popular. Trump has boasted that he has a high IQ,[3] and that he was top of his class when he attended the Wharton School of Business.[4] Both of these claims are pure assertion and carry little credibility with non-Americans who tend to view Trump as an uncouth anti-intellectual. Trump, with his simplistic solutions, his lowest common denominator attacks on his political opponents, and his constant disregard for experts and their findings, is in fact top of the class of loud-mouthed American bloviators for many. In the mid-19th century, similar nativist rhetoric was associated with the Know-Nothing anti-immigration movement. The third stereotype – that Americans are sameish and live bland lives – would seem at first glance to miss the mark with Trump. This view of Americans is that their lives, to quote Alexis de Tocqueville, are particularly "unpoetic" and that they live by clichés and hollow catchphrases like "have a nice day" and "you're fired". If one takes a deeper look at Trump and his enterprises, he has a remarkable talent for making glamour bland and soulless. The fact that Rebecca Sonit's essay the "The Loneliness of Donald Trump" was widely shared on the Internet exemplifies the strength of this perception of the soulless Trump. Solnit presents a man that is the personification of what Hannah Arendt called the "banality of evil" because of his total lack of self-perception and self-reflection.[5]

Behind all the bluster and his claims that he is "very highly educated, I know words, I have the best words,"[6] Trump's vocabulary is repetitive and dull as he recites the same platitudes and self-praise over and over.[7] And for all of his money, the Trump diet consists of plenty of McDonald's, extremely well done crispy steak, diet cola, and no alcohol.[8] In a world where eating a variety of food has become commonplace, Trump's diet lacks sophistication and imagination. It is not only unhealthy, but many around the world would see it as trashy. I wrote about Trump's diet and the perception that he has bland and unadventurous tastes in a 2016 newspaper article and received a lot of criticism from various conservative commentators that my comments were snobbish and anti-American. My point is that lots of people see Trump this way, not that it is necessarily a particularly insightful way of critiquing Trump or those who eat at McDonald's.

When it comes to boasting, Trump is constantly self-congratulatory and arguably the biggest self-promoter in living memory. His "America first" patriotism was expressed during the 2016 campaign with his oft-made claim that America will get so used to "winning" everything under a Trump presidency that it would get "so sick and tired of winning".[9] Trump brags about his wealth, properties, celebrity status, ability to sexually molest women with impunity, the size of his crowds, his poll numbers, his election victory, and his deal-making ability. In 2018, Trump famously told the leaders of the NATO nations that he was a "stable genius" before running Theresa May down to the British tabloid *The Sun*, while in the UK.[10] He then moved on to a summit press conference with Putin in Helsinki where he got his "nots" tied up when asked a question about Russian interference in the 2016 presidential election.[11]

Trump's status as a successful businessman was central to Trump's appeal to many Americans that one saw interviewed on television during the presidential election campaign. However, outside of America, boasting about your wealth and fame is still largely seen as gauche. The Wharton School was the first university Business School in America established in 1881, whereas Oxford University did not offer an MBA until 1996 when the Said Business School was established. As Tony Judt writes in *Ill Fares the Land*, well into the 20th century the brightest British students wanted to be diplomats and study philosophy and history, not business or law, which were long considered technical subjects chosen by the less academically gifted. In America money always talked and had a more revered place in society. This was noticed regularly by travel writers in the early 19th century. In *American Notes* Charles Dickens writes: "The love of trade is a reason why the literature of America is to remain forever unprotected [lacking respect for copyright]: 'For we are a trading people, and don't care for poetry.'"[12] Captain Frederick Marryat, another widely read travel writer of the 19th century, wrote of American commerce that:

> Trade demoralizes; there are so many petty arts and frauds necessary to be resorted to by every class in trade, to enable them to compete with each other; so many lies told, as a matter of business, to tempt a purchaser, that almost insensibly and by degrees the shopkeeper becomes dishonest.[13]

The single greatest threat to American morality and values in Marryat's view was the fact that "money is in America everything, and everything else nothing; it is the only sure possession, for character can at any time be taken from you, and therefore becomes less valuable than in other countries."[14] Two decades before Dickens' or Marryat's books appeared, the British traveller W. Faux wrote:

> It is the pride and pleasure of Americans to get into debt, and then by avoiding payment, show how adroitly they can cheat and wrong each other. Few look upon knavery with disgust, but rather with a smile of approbation. It is indeed difficult to trade with the people in an old plain honest way. Knavery damns the North, and slavery the South.[15]

These comments about money obsession could have been written about Trump's America two centuries later. The enduring strength of the idea of Americans as money-obsessed and swindlers is longstanding and powerful.

Lastly, the saying that "those in glasshouses should not throw stones" never seems to occur to Trump. Being a hypocrite clearly does not concern him and this is one of those infuriating traits that makes him so strongly disliked around the world. In the 19th century it was slavery (and to a lesser extent the poor treatment of native Americans) that travellers most noted as they called Americans out for their hypocrisy. Frances Trollope in her widely read *Domestic Manners of Americans* wrote that America's "eternal boast of liberty and their love of freedom" was empty. She states in strong language that she was

> revolted by the contradictions in their principles and practice... you will see them with one hand hoisting the cap of liberty and with the other flogging their slaves. You will see them one hour lecturing their mob on the indefensible rights of man, and the next driving from their homes the children of the soil, whom they have bound themselves to protect by the most solemn treaties.[16]

Racism continues to stain America's much proclaimed belief in freedom and the inalienable rights of all. High levels of poverty and inequality are also stains on the reputation of this wealthy nation.[17] From the Cold War onwards it has been American militarism that has most garnered the claim of hypocrisy. The phrase the "ugly American" dates to the Cold War era and brings to mind Americans in Vietnam proclaiming to be fighting to secure freedom and democracy while killing non-combatants and defoliating the countryside with napalm. America's Cold War hypocrisy was kept alive by Reagan calling the murderous Contra rebels in Nicaragua "freedom fighters" and even more peculiarly he also dubbed the anti-Soviet

Muslim mujahidin in Afghanistan "freedom fighters".[18] At the same time Reagan was calling the Ayatollah Khomeini the great Satan, his administration was selling military weapons to the Iranian regime. In the 21st century, American hypocrisy was firmly associated with the invasion and occupation of Iraq. Trump has eschewed the normal exceptionalist language of presidents, but nonetheless claims of hypocrisy have still surrounded him for his hypocrisy about sexual harassment,[19] naturalising his wife's parents via "chain migration", members of his administration using private email accounts for government business, and a wide range of other accusations of hypocrisy.

It is tempting to proclaim that Trump is very familiar to us because he embodies the worst things about Americans. However, these traits are apparent across the world. Trump therefore is not merely an "ugly American" but an amplification of commonplace global cultural trends. Those characteristics that Trump exemplifies, such as narcissism, self-centredness, gnat-like attention spans, obsessive self-regard,[20] ignorance,[21] preoccupation with the number of followers one has and a lack of interest in listening to others, are trends that are easy to pass off as particularly "American." But if we are honest, this behaviour is far from being exclusive to America. Preventing the next Trump – and there will be more – requires challenging the sources of selfishness in much of modern culture that are seemingly on the rise. If seeing Trump as the ugly American personified does not help us understand him, what is a better approach? I would argue that it is more useful to see Trump as the product of a therapeutic culture where creating resentment to be soothed has become a common approach to politics. As a result, providing realistic policy solutions is eschewed; instead, politics as mass therapy and entertainment has come to the fore.

In *The Culture of Narcissism* (1979) Christopher Lasch claimed that: "Having displaced religion as the organising framework of American culture, the therapeutic outlook threatens to displace politics as well."[22] In the early 21st century electoral politics has become a combination of therapy and entertainment. The liberal democratic understanding of politics as a rational debate over who gets what, when and how is generally overshadowed in electoral politics by spectacle and emotionally charged rhetoric which is aimed at making Americans feel better about themselves and their nation. Presidential candidates play the role of applicants for the position of Therapist in Chief (as much as Commander and Chief). "Make America Great Again" is as much about feelings as it is about changing material realities. The therapeutic approach to politics had been evident well before Trump emerged. Reagan and Obama both evoked the idea of American exceptionalism to sooth a restless nation. They presented their own lives as the modern version of Lincoln's Log Cabin to White House story of exceptionalism. Obama liked to say that "in no other country on Earth is my story even possible". This was purely assertion that is not accurate, which can be seen if one examines the record in other democracies. Henry Louis Gates asks, was "Barack Obama the first black president in the New World?" His answer is "No way. Vicente Guerrero in 1829. Mulatto, just like Barack Obama. First President of Mexico."[23] Peru has had two Chinese-Peruvian Prime Ministers and a Japanese-Peruvian President.[24] Many other nations have had mixed-race and minority leaders.[25]

Before Trump, the comforting message American politicians constantly sent their citizens was that America is exceptional and special. Obama, like Reagan, believed in the promise of America and this hope was largely what they sold disillusioned voters and young Americans. This is the politics of motivational speaking: "we want you to feel hopeful about America because we do". American exceptionalism operates in this mode of politics as a term of national self-help, which is repeated over and over to help voters believe that it is in fact true. This is how mythology and religious liturgy works, politics has gone down this route with mantras like "it's morning again in America," "America is the greatest country in the world," and "hope and change".[26] Trump, as I will argue below, has used blunt shock-therapy rather than trying to dispense the type of national motivational therapy favoured by Reagan and Obama. Rather than drawing heavily on exceptionalist mythology, the largely ahistorical Trump has drawn on the logic of popular culture to gain attention of, entertain, and distract American voters. He has called for greatness to be restored, but in a surprising move for a presidential candidate and then president he has dispensed with talk of America being exceptional. In his rhetoric and actions, far from showing America to be the "greatest" nation on earth, he has torn asunder the illusion that America is immune to the follies of myopic nationalism, which in fact have always plagued all nation-states. As I will argue below, Trump has also shown American politics to be increasingly a product of popular culture and populism, as politics is in many other places. These factors have starkly revealed the long-standing reality that America is not exceptional, but rather a nation with extraordinary power and influence yet commonplace problems and concerns.

An ugly world: popular culture and populism

During the 2016 presidential campaign Trump lived by the entertainment industry maxim that you can get away with almost anything as long as you are not boring.[27] In many ways the Trump campaign was politics catching up with popular culture. The music journalist James Parker has argued that Trump is something different in politics, but utterly familiar in popular culture. Trump's "punk-rock appeal," as Packer puts it, is to be found in the way he breaks the rules of political presentation over and over again without regret or contrition.[28] Instead of screaming "Anarchy in the UK," Trump's sardonic message is "law and order in the USA". However, as it was with the Sex Pistols, Trump used shock tactics to enhance his brand rather than offering a coherent new manifesto.[29] What is fascinating in both cases, is how their frustrated and bored followers embraced their anti-establishment diatribes with a certain nihilistic glee.[30] As Parker writes of Trump:

> he has co-created a space in American politics that is uniquely transgressive, volatile, carnivalesque, and (from a certain angle) punk rock. He's done it by harping on America's most conservative intuitions — "chaos in our communities," barbarians at the border — while addressing us in a style that thrillingly breaches every convention of political presentation. It's as if the Sex Pistols

were singing about law and order instead of anarchy, as if their chart-busting (banned) single, "God Save the Queen," were not a foamingly sarcastic diatribe but a sincere pledge of fealty to the monarch....he's not doing politics at all. He's doing bad art. *Terrible* art. He can't go off message, because his message is "Look at me! I'm off message!"[31]

In popular culture being offensive, attention-seeking, and incoherent is commonplace. If we view Trump as a product of popular culture, then he is clearly a symptom of a cultural malaise rather than the cause of the end of the world as we know it. Furthermore, American electoral and presidential politics, with its emphasis on symbolism and public relations, was long before Trump often an element of popular culture, rather than something that stands above popular culture with more exalted standards and principles. Given these relatively obvious points it has been intriguing to watch the *New York Times, CNN* and many other established media outlets around the world react with endless shock and horror during and since the 2016 campaign, as if they had never seen anything like Trump before. Trump was treated as though he was the first person to appear on television wearing no clothes, when in fact naked people have been appearing on television for decades.

In *The Shock of the New* (1980) Robert Hughes examined how modernist art mirrored the rapid and disruptive developments in technology, capitalism, and ideas in the late 19th and 20th century. According to Hughes by the late 20th century art was losing its capacity to encapsulate reality as it was being overtaken by photography, film, and television. It was also losing its ability to shock, as was literature. Two of the last truly attention-grabbing examples of these cultural forms were Andres Serrano's *Piss Christ* (1987) and Salman Rushdie's *Satanic Verses* (1988). In the 21st century high art continued to be transgressive, however, most politicians, censors, and the media failed to pay it much attention or respect. In this century, as Alex Ross has written: "The old hierarchy of high and low [culture] has become a sham: pop is the ruling party." This of course was not always the case, modernist art and literature had often led the way in terms of shock, revelation, and constantly pushing the boundaries, with the pushback generally being temporary. Artists and writers like Édouard Manet,[32] D. H. Lawrence, Allen Ginsberg, and Anne Desclos were all censored for obscenity, whereas now their artistic expressions seem far less shocking in contrast to the thousands of pornographic films that have been watched billions of times. PornHub for example gets 80 million daily visits.[33] This reality makes Trump's secret sexual affair with a porn star a mundane male fantasy being realised, rather than a cause for great surprise. Stormy Daniels is the Marilyn Munroe of our age. This does not make Trump's relationship with Ms Daniels morally without question, it just is not as surprising to many Americans as the media coverage tends to suggest (or at least pretends to suggest possibly to boost ratings). Even evangelical Christians seem less outraged by Trump's relationships, sex life, and misogyny than is often assumed. The moral outrage of evangelicals is politically calibrated like it is for most people unfortunately. This was starkly illustrated by a Marist poll that found that 48% of white evangelicals said they would support the nomination of Brett Kavanaugh to the Supreme Court "even if the allegations against him were true".[34]

Popular culture and the internet have made the once unacceptable fairly commonplace – many people are blasé about things that not that long ago would have seemed totally outrageous. The fact that Trump could survive in the GOP primaries after saying of John McCain, "He's not a war hero. He's a war hero because he was captured. I like people that weren't captured" was an early sign that respect is not what it used to be, even amongst Republicans about the US military (tick, another taboo broken!). On the Access Hollywood tape Trump brags that if you are a celebrity you can get away with groping and sexually assaulting women; it was appalling and revealing that many voters let Trump get away with this behaviour by not punishing him at the ballot box as if the laws of the land, and of decency, did not apply to celebrities and politicians. The widespread popularity of hardcore pornography and gangsta rap[35] should remind us just how crass, transgressive, and unruly popular culture in the 21st century has become. The gatekeepers of political discourse appear incapable of remembering this; instead they often seem to believe that culture and politics are two separate spheres that are mutually exclusive and do not affect how people judge behaviour in the other sphere. Trump's ascent to the presidency showed how faulty this thinking was. The films *Bob Roberts* (1992) and *Bullworth* (1998) predicted this fusion in the late 20th century.

Since the 1950s the most depraved and disturbing aspects of human behaviour have been explored in commercial music by bands like Guns N' Roses, Alice Cooper, Black Flag, and Body Count.[36] Comedy, cartoons, and films are constantly pushing the limits of what is acceptable by playing with what is still apparently shocking. Given the amount of obscenity and norm breaking the average person in the 21st century with access to the internet has heard or seen it is remarkable that Trump was viewed as such an aberration. However, for the gatekeepers of American politics – professional politicians, party leaders and most mainstream journalists and political commentators – Trump was totally aberrant because politicians have tended not to behave on camera as brazenly contemptuous of their opponents and the mainstream media as Trump.[37] As it turned out, Trump was far less shocking and beyond the pale to American voters than most of these gatekeepers assumed. Trump's bad political manners, racism, misogyny, unethical past, and unpredictability were mistakenly deemed by these gatekeepers to make him unelectable. Instead, it was the vastly more knowledgeable and politically experienced Hillary Clinton that was viewed as alien and unacceptable by too many American voters in key states. This is not an "only in America" story: pop and populism have been working in unison elsewhere as well. Ugly American cultural traits were never solely American failings and they are even less so in the 21st century. Politics in many other nations has been deeply affected by the desensitising, demoralising, and dumbing-down aspects of popular culture which has helped create a pervasive cynicism about politics and much else. If the shock of the new was a quintessential element of modernist culture, irony and cynicism are core elements of post-modern culture.

The popular culture icons that Trump most resembles are right-wing radio shock-jocks. America's first popular shock-jock Ralph Waldo "Petey" Greene was a liberal African-American who inspired a young Howard Stern. In the 1990s Stern's daily radio show at the peak of its popularity had 20 million daily listeners, making it the most popular radio show in American history. Donald Trump was a guest over a period of two decades around two dozen times on *The Howard Stern Show*. These appearances involved making derogatory comments about women's looks. Stern's show is a mix of music, sex talk, blue banter, and at times conspiracy theories. The untrue conspiracy theory told by Donald Trump during the 2016 campaign that after the terrorist attacks of 9/11, Muslim Americans were celebrating in the streets of New Jersey and that he saw this broadcast on television, has been linked to a comment that aired on Howard Stern's show. A new wave of conservative talk radio hosts learnt from the shock-jocks of the 1980s and they became the most popular shows on radio by the 1990s. The king of American talk radio is the extremely conservative Rush Limbaugh, who still has the most popular talk radio show in America with 14 million weekly listeners. At the height of its popularity in the 1990s the Rush Limbaugh Show had a weekly audience of over 20 million. Today, talk radio shows by Sean Hannity, Michael Savage, and Glenn Beck each have over 10 million listeners per week. Outrage, distortion, and misinformation are commonplace on all of these shows. Limbaugh's Show and other conservative talk radio shows provided the blueprint for *Fox News* which was launched as a cable channel in 1996. Arguably Trump's political persona is a mix of Howard Stern's say-anything cavalier attitude and Limbaugh's rage against "liberal establishment" politics. Listeners to Stern and Limbaugh were unlikely to have been shocked by Trump's rough language and exaggerations. As for those who still think Trump's political success is totally aberrant, they should probably spend some time listening to Stern and Limbaugh, and even Glenn Beck. Once again, shock-jocks and right-wing gadfly talk radio hosts are not just an American tradition, they are commonplace in Australia and other nations.

Trump clearly also draws upon the shock tactics and cynicism of anti-PC comedy, seen in shows like *South Park*. The overlap with Trump is the use of extreme comments to get attention and laughs/votes. In her brilliant essay "How Jokes Won the Election" Emily Nussbaum highlights the protection that joking provides and how you lose by taking offensive "humour" too seriously.[38] Anti-PC comedy also often jokes about its own complicity in that too clever by half post-modern way. In a September 2015 episode of *South Park*, which uses the Trump campaign for its storyline, an earnest Canadian political refugee father who has fled his country to live in the US explains the recent election of a Canadian President Trump in the following manner:

> There were several candidates during the Canadian elections. One of them was this brash asshole who just spoke his mind. He didn't really offer any solutions, he just said outrageous things. We thought it was funny. Nobody really thought he'd ever be President. It was a joke! But we just let the joke go on for too long. He kept gaining momentum, and by the time we were all

ready to say "Okay, let's get serious now. Who should really be President?" he was already being sworn into office. We weren't paying attention.

Soon after this speech in the episode we see President Trump wrestling on the presidential mat with an even more demagogic American populist who rapes Trump to death. Shocking "eh"? Maybe not: for regular *South Park* viewers it was just another extreme punch-line in a very long production line of them, after all it was the 259th episode of this hugely popular comedy show. My point about *South Park* is my more general claim here that such entertainment helps make the outrageous and offensive normalised, and opposition to such remarks and attitudes is treated as boring and prissy. Conventional politicians and policies in this environment are increasingly ignored.

Trump's anti-PC comments are not simply viewed as offensive by his supporters but also appreciated for being unusually honest, authentic, and unscripted for a politician. Just as an inability to play musical instruments with technical prowess was forgiven in punk rock performances, Trump's lies, rambling speeches and interviews that lack basic policy knowledge, and the implausibility of his solutions are seen as fairly irrelevant because more important to his supporters is the way he constantly affronts status quo politics. The popularity of this attack tells us something significant about the levels of frustration and desperation amongst his supporters and about their sheer boredom with conventional politics. Stuart Jefferies has argued that:

> If you listen to Trump speak, it's all stream-of-consciousness gibberish. There's no real thought, no real intellectual process, no historical memory. It's a rhetorical sham, but a kind of brilliant one when you think about it. He's a projection of his supporters, and he knows it. He won by capturing attention, and he captured attention by folding pop entertainment into politics, which is something the critical theorists anticipated.[39]

This too is nothing new: in the 1970s the hall of mirrors, echo chamber, aspect of popular culture and the contemporary personality was lampooned by Tom Wolfe in "The 'Me' Decade and the Third Great Awakening" and lamented by Christopher Lasch in *The Culture of Narcissism* (1979).[40]

Just as popular music, internet pornography, shock-jocks, and anti-PC comedy has paved the way for Trump and other populists, so have "pushing the envelope" films and television shows. Extremely violent films like the *Clockwork Orange*, *Scarface*, *Natural Born Killers*, and *Kill Bill* open our culture up to viewing the world far less literally, to seeing screen violence as just entertainment, which has been part of a process of watering down conventional universalist ethics. Everything becomes situational. Similarly, television programs like *The Jerry Springer Show*, *Jackass*, and *World Wrestling Entertainment* (WWE) desensitise us to outrageous claims and behaviour. Such shows were important in making the Trump presidency possible. Those familiar with *Fox News*, the WWE and Springer's show would understand a lot more instinctively about Trump's appeal than many political scientists. The world of fake wrestling is one that Trump has appeared in as a star, humiliating one of the owners of the WWE, Vince McMahon, in a famous episode where he shaves McMahon's hair off. Trump's political rallies with their haranguing of the media section, and Trump's abuse of protestors that are being ejected from arenas, mirrors the very intense mock threats and mood of WWE events.[41] Trump's stunt of bringing three women that have accused Bill Clinton of sexual assault to the second presidential debate against Hillary Clinton was reminiscent of the way *The Jerry Springer Show* dealt with issues in an attention-seeking and shock-value manner rather than with a particular aim to seek the truth or justice. Springer, a former Cincinnati Democratic Party Mayor, called it quits in June of 2018 with the airing of the 4,000[th] and final episode of *The Jerry Springer Show*. [42]

Although my examples above of popular culture that paved the way for Trump are largely American, there are plenty of non-American forms of popular culture that are equally as degrading, shock-oriented, and amoral. For example, the *Big Brother* franchise (which originated in the Netherlands), European films like *The 120 Days of Sodom, Caligula*, or *The Idiots*, and recently the UK drill rappers who have not just glorified violence in their songs but gone on to commit violent crimes possibly inspired by their music culture.[43] Such cultural forms that are desensitising, degrading, and have a life imitating art aspect to them helped get Trump elected but also have made the success of politicians like Berlusconi, Duterte and Boris Johnson possible. The impact of popular culture on populist politics is not an "only in America" story. The proliferation of extreme cultural products almost everywhere is part of a world with less of a moral compass. Such cultural forms have spread in a world where legitimate authority is not as powerful as it once was. It is of course more than just shock tactics, the dumbing down of culture, and jettisoning of conventional ethics that brings populist leaders to power. Their fearmongering and lies have also been crucial to their success,[44] as has their ability to distract,[45] and their authoritarian appeal.[46] Steve Bannon has said that: "We got elected on Drain the Swamp, Lock Her Up, Build a Wall...This was pure anger. Anger and fear is what gets people to the polls."[47] My second qualifier here is that, just as it was more than popular culture that put Trump in the White House, I recognise that not all popular culture leads to a race to the bottom. Popular culture can also inform and enrich our lives. My point is that popular culture is powerfully and intimately connected to modern politics.

Underlying the attack on ugly American culture was a fear about what mass culture everywhere might become in the future without political and cultural gatekeepers. Nineteenth-century European travel writers often left their homes as radicals or liberals and returned from America a lot more conservative. What frightened them into becoming more conservative was a sense that they had seen an inferior future in America's democratic popular culture that they did not approve of. For writers like Alexis de Tocqueville, Frances Trollope and Charles Dickens, American popular culture was too oriented towards instant gratification, pandered too much towards the lowest common denominator, and lacked basic ethics because it was largely driven by commercial imperatives. This critique was often rather selective in what it focused on. For instance, Tocqueville said there was no American literature of note – ignoring the work of Edgar Allan Poe, Henry Wadsworth Longfellow, Washington Irving, and James Fenimore Cooper.[48] In Dickens' case his contempt towards American commercial culture was driven by his disgust at the general disregard for British copyright laws in America (meaning he ended up with a lot less money than he otherwise would have). More insightfully, Dickens was one of the first writers to recognise the negative impact that celebrity culture would have on the public's behaviour when they were faced with celebrities (like himself). Dickens complained that much of the general public he met quickly turned into fawning sycophants. This longstanding response to the famous undoubtedly benefited Trump whose lack of political experience and policy knowledge (as well as his highly questionable personal behaviour) were excused by many voters because he is a celebrity businessman. Once again, the parallels with Berlusconi's career are unmistakable.

In the mid-20th century Frankfurt School critical theorists added to the European intellectuals' ongoing dismissal of American popular culture – what they damningly called the "cultural industry" – by arguing it "blurred the distinction between truth and fiction, between the commercial and the political,"[49] and that it "enforces conformity, quiets dissent, mutes thought".[50] Like the European travel writers of the 19th century their critique was partially correct but it significantly underplayed the sheer variety of American cultural forms which contain the good, the bad, and the ugly. Or in the words of Fredric Jameson popular culture contains "catastrophe and progress all together."[51] However, the Frankfurt School's general belief that American popular culture was categorically different from popular culture elsewhere lacks credibility as it misses the globally interbred nature of popular culture and the ways in which popular culture everywhere tends to push the boundaries of morality, good taste, and mindlessness. The race to the bottom is evident in many places, so is the sheer variety of popular culture. The impact of the entertainment industry on politics is more obviously evident in America than elsewhere but it is useful to remember that the Italian media tycoon Silvio Berlusconi was a forerunner to Trump, with similar entertainer's theatrics and a disdain for the judiciary. The anti-American instinct is to see America as not part of multidirectional worldwide trends but as a monodirectional proliferator of the most negative ideas and trends. America is best understood in a transnational manner rather than being viewed as either an inferior or superior nation that is somehow a world unto itself.[52] Moreover, "ugly American" traits are apparent all around the world if we care to look closely enough.

American exceptionalism in the age of Trump

One of the obvious challenges to understanding what Trump "really thinks" about political issues, is that he uses words in such a cavalier manner. David Roberts has astutely argued that:

For most people, words are both representations and tools; for Trump, they're only the latter. When Trump utters words, his primary intent is not to *say* something, to describe a set of facts in the world; his primary intent is to *do* something, to position himself in a social hierarchy. This essential distinction explains why Trump has so flummoxed the media and its fact-checkers.[53]

Nonetheless, Trump's words still need to be analysed because, as with more conventional politicians, they offer insight into his thinking and worldview. Since the 1980s Trump has rallied against America having trade deficits with other nations: on this issue his statements over time are remarkably consistent. On many other topics there is considerable flux in the stances Trump has adopted since the 1980s. When it comes to understanding Trump's views on American exceptionalism there are very direct statements to parse and try to make sense of. At a conservative convention in Texas in 2015, when Trump was asked this question by a local businessman: "Define American exceptionalism. Does American exceptionalism still exist? And what do we do to grow American exceptionalism?" His response apparently stunned the audience into silence:

> I don't like the term. I'll be honest with you. People say, "Oh he's not patriotic." Look, if I'm a Russian, or I'm a German, or I'm a person we do business with, why, you know, I don't think it's a very nice term. We're exceptional; you're not. First of all, Germany is eating our lunch. So they say, "Why are you exceptional. We're doing a lot better than you." I never liked the term. And perhaps that's because I don't have a very big ego and I don't need terms like that. Honestly. When you're doing business—I watch Obama every once in a while saying "American exceptionalism," it's [Trump makes a face]. I don't like the term. Because we're dealing—First of all, I want to take everything back from the world that we've given them. We've given them so much. On top of taking it back, I don't want to say, "We're exceptional. We're more exceptional." Because essentially we're saying we're more outstanding than you. "By the way, you've been eating our lunch for the last 20 years, but we're more exceptional than you." I don't like the term. I never liked it. When I see these politicians get up [and say], "the American exceptionalism"—we're dying. We owe 18 trillion in debt. I'd like to make us exceptional. And I'd like to talk later instead of now. Does that make any sense? Because I think you're insulting the world. And you, know, Jim, if you're German, or you're from Japan, or you're from China, you don't want to have people saying that.[54]

This is not what many would expect from Trump. The argument that other nations have been "eating our lunch for the last 20 years" and that America should no longer put up with this and should fight back is totally familiar from Trump, but the need to be humble and not "insult" other nations sounds more like most people's view of Obama than Trump. As I stated in an earlier chapter we need to be cautious about overplaying what politicians say on the campaign trail, after all they end up saying many things given the endless debates and long primary process. George W. Bush said in the second presidential debate in 2000 that America needed a "humble" foreign policy, because "one way for us to end up being viewed as the ugly American is for us to go around the world saying, 'we do it this way, so should you.'"[55] This a long way from how Bush behaved in office as Commander and Chief of the Armed Forces. However, Trump's views on American exceptionalism expressed in 2015 are consistent with an earlier position he advanced on Fox News in September 2013, when he was praising an article Vladimir Putin had written criticising Obama's promotion of America's "exceptional" role in the world.

On September 11, 2013 the *New York Times* published an op-ed by President Putin where he rebutted a speech by President Obama the day before on the role the US should play in the Syrian conflict. After Putin points out that the US had had an unsuccessful record of intervening in Afghanistan, Iraq and Libya, he suggested that the US therefore should stay out of military intervention in Syria. He then wrote that:

> I carefully studied his [Obama's] address to the nation on Tuesday. And I would rather disagree with a case he made on American exceptionalism, stating that the United States' policy is 'what makes America different. It's what makes us exceptional.' It is extremely dangerous to encourage people to see themselves as exceptional, whatever the motivation. There are big countries and small countries, rich and poor, those with long democratic traditions and those still finding their way to democracy. Their policies differ, too. We are all different, but when we ask for the Lord's blessings, we must not forget that God created us equal.[56]

Trump went on Fox News the next day congratulating Putin for his op-ed. This occurred two months before Trump's widely discussed trip to Moscow for the Miss Universe Pageant that was a central element of Christopher Steele's dossier. Trump starts the Fox News interview by saying that Putin's article "was amazingly well crafted. I've read it a number of times." When asked a question on Putin's rejection of the notion of American exceptionalism Trump again praises Putin and offers an outlook similar to what he would say 20 months later in Texas:

> it really makes him [Putin] look like a great leader, frankly. And when he criticizes the president for using the term "American exceptionalism," if you're in Russia, you don't want to hear that America is exceptional. And if you're in many other countries, whether it's Germany or other places, you don't want to hear about American exceptionalism because you think you're exceptional. So I can see that being very insulting to the world. And that's basically what Putin was saying is that, you know, you use a term like "American exceptionalism," and frankly, the way our country is being treated right now by Russia and Syria and lots of other places and with all the mistakes we've made over the years, like Iraq and so many others, it's sort of a hard term to use. But other nations and other countries don't want [to] hear about American exceptionalism. They're insulted by it. And that's what Putin was saying.[57]

These statements by Putin and then Trump are not entirely wrong, even if the intentions behind them are questionable and in Trump's case downright murky.[58] What is interesting is that Trump has in a variety of ways taken the energy out of the claims of American exceptionalism, a concept that was once so central to Republican Party rhetoric on foreign policy. In the 2012 presidential election "American exceptionalism" was one of the six planks of the GOP platform. The section begins with the statement that: "Professing American exceptionalism—the conviction that our country holds a unique place and role in human history—we proudly associate ourselves with those Americans of all political stripes who, more than three decades ago in a world as dangerous as today's, came together to advance the cause of freedom."[59] Hillary Clinton in the 2016 election tried to use Trump's turn against Republican Party orthodoxy against him as she claimed to be the true defender of the exceptionalist tradition. She stated in August of 2016 that: "My opponent misses something important. When we say America is exceptional, it doesn't mean that people from other places don't feel deep national pride, just like we do. It means that we recognize America's unique and unparalleled ability to be a force for peace and progress, a champion for freedom and opportunity."[60] Hillary Clinton was championing what many scholars describe as America's role in creating and maintaining the liberal international order. To the chagrin of Hillary Clinton and many liberal international relations scholars, defending that order was not a priority for many American voters. Many voters instead sympathised with Trump's frontal assault on the liberal international order that he described as too expensive for America to maintain for too little reward. Trump advocated a more transactional approach to international affairs, or what others not unfairly called a mercantilist outlook. Trump's approach rejected both free trade policies and America's self-appointed role of being a vocal champion of democracy and freedom around the world. He also questioned long-standing US alliances. These views were antithetical to the beliefs of most of the existing leadership of the Republican Party and most conservatives working for Washington DC think tanks. An example of the divergent views of the Party and candidate Trump is the 2016 Republican platform which opens with this declaration: "We believe in American exceptionalism. We believe the United States of America is unlike any other nation on earth. We believe America is exceptional because of our historic role — first as refuge, then as defender, and now as exemplar of liberty for the world to see." Later in the 2016 platform it is stated: "We believe that American exceptionalism — the notion that our ideas and principles as a nation give us a unique place of moral leadership in the world — requires the United States to retake its natural position as leader of the free world."[61] This was Trump's platform, which he clearly did not write or believe in. Within the Trump Administration the exceptionalist view of America's role in the world is supported by certain high-ranking officials, whereas the president himself takes a much more limited view of America's role as the so-called leader of the free world.

How have international relations scholars and commentators reacted to these confusing times? Trump's disruptive disregard for the norms of diplomacy and international relations has forced scholars to not just offer critiques of his potentially dangerous approach, it has also required them to defend the principles and results of their advocated approach to international relations. This has particularly been the case for liberals who see Trump's approach to foreign policy as an existential threat to the rules-based liberal international order that America has stood at the helm of since WWII. For scholars like John Ikenberry, this order is not perfect but the best approach to world affairs we can reasonably expect.[62] For realist scholars like Graham Allison and Stephen Walt, the liberal response to Trump is another case of liberal over-congratulations, whitewashing, and misinterpretation.[63] Recently Allison has argued that the Cold War international system largely discouraged Great Power wars not because of liberal international institutions, norms, and laws but because there was a bi-polar balance of power between the USSR and the US. Allison argues that the collapse of the USSR has led to a more unrestrained US in the Middle East, which has been disastrous.[64] Andrew Bacevich has persuasively set out this critique of post-Cold War overreach in a number of books and articles; as did Anatol Lieven in his excellent *America Right or Wrong*.[65] Realists like Walt, Bacevich and Lieven advocate a more restrained US foreign policy and one that recognises American exceptionalism to be a myth that leads America into hubris and folly in its foreign policy. They are explicitly critical of the way American policy makers have seen Israel as an "exceptional" partner that America needs to defend at the cost of consistency and in fact America's national interests. Very similar arguments about American exceptionalism, the unjust defence of Israel, and the dangers of liberal internationalism have been made by scholars and commentators on the left such as Perry Anderson,[66] Patrick Smith,[67] and Samuel Moyn.[68] All of these thinkers fall broadly within the tradition that Walter Russell Mead has called Jeffersonian,[69] as they want America to avoid fighting wars of choice abroad and instead focus on putting its own house in order. Most of these scholars advocate a de-militarisation of US foreign policy. Specifically both Bacevich and Moyn advocate spending less on the US military as a way to avoid seeing every international conflict as a nail that the hammer force of the US military needs to consider hitting. Noam Chomsky in a more extreme and thoroughgoing manner fits within this broad but seldom practiced Jeffersonian position.

That these scholars hold a very critical view of American exceptionalism that is consistent with that of Trump and Putin on exceptionalism should not be a reason to take the opposite view.[70] Just because these two abhorrent politicians are broadly right on this issue does not mean their approach to foreign policy is commendable. Trump is not a Jeffersonian, he is much more of a Jacksonian (and a militarist) as I will conclude below.[71] Before examining Trump's general outlook I will return to liberal defences of American hegemony and the so-called rules-based international order. It will be argued that American liberals often undermine their argument that this order is a multilateral and mutually beneficial system by implicitly or explicitly simultaneously promoting American exceptionalism.

In a 2017 article in *Dissent* Samuel Moyn wrote: "When asked what he thought of 'Western civilization,' Mohandas Gandhi is said to have replied that it sounded like a good idea. I think the same is true of 'liberal internationalism,' which has often served as the Democratic Party's preferred label for its vision of American foreign policy."[72] Moyn goes on to argue that the American practice of liberal internationalism has generally neither been particularly liberal nor that internationalist. Instead it has served as the ideological way America "soft sells" being an Empire.[73] The attachment of leading American liberals like John Ikenberry, Anne Marie Slaughter and Charles Kupchen to American exceptionalism leads to them promoting two essentially imperial views: firstly the belief that because America has more hard and soft power than any other nation it has a duty to play an expansive role in global affairs. Peter Beinart has called this "responsibility" exceptionalism.[74] This could be labelled the Spiderman approach to foreign policy: with great power comes great responsibility. Stephen Walt has been at the forefront of pushing back against this attitude that in any crisis the US is compelled to "do something" including intervening militarily "as a last resort."[75] The second exceptional tenet these liberals hold to is that America's crooked path to becoming (and sustaining) a liberal democracy provides America with a broad blueprint on how to conduct international affairs. We see this in Slaughter's book *The Idea that Is America: Keeping Faith with Our Values in a Dangerous World* and in Kupchan's recent article "The Clash of Exceptionalisms."[76]

In Kupchan's "The Clash of Exceptionalisms" he outlines two periodised versions of American exceptionalism 1.0 and American exceptionalism 2.0. The first version lasted from America's founding to the Pearl Harbor attacks and emphasised America as an "exemplar" to other nations, whereas American exceptionalism 2.0 was based on "global engagement." This second approach coheres with Beinart's "responsibility exceptionalism." Kupchan claims that Trump's "America first" politics "reveals serious cracks in American Exceptionalism 2.0, which still dominates the US foreign policy establishment." Although he sees faults in the later version of exceptionalism, Kupchan argues that a new exceptionalist vision is necessary to hold together a consensus amongst the American people so that we do not "risk the return of a Hobbesian world, violating not just the United States' principles but also its interests."[77] In outlining his American exceptionalism 3.0, Kupchan advocates a return to a less interventionist exceptionalism but in a way that sends mixed messages. He writes: "Although the United States' messianic mission should remain at the core of its exceptionalist narrative, the country must transition from crusader back to exemplar."[78] And similarly, he ends the article with the rousing assertion that: "Looking beyond Trump, the United States will need a new exceptionalism to guide its grand strategy and renew its unique role as the world's anchor of liberal ideals."[79] As Hilde Eliassen Restad convincingly argues in *American Exceptionalism*, a false dichotomy between the exemplar and engagement versions of exceptionalism has long been propagated when in fact both were underpinned by a unilateral and imperial logic. Furthermore, she argues that the centrality of exceptionalism to American identity has led to an exaggerated sense of American self-importance and self-righteousness.

To challenge the exemplar/engaged dichotomised understanding of US foreign policy history, Restad draws on Anders Stephanson's *Manifest Destiny: American Expansionism and the Empire of Right* to argue that American isolationism has long been much overstated. Indeed, Restad points out that in the period where America was supposedly an "exemplar," it was also unjustly killing native Americans, Mexicans and others as it expanded first south and westwards and then into the Caribbean and Pacific. She similarly challenges the rose-tinted view that in the 20th century the US was a benevolent liberal hegemony. Her central argument is that the exceptionalist underpinnings of US foreign policy lead to unilateral goals and behaviour, which are sold as universalist goals that are supposedly supported by multilateral coalitions. This is another way of saying that the liberal narrative of US foreign policy as multilateralist is a myth.[80] If one is acquainted with death tolls from the Korean and Vietnam wars, and the civil wars of Guatemala and the Congo in the mid-to-late 20th century, it is hard to see the role the US played in these interventions as benevolent or a positive reflection on its own liberal values. My point here in recounting these debates is not to suggest liberalism is not without certain merits as an approach to international relations but rather to argue that American liberalism would offer a far more just and commendable approach to world politics if it separated itself from American exceptionalism. This needs to occur because exceptionalist thinking is undergirded by a sense of superiority. Liberals are right that America's power allows it to play a major role in the world but the outcomes of this reality need to be acknowledged as being both positive and negative. Before claiming that on balance American interventions are more positive than negative, as Ikenberry too quickly tends to do, a lot more evidence needs to be presented and many more non-American voices particularly from the Global South need to be heard in this debate. To repair the reputation of American liberalism in the face of the invasion of Iraq and the amount of global inequality that can be associated with "liberalism" broadly understood, American liberal politicians need to start humbly working with other nations on important global problems like climate change, poverty, famine, the refugee crisis and terrorism. American retreat is not the answer to many international problems, in my view a less imperial form of engagement is what is required. This brings us back to Trump who is neither an exceptionalist nor is he taken by the idea of engaging globally for the greater good of humanity.

Trump's commitment to internationalism is far more limited and contingent than any other post-WWII president. Some have described this worldview as neo-isolationism. However, isolationism is rather difficult for a nation that has military bases in at least 70 countries,[81] and intelligence gathering installations in many nations as well as companies, investments, and aid projects spread across the globe. Despite the broad private and public commitments of America across the globe, Trump is certainly more isolationist in his attitudes and inclinations than George W. Bush or Barack Obama. Nonetheless, given Trump's militaristic and nationalist instincts, calling him an isolationist does not give us the full picture of his outlook towards the world.[82] A more useful label is to call him a foreign policy Jacksonian, to use language employed by Walter Russell Mead and Anatol Lieven. This label fits with the longstanding foreign policy concerns Trump has voiced that dates back to the 1980s when he "began to appear on television shows and in print interviews complaining about Japan dumping cheap cars and electronic devices in the United States and defeating America economically."[83] In 1987 he paid for full page ads in a number of major newspapers which were billed as "an open letter from Donald J. Trump" in which he called for Japan, Saudi Arabia and others to pay for the protection that being an ally of the US afforded them; in other words to pay for their freedom being defended.[84] This sounded rather like seeing US alliances as protection rackets that America needed to get kickbacks from. On these issues of protecting American manufacturing firms and jobs from foreign trade and alliances being largely zero-sum engagements rather than mutually beneficial, Trump's opinions are remarkably consistent (on many other issues he is far less consistent). Moreover, these long-standing protectionist and unilateralist instincts of Trump aligned with his former Svengali Steve Bannon the committed anti-globalist. Apparently, it was Bannon who suggested that Trump put a portrait of Andrew Jackson on his wall in the Oval Office, which he did.

Jacksonians are strong nativists and populists who believe that American settlers rejected Europe for the US for good reasons and that Americans should not look to get caught up in the endless problems of Europe or anywhere else. In short, their outlook is that the rest of the world should largely be ignored and avoided unless the US is threatened. To pre-empt threats to America, Jacksonians believe the US should have a very well-funded and extremely powerful military that its leaders make clear it is willing to use if necessary. Furthermore, if the US is attacked or provoked they believe America should destroy its enemy. Trump's claim that "North Korea best not make any more threats to the United States" or else "they will be met with fire and fury like the world has never seen" is very much in keeping with the Jacksonian mindset.[85] So is Trump's questioning of long-standing alliances and general negative view towards international institutions and laws. Walter Russell Mead in *Special Providence* outlines the Jacksonian worldview and ever since has been predicting its likely return to prominence in American politics. Acknowledging that things had turned out as he had predicted, Mead wrote in early 2017 that: "Donald Trump sensed something that his political rivals failed to grasp: that the truly surging force in American politics wasn't Jeffersonian minimalism. It was Jacksonian populist nationalism."[86] Mead calls the Jacksonians "the core of Trump's passionately supportive base" who reject the Wilsonian notion that America has a missionary calling to spread the enlightenment ideal that underpins American identity around the world. For Jacksonians they see identity quite differently; for them America "is a nation-state of the American people, and its chief business lies at home."[87] This understanding of nationalism has been commonplace in Europe since the nineteenth century. Mead makes the important point that: "Jacksonian populism is only intermittently concerned with foreign policy, and indeed it is only intermittently engaged with politics more generally."[88]

In other words, political engagement for those with Jacksonian views is occasional therefore it took an unusual range of forces to get these Jacksonian Americans out in large numbers to vote. Mead argues these voters felt America was "under siege, with its values under attack and its future under threat."[89] One of the weaknesses of Mead's analysis is a failure to emphasise that Trump often provoked and helped create this siege mentality with false information and xenophobic rhetoric. More insightfully Mead claims that Jacksonians "are not obsessed with corruption, seeing it as an ineradicable part of politics."[90] Mead also claims that they have tended to see powerful elite forces "including the political establishments of both major parties, in cahoots against them."[91]

In Summation

Lorna Finlayson in the *London Review of Books* recently observed that: "British liberals like to believe that Americans are a different species".[92] Throughout this book I have argued against seeing Americans and America as either exceptionally superior or inferior. Both the American exceptionalist and anti-American mindsets exaggerate differences. Exceptionalist thinking fuels American hubris, whereas an anti-American outlook leads to faulty analysis of the weaknesses of American society and policy. This faulty thinking is often the result of America being analysed as though it were a world unto itself, with the study of American politics, history and culture often conducted with little reference to, or knowledge of, developments in other nations.[93] A more comparative approach is the crucial first step to overcoming the anti-American or exceptionalist outlook.[94] The second and most important step is to see America in a transnational manner. As scholars like Godfrey Hodgson and Richard Pells have argued,[95] much of what are commonly thought of as American ideas, anthems, and culture are in fact European beliefs and products. Puritan exceptionalist ideas, the Star-Spangled Banner, and hot dogs, are some of the many examples of European exports to America that are now thought of as quintessentially American.[96] The process of globalisation is centuries old and America has long been at the crossroads of global exchanges. For example, the iconic Levi's Jeans were first produced by a German born American, Levi Strauss. Ian Tyrrell recounts this hybrid reality very effectively in his highly commendable *Transnational Nation: United States History in Global Perspective Since 1789.*[97] Hopefully scholars and commentators in the future will heed this advice to see America as part of the world, not separate, unique, or alien from it. However, it is too much to expect the ideologies that fuel American exceptionalism and anti-Americanism to be more circumspect in the future as pleasant as this thought is. American exceptionalism as I have argued is a powerful and longstanding component of American nationalism. Most expressions of nationalism promote a belief that their nation is better than others; American exceptionalist nationalism is particularly inclined to see America as superior to all other nations. Obama added a multicultural dimension and a degree of modesty to the American exceptionalism he promoted, but he still talked of America being the "indispensable nation" in world politics and one that could confront the hard problems that other nations did not have the capacity and values to address.[98] In the case of Syria this talk did not lead to as much action as it foretold. In the case of Afghanistan and Pakistan the exceptionalism that Obama practiced was not the "responsibilities" exceptionalism he talked of but a "rights" exceptionalism.[99] This apparently allowed America to operate outside of international law as the Obama administration did with the use of drones (to kill American enemies) and by breaching the sovereignty of other nation states. This unilateralist approach should lead all of us to be sceptical of claims that America is the bastion of the rules based liberal international order. The power of American exceptionalist nationalism, despite Trump's dismissal of the term, is ongoing and imperial. Trump too seems to think America has exceptional rights to act as a lone wolf in international affairs – his threats towards North Korea and then Iran are obvious examples of this. Nationalism is dangerous, but exceptionalist nationalism is doubly dangerous as it frequently leads either to self-righteousness or a sense that America is a law unto itself. Nationalism needs to be restrained by ideas like realism, liberalism, libertarianism, and socialism. The richest and most multidimensional of these traditions in America is liberalism, but when liberals embrace exceptionalism they make a grave mistake.

The state of affairs regarding the ideology of anti-Americanism is more complicated. In the post-George W. Bush era anti-Americanism has declined as opposition to Trump has tended to separate the man from his people and nation. In other words, loathing Trump is more obviously disconnected from anti-Americanism than loathing George W. Bush was. Nonetheless as I have outlined in this concluding chapter the way Trump is analysed as the quintessential "ugly American" typifies a tendency to see American popular culture, capitalism and electioneering as uniquely malignant and malign. Just as we accept that nationalism and populism are often dangerous forces in many nations we should accept that capitalist culture (that has clearly infected political campaigning) has an ugly attention-seeking logic to it not just in America but globally. Undoubtedly some of the most disturbing examples of this puerile, inhumane, and desensitising culture can be found in America, but if you look closely they are commonplace elsewhere as well. Just as we should be highly critical of American racism, while not overlooking racism in our own nation, we should recognise the obnoxious and noxious aspects of popular culture in our own societies as well. Anti-Americanism has long been a way of feeling superior to America, making it the reverse of American exceptionalism. This book stands in opposition to both ideologies. America is neither intrinsically superior or inferior. Americans are not a different species, they are just people like the rest of us. Holding power to account is an honourable tradition and there is much to criticise about American culture, society, politics and foreign relations. This criticism, however, should proceed based on evidence and with a keen sense that America, while often a leader of many global trends, is more crucially part of a world where ideas, products and people circulate widely and in a multidirectional manner. In this transnational world, anti-Americanism makes little sense, therefore we are far better off to identify the root causes of global ills in universal forces such as imperialism, nationalism, capitalism, consumerism, militarism, populism, and the technological imperative.

Notes

1 WIN & Gallup, "WIN/Gallup International's Global Poll on the American Election," *Gallup International*, 2016, <http://gallup.com.pk/wp-content/uploads/2016/10/FINAL-Global-Press-Release-Global-Poll-on-US-Election2.pdf>.

2 James Parker, "Donald Trump, Sex Pistol," *The Atlantic*, October 2016, <https://www.theatlantic.com/magazine/archive/2016/10/donald-trump-sex-pistol/497528/>. Moffat and Tormey argue that "bad manners" are a key to the political style of populist politicians in Benjamin Moffitt and Simon Tormey, "Rethinking Populism: Politics, Mediatisation and Political Style," *Political Studies* 62, 2 (2013).

3 Owen Amos, "Can we Tell if Donald Trump has a High IQ?" *BBC*, October 11, 2017, <https://www.bbc.com/news/world-us-canada-41573846>; David Nakamura and Karen Tumulty, "Trump Says he is a 'Genius' as he Defends Mental Fitness," *The Sydney Morning Herald*, January 07, 2018, <https://www.smh.com.au/world/trump-says-he-is-a-genuis-as-he-defends-mental-fitness-20180107-h0eiip.html>.

4 Elisa Lala, "Penn Student Newspaper Debunks Trump's Reported Claims of Graduating Top of his Class," *PhillyVoice*, February 16, 2017, <https://www.phillyvoice.com/penn-student-newspaper-debunks-trumps-claims-graduating-top-his-class/>.

5 Rebecca Solnit, "The Loneliness of Donald Trump," *Literary Hub*, May 30, 2017, <https://lithub.com/rebecca-solnit-the-loneliness-of-donald-trump/>.

6 Kate Feldman, "President Trump has the Best Words, says 'The Daily Show'," *New York Daily News*, December 07, 2017, <http://www.nydailynews.com/entertainment/tv/president-trump-best-words-daily-show-article-1.3682271>.

7 This article studied Trump's speeches and found them to contain shorter words and sentences when compared to other major candidates in the 2016 election: J. Eric Oliver and Wendy M. Rahn, "Rise of the Trumpenvolk: Populism in the 2016 Election," *Annals of the American Academy of Political and Social Science* 667, 1 (2016), 189–206.

8 It is claimed Trump consumes a dozen Diet Cokes per day. Maggie Haberman, Glenn Thrush and Peter Baker, "Inside Trump's Hour-by-Hour Battle for Self-Preservation," *New York Times*, December 09, 2017, <https://www.nytimes.com/2017/12/09/us/politics/donald-trump-president.html>; Ashley Parker, "Donald Trump's Diet: He'll Have Fries with That," *New York Times*, August 08, 2016, <https://www.nytimes.com/2016/08/09/us/politics/donald-trump-diet.html>.

9 Lilliana Mason, "Trump's "Winning" is America's Losing," *The New York Times*, June 06, 2018 <https://www.nytimes.com/2018/06/06/opinion/trump-winning-america-.html>.

10 Mary Dejevsky, "Does Trump's *Sun* Interview signal the End of Diplomacy," *The Guardian*, July 13, 2018, <https://www.theguardian.com/commentisfree/2018/jul/13/donald-trump-sun-diplomacy-theresa-may-insults>.

11 Fred Kaplan, "Trump Digs the Hole Deeper," *Slate*, July 17, 2018, <https://slate.com/news-and-politics/2018/07/trumps-excuses-and-justifications-for-his-performance-in-helsinki-were-almost-as-bad-as-the-debacle-itself.html>.

12 Charles Dickens, *American Notes* (London: Chapman & Hall, 1842).

13 Frederik Marryat, *Diary in America, With Remarks on its Institutions* (Canada: W. H. Colyer, 1839), 152

14 ibid. 144–145

15 William Faux, *Faux's Memorable Days in America, November 27, 1818–July 21, 1820.* Vols. 1 & 2. (London: Printed for W. Simpkin and R. Marshall, 1823), 117–118.

16 Francis Milton Trollope, *Domestic Manners of the Americans* (London: Printed for Whittaker, Teacher, & Co., 1832); Americans too have been keenly aware of this contradiction. Herman Melville is quoted by Arthur Schlesinger Jr to strong effect on this point:

> We must face the shameful fact: historically America has been a racist nation. White Americans began as a people so arrogant in convictions of racial superiority that they felt licensed to kill red people, to enslave black people, and to import yellow and brown people for peon (servant) labor. We white Americans have been racist in our

laws, in our institutions, in our customs, in our conditioned reflexes, in our souls. The curse of racism has been the great failure of the American experiment, the glaring contradiction of American ideals and the still crippling disease of American life – "the world's fairest hope" wrote Herman Melville, "linked with man's foulest crime.'"

(Arthur Schlesinger Jr, The Disuniting of America: Reflections on a Multicultural Society (Revised and Enlarged Edition) (New York: Norton, 1998))

17 See Rod Tiffen et al., *How America Compares* (Melbourne: Springer, 2019).
18 Reagan called for supporting the Afghan "freedom fighters" as a candidate. See: Ronald Reagan, "Address Accepting the Presidential Nomination of the Republican National Convention in Detroit," *Reagan Library*, July 17, 1980 <https://www.reaganlibrary.gov/7-17-80>; Ronald Reagan, "Address to the Nation on United States Policy in Central America," *Reagan Library*, May 09, 1984, <https://www.reaganlibrary.gov/research/sp eeches/50984h>; Ronald Reagan, "Address to the Nation on Aid to the Nicaraguan Democratic Resistance," *Reagan Library*, February 02 1988 <https://www.reaganlibrary.gov/research/speeches/020288e>; James M. Scott, *Deciding to Intervene: The Reagan Doctrine and American Foreign Policy* (North Carolina: Duke University Press, 1996).
19 David A. Graham, "It's Not an Act," *The Atlantic*, November 29, 2017, <https://www.theatlantic.com/politics/archive/2017/11/its-not-an-act/547010/>.
20 Jacob Weisberg, "We Are Hopelessly Hooked," *The New York Review*, February 25, 2016, <https://www.nybooks.com/articles/2016/02/25/we-are-hopelessly-hooked/>.
21 Many examples could have been chosen here, but this is particularly alarming. Elizabeth Kolbert writes: "Asked about the [2018 IPCC] report last week, Donald Trump said, 'I want to look at who drew it—you know, which group drew it.' The answer seemed to indicate that the President had never heard of the I.P.C.C., a level of cluelessness that, while hardly a surprise, was nevertheless dismaying." Elizabeth Kolbert, "What is Donald Trump's Response to the U.N.'S Dire Climate Report?" *The New Yorker*, October 22, 2018, <https://www.newyorker.com/magazine/2018/10/22/what-is-dona ld-trumps-response-to-the-uns-dire-climate-report>.
22 Christopher Lasch, *The Culture of Narcissism* (London: W. W. Norton & Company, 1979).
23 Henry Louis Gates, Jr. "Q&A with Professor Henry Louis Gates, Jr.," *PBS*, 2011, <http://www.pbs.org/wnet/black-in-latin-america/featured/qa-with-professor-henry-louis-gates-jr/164/>.
24 Odd Arne Westad, *Restless Empire* (New York: Basic Books, 2012), 227.
25 Jerry John Rawlings (Prime Minister of Ghana) and Michael Manley (PM of Jamaica) are two elected leaders that had a black parent and a white parent. Edward Seaga a Lebanese-Jamaican minority was also elected PM of Jamaica and a number of minorities and discriminated against caste members have been elected to leadership positions in India. Sadiq Aman Khan the current Mayor of London is British Pakistani and a Muslim.
26 This statement is constantly repeated by American politicians. Two examples are: "We are surely blessed to be citizens of the greatest nation on earth." Barrack Obama, "President Obama's Convention Speech," *NPR*, September 06, 2012, <https://www.npr.org/2012/09/06/160713941/transcript-president-obamas-convention-speech> "our pride and gratitude in the United States of America, the greatest, freest nation in the world—the last, best hope of man on Earth." Ronald Reagan, "Remarks at the Presentation Ceremony for the Presidential Medal of Freedom," *The American Presidency Project*, January 19, 1989, <http://www.presidency.ucsb.edu/ws/?pid=35402>.
27 Corey Robin, *The Reactionary Mind: Conservatism from Edmund Burke to Sarah Palin* (Oxford: Oxford University Press, 2011).
28 Parker, "Donald Trump, Sex Pistol".
29 The authoritarian roots of punk are explored in Simon Reynolds' *Retromania: Pop Culture's Addiction to Its Own Past* (London: Faber & Faber, 2010). However, there is a lot more to punk than just the Sex Pistols and many other punk bands left a more admirable legacy. The proto-punk band the Velvet Underground opened up important ways

of thinking about art, sexuality and life (See Michael Banister, "'I'm set Free…': The Velvet Underground, 1960s Counterculture, and Michel Foucault," *Popular Music and Society* 33, 2 (2010)). The Clash are the best example of progressive punk that was anti-authoritarian and anti-racist. The punk musician Ian Dury is a good example of punk at times being way ahead of its time in meaningful ways: in 1981 when his song "Spasticus Autisticus" – a critique of what he saw as the patronising tone of the International Year of Disabled Persons – came out he was widely condemned and denied airplay by the BBC and other radio stations; in 2012 it was performed live as part of the opening ceremony of the Paralympics. Lastly, there is much to be admired about the DIY non-conformist punk ethos of performers like Chris Knox and the band The Clean.

30 Alex Ross has written:
"Of the clouds and shadows that hung over Clinton in the press, the darkest, perhaps, was the prospect of boredom. Among voters, a kind of nihilistic glee may have been as much a factor in Trump's election as economic dissatisfaction or racial resentment. The mechanism by which people support a political program 'largely incompatible with their own rational self-interest,' as Adorno wrote, requires many kinds of deception."
(Alex Ross, "The Frankfurt School Knew Trump was Coming," *The New Yorker*, December 05, 2016. <https://www.newyorker.com/culture/cultural-comment/the-fra nkfurt-school-knew-trump-was-coming>)

31 Parker, "Donald Trump, Sex Pistol".

32 Manet's controversial nudes were rejected by galleries in the mid-18th century Paris.

33 Jane Gilmore, "Latest Porn Statistics are Surprising," *The Sydney Morning Herald*, April 24, 2018, <https://www.smh.com.au/lifestyle/life-and-relationships/latest-porn-statis tics-are-surprising-20180424-p4zbd8.html>.

34 Tara Isabella Burton, "Poll: 48% of White Evangelicals Would Support Kavanaugh even if the Allegations against him Were True," *Vox*, September 27, 2018, <https://www. vox.com/policy-and-politics/2018/9/27/17910016/brett-kavanaugh-christine-blasey-ford-white-evangelicals-poll-support>.

35 Rap music and its impact is of course not monolithic. It has positive as well as negative consequences. I agree with many of the claims made by Robin Kelley about the impact and joys of listening to rap that he stylishly outlines in *Race Rebels* where he argues that: "When gangsta rappers do write lyrics intended to convey a sense of social realism, their work loosely resembles a sort of street ethnography of racist institutions and social practices." Robin Kelley's *Race Rebels: Culture, Politics, and the Black Working Class* (New York: Free Press, 1994), 190.

36 In the realm of music, punk rock mined the thrill (or uncomfortable feeling) of being shocked to the nth-degree, and when that wore off it just played to the public's nihilism, disillusionment and disengagement. It spoke to a sense that someone somewhere else has a better deal or better life, and that you have been cheated and unfairly passed over. That you were stranded (to quote The Saints) in circumstances that were neither fair or no fun (to quote The Stooges). Resent-ment fuels much in popular culture, in politics and on the internet, and Trump has tapped into the rivers of American resentment as right-wing populist leaders in Europe have similarly done. The political scientist Stanley Feldman has shown that many Trump supporters have a want for more authoritarian styled leadership (Christopher Weber and Stanley Feldman, "How Authoritarianism is shaping American Politics (and it's not just about Trump)," *Washington Post*, May 10, 2017. <https://www.washingtonpost.com/news/monkey-cage/wp/2017/05/10/ how-authoritarianism-is-shaping-american-politics-and-its-not-just-about-trump/?utm_ term=.404fe30e92c8>). This is rightly one of the central concerns about where populist lea-ders might be emboldened to head if they gain power. At first the idea of authoritarian popu-lism might seem antithetical to Trump's anything-goes lifestyle and norm breaking ways. Nonetheless his authoritarian impulses are lurking behind his actions on immigration and an independent judiciary, and his treatment of the press and the federal intelligence agencies. If we take a close look at popular culture, we can also spot this mix of the libertine and authoritarian instincts. Punk rock is a good example of this: as Simon Reynolds and Dick Hebdige have demonstrated punk had authoritarian roots in the 1950s Teddy Boy culture (a subculture that

was most graphically illustrated in the film the *Clockwork Orange*). In certain instances punk and post-punk has been vocally anti-racist (think the Clash's *White Riot* and Siouxsie and the Banshees' *Hong Kong Garden*), on other occasions it has been brazenly taken by the shock value of Nazism (think Sid Vicious and Siouxsie Sioux wearing swastikas in public and band name Joy Division taken from the name the Nazi's gave to the Jewish women they sexually assaulted in concentration camps). The point here is there is nothing new to using shock to gain attention, classic music did this well before punk. And that shock can be used for a variety of purposes. See, Dick Hebdige, *Subculture: The Meaning of Style* (New York: Routledge, 1988) and Simon Reynolds" *Retromania: Pop Culture's Addiction to Its Own Past* (London: Faber & Faber, 2010).

37 Trump's brazen attacks on the media of course generally excluded conservative media outlets like Fox News. Trump was certainly not the first politician to have largely symbolic and impractical policy positions.

38 Emily Nussbaum "How Jokes Won the Election," *The New Yorker*, January 23, 2017, <https://www.newyorker.com/magazine/2017/01/23/how-jokes-won-the-election>.

39 Sean Illing, "If you Want to Understand the Age of Trump, Read the Frankfurt School," *Vox*, December 26, 2017, <https://www.vox.com/conversations/2016/12/27/14038406/donald-trump-frankfurt-school-brexit-critical-theory>.

40 Christopher Lasch, *The Culture of Narcissism* (London: W. W. Norton & Company, 1979), 47.

41 Eric Lach, "Donald Trump Celebrates Violence against Journalists," *The New Yorker*, October 20, 2018, <https://www.newyorker.com/news/current/donald-trump-celebrates-violence-against-journalists>.

42 *ABC*, "The Jerry Springer Show Comes to an End After 27 Years, 4,000 Episodes," *ABC News*, June 21, 2018 <https://www.abc.net.au/news/2018-06-21/jerry-springer-show-ends-after-27-years-on-television/9893606>.

43 Ben Beaumont-Thomas, "Is UK Drill Music Really Behind London's Wave of Violent Crime?" *The Guardian*, April 10, 2018, <https://www.theguardian.com/music/2018/apr/09/uk-drill-music-london-wave-violent-crime>.

44 Most insightfully Christopher Lasch wrote in 1979 that: "as the more penetrating critics of mass culture have pointed out, that the rise of mass media makes the categories of truth and falsehood irrelevant to an evaluation of their influence. Truth has given way to credibility, facts to statements that sounds authoritative without conveying any authoritative information." Christopher Lasch, *The Culture of Narcissism* (London: W. W. Norton & Company, 1979), 74.

45 "If you read Herbert Marcuse's *One-Dimensional Man*, you see him struggling with this problem. He sees in 1964 that everyone is getting too comfortable to revolt against oppression of any kind. People are distracted by the sexual revolution, by popular music, by virtually every aspect of mass culture."
   (Illing, *"If you want to understand the age of Trump, read the Frankfurt School"*)

46 Amanda Taun, "The Rise of American Authoritarianism," *Vox*, March 01, 2016, <https://www.vox.com/2016/3/1/11127424/trump-authoritarianism>.

47 Michael Lewis, "Has Anyone Seen the President?" *Bloomberg*, February 09, 2018, <https://www.bloomberg.com/view/articles/2018-02-09/has-anyone-seen-the-president>.

48 Garry Wills, "Did Tocqueville "Get" America?', *New York Review of Books*, April 29 2004, <https://www.nybooks.com/articles/2004/04/29/did-tocqueville-get-america/>.

49 Illing, "If you want to understand the age of Trump, read the Frankfurt School".

50 Ross, "The Frankfurt School Knew Trump was Coming";

   Adorno and the other critical theorists saw culture as inherently totalitarian, and this was particularly true in America. This, of course, didn't go over well with the public. You have these Germans coming to your country with their old attitudes and their defense of bourgeois art, and they're critical of every aspect of American culture and regard it as an artistic wasteland.
   (Illing, *"If you want to understand the age of Trump, read the Frankfurt School"*)

51 Alex Ross, "The Naysayers," *The New Yorker*, September 15, 2014, <https://www.newyorker.com/magazine/2014/09/15/naysayers>.

52 See Ian Tyrrell's excellent transnational history of America, which is a model for the type of research that should be encouraged. Ian Tyrrell, *Transnational Nation* (New York: Palgrave, 2007).

53 David Roberts, "The Question of what Donald Trump 'Really Believes' Has no Answer," *Vox*, September 29, 2016, <https://www.vox.com/2016/9/29/13086236/trump-beliefs-category-error>.

54 David Corn, "Donald Trump Says he Doesn't Believe in 'American Exceptionalism,'" *Mother Jones*, June 07, 2016, <https://www.motherjones.com/politics/2016/06/donald-trump-american-exceptionalism/>.

55 George W. Bush, "The Second Gore-Bush-Presidential Debate," *Commission on Presidential Debates*, October 11, 2000, <https://www.debates.org/voter-education/debate-transcripts/october-11-2000-debate-transcript/>.

56 Vladimir Putin, "A Plea for Caution from Russia," *New York Times*, September 11, 2013, <http://www.nytimes.com/2013/09/12/opinion/putin-plea-for-caution-from-russia-on-syria.html?_r=1>.

57 Donald Trump, "Trump: 'Embarrassing' how Putin has 'played' Obama," *Fox News*, September 12, 2013, <http://www.foxnews.com/transcript/2013/09/13/trump-embarrassing-how-putin-has-played-obama.html>.

58 Bill Powell, "Donald Trump Associate Felix Sater is Linked to the Mob and the CIA – What's His Role in the Russia Investigation?" *Newsweek Magazine*, 07 June, 2018, <https://www.newsweek.com/2018/06/15/sater-963255.html>; Matt Bevan, "Donald Trump has Always Denied Deals with Russia, but how True is That?" *ABC News*, May 14, 2018, <http://www.abc.net.au/news/2018-05-14/donald-trump-denies-deals-with-russia-but-is-that-true/9751876>; Michael Isikoff and David Corn, *Russian Roulette: The Inside Story of Putin's War on America and the Election of Donald Trump* (New York: Grand Central Publishing, 2018).

59 Republican Party Platforms, "2012 Republican Party Platform Online," *The American Presidency Project*, August 27, 2012, <https://www.presidency.ucsb.edu/documents/2012-republican-party-platform>.

60 Tim Hains, "Hillary Clinton: Trump Thinks 'American Exceptionalism' is Insulting to the Rest of the World," *RealClear Politics*, August 31, 2016, <https://www.realclearpolitics.com/video/2016/08/31/hillary_clinton_trump_thinks_american_exceptionalism_is_insulting_to_the_rest_of_the_world.html>.

61 Republican Party Platforms, "2012 Republican Party Platform Online," *The American Presidency Project*, August 27, 2012, <http://www.presidency.ucsb.edu/ws/index.php?pid=101961#american>.

62 John Ikenberry "The Plot against American Foreign Policy: Can the Liberal Order Survive," *Foreign Affairs* 96 (2017), 3–4.

63 Stephen Walt, *The Hell of Good Intensions* (New York: Farrar, Straus and Giroux, 2018); Stephen M. Walt, "Why I Didn't Sign Up to Defend the International Order," *Foreign Policy*, August 01, 2018, <https://foreignpolicy.com/2018/08/01/why-i-didnt-sign-up-to-defend-the-international-order/>.

64 Graham Allison, "The Myth of the Liberal Order: From Historical Accident to Conventional Wisdom," *Foreign Affairs* 97 (2018).

65 Anatol Lieven, *America Right or Wrong: An Anatomy of American Nationalism* (Oxford, UK: Oxford University Press, 2012).

66 Perry Anderson, *American Foreign Policy and Its Thinkers* (New York: Verso, 2015).

67 Patrick Smith, *Time No Longer: Americans After the American Century* (New Haven: Yale University Press, 2013).

68 Samuel Moyn, "Beyond Liberal Internationalism," *Dissent Magazine*, Winter 2017, <https://www.dissentmagazine.org/article/left-foreign-policy-beyond-liberal-internationalism>.

69 See Walter Russell Mead, *Special Providence: American Foreign Policy and how it Changed the World* (New York: Routledge, 2002).

70 As Dani Rodrik has argued on trade, at times Trump is right, although he has strongly questioned his solutions. See Dani Rodrik, *Straight Talk on Trade: Ideas for a Sane World Economy* (Princetown: Princetown University Press, 2017).

71 Susan B. Glasser, "Walter Russell Mead: The Full Transcript," *Politico Magazine*, January 22, 2018, <https://www.politico.com/magazine/story/2018/01/22/walter-russell-mead-the-full-transcript-216492>; Susan B. Glasser, "The Man who put Andrew Jackson in Trump's Oval Office," *Politico Magazine*, January 22, 2018, <https://www.politico.com/magazine/story/2018/01/22/andrew-jackson-donald-trump-216493>.

72 Moyn, "Beyond Liberal Internationalism".

73 Samuel Moyn "Soft Sells: On Liberal Internationalism," *The Nation*, September 14, 2012, <https://www.thenation.com/article/soft-sells-liberal-internationalism/>; Like Moyn, Bacevich also refers to America as an empire. See Andrew J. Bacevich, *American Empire: The Realities and Consequences of U.S. Diplomacy* (Cambridge, MA: Harvard University Press, 2002).

74 Peter Beinart, "The Iran Deal and the Dark Side of American Exceptionalism," *The Atlantic*, May 09, 2018, <https://www.theatlantic.com/international/archive/2018/05/iran-deal-trump-american-exceptionalism/560063/>.

75 Stephen Walt, *The Hell of Good Intentions* (New York: Farrar, Straus and Giroux, 2018).

76 Charles Kupchan, "The Clash of Exceptionalisms: A New Fight over an Old Idea," *Foreign Affairs* 97 (2018).

77 Ibid., p. 146.

78 Ibid., p. 147.

79 Ibid., p. 148.

80 Hilde Eliassen Restad, *American Exceptionalism: An Idea that Made a Nation and Remade the World* (New York: Routledge, 2014).

81 David Vine, "Where in the World is the U.S. Military?" *Politico Magazine*, July/August 2015, <https://www.politico.com/magazine/story/2015/06/us-military-bases-around-the-world-119321>.

82 Peter Baker, "'Use that Word!': Trump Embraces the 'Nationalist' Label," *The New York Times*, October 23, 2018, <https://www.nytimes.com/2018/10/23/us/politics/nationalist-president-trump.html>.

83 Liu Zhen, "What's Donald Trump Planning? 1987 Advertisement Offers Clues," *South China Morning Post*, 04 December, 2016, <https://www.scmp.com/news/china/diplomacy-defence/article/2049751/whats-donald-trump-planning-1987-advertisement-offers>.

84 Ibid.

85 Peter Baker, Choe Sang-Hun, "Trump Threatens 'Fire and Fury' Against North Korea if it Endangers U.S.," *The New York Times*, September 12, 2013, <https://www.nytimes.com/2017/08/08/world/asia/north-korea-un-sanctions-nuclear-missile-united-nations.html>.

86 Walter Russell Mead, "The Jacksonian Revolt: American Populism and the Liberal Order," *Foreign Affairs*, 96, 3 (2017).

87 Ibid., p. 3.

88 Ibid., p. 4.

89 Ibid., p. 4.

90 Ibid., p. 4.

91 Ibid., p. 4.

92 Lorna Finlayson, "Corbyn Now," *London Review of Books*, 40, 18 (2018), <https://www.lrb.co.uk/v40/n18/lorna-finlayson/corbyn-now>.

93 Raewyn Connell, "Social Science on a World Scale" *Sociologies in Dialogue* 1, 1 (2015).

94 Alfred Setpan and Juan J. Jinz, "Comparative Perspectives on Inequality and the Quality of Democracy in the United States," *Perspectives on Politics* 9, 4 (2011).

95 Godfrey Hodgson, *The Myth of American Exceptionalism* (New Haven: Yale University Press, 2009); Richard Pells, *Not Like Us: How Europeans Have Loved, Hated, And Transformed American Culture Since World War II* (New York, Basic Books, 1997).

96 Huffington Post, "13 Things You Thought Were American But Really Aren't," *Huffington Post*, December 27 2013, <https://www.huffingtonpost.com/2013/12/27/classic-american-things-not-from-us_n_4440784.html?slideshow=true#gallery/329636/12>.
97 Ian Tyrrell, *Transnational Nation: United States History in Global Perspective Since 1789* (London: Palgrave MacMillan, 2015).
98 Barrack Obama, "Remarks by the President at the United States Military Academy Commencement Ceremony," *The White House*, May 28 2014, <https://obamawhitehouse.archives.gov/the-press-office/2014/05/28/remarks-president-united-states-military-academy-commencement-ceremony>.
99 Beinart, "The Iran Deal and the Dark Side of American Exceptionalism".

INDEX

Note: Information in figures and tables is indicated by page numbers in *italics* and **bold**.

Wilson, Woodrow xvii, 127, 134
With Us or Against Us (Judt and Lacorne) 35
Wolfe, Tom 170
Women's March 116
Woodward, Bob 108, 118n20
World Trade Center xii, xiii
World War II 69–70, 135

wrestling, professional 170–171

Zakaria, Fareed 143
Zeldin, Theodore 39
Zelig (film) 99n21
Zhou Enlai 93

Made in the USA
San Bernardino, CA
05 May 2020

70853809R00120